*New Religions as Global Cultures*

# EXPLORATIONS
*Contemporary Perspectives on Religion*

# New Religions as Global Cultures

## MAKING THE HUMAN SACRED

### Irving Hexham
### Karla Poewe

University of Calgary

WestviewPress

*A Division of* HarperCollins*Publishers*

*Explorations: Contemporary Perspectives on Religion*

Published in 1997 in the United States of America by Westview Press, 5500 Central Avenue, Boulder, Colorado 80301-2877, and in the United Kingdom by Westview Press, 12 Hid's Copse Road, Cumnor Hill, Oxford OX2 9JJ

Library of Congress Cataloging-in-Publication Data
Hexham, Irving.
    New religions as global cultures : making the human sacred
/ by Irving Hexham & Karla Poewe.    — (Explorations)
        p.    cm.    — (Explorations)
Includes bibliographical references and index.
    ISBN 0-8133-2507-2 (hc). — ISBN 0-8133-2508-0 (pbk.)
    1. Cults—History—20th century.    2. Cults—Study and teaching—
History—20th century.    3. Anti-cult movements—History—20th
century.    4. Religion and culture—History—20th century.
5. Religion and sociology.    I. Poewe, Karla O.    II. Title.
III. Series: Explorations (Boulder, Colo.)
BP603.H48    1997
291.046—dc21
                                                                        96-51758
                                                                        CIP

The paper used in this publication meets the requirements of the American National Standard for Permanence of Paper for Printed Library Materials Z39.48-1984.

10    9    8    7    6    5    4    3    2

# Contents

# *Foreword*

## RODNEY STARK

$T$o better appreciate why the authors wrote this book and what readers can hope to learn from them, consider a particular new religion. Like most of these groups, it can be identified as a cult because it displays three typical cultic features. First, it claims to have extensive new religious truths—a set of unique doctrines that are very different from those taught by the conventional churches. Second, the source of these new teachings is a young man who claims to have received them directly from God. Third, the leader requires obedience and encourages his followers to abandon their current lives and become full-time members.

Understandably, the parents of many of these followers are upset and angry about the exploitation of their children by this self-proclaimed messiah. Their worst fears are confirmed by well-known clergy who issue public warnings about the dangers of this cult and the dangers of all authoritarian religions led by deluded fanatics. The growing public outcry soon forces the government to act: The leader is crucified between two thieves.

This may seem a rather melodramatic introduction, but I intended it to force you to think about the word "cult" and about new religions. All of the world's major, respectable religions, including Christianity, began in obscurity. Each aroused angry opposition. Each would have been classified as a cult according to the three criteria outlined above.

The moral of this lesson should now be clear: One person's true faith is another's sinful heresy, and there is no easy answer to the question whether cults are dangerous. The pagan priests of ancient Rome thought the Christians were dangerous, and from their point of view they were absolutely right. The triumph of Christianity spelled the doom of paganism; in fact most pagan temples were remodeled into Christian churches or destroyed. Of course most Christians applaud this outcome, believing Christianity was destined to triumph because it is true. But all religious groups, old as well as new, think they are true. They can't all be right. So what's a person to believe?

These are issues that lie at the core of this book as it assesses new religious movements around the world. There may be many works on this topic, but this one offers a unique and extremely valuable perspective. The authors have spent years examining new religious movements. They are fully aware of the immense variety of groups and know the factual and moral complexities involved in characterizing them.

They wrote this book for students, especially those from Judeo-Christian backgrounds. In all times and places, young people are the primary source of converts to new religious movements. Partly for this reason, students have been the targets of a great deal of propaganda on the subject. To pursue this point, let's examine the "cult" section of any bookstore or, better yet, of a religious bookstore. Here we find dozens of books about new religions. Many offer descriptive accounts of new religious groups, their teachings, practices, history, and lifestyles. Some were written by scholars who were moderately attracted to the group—most new religions attract a fringe of groupies. Others were written by former members, many of whom were out to get even. Still others were written in hopes of making money from sensational revelations about secret rites or other goings-on—and these accounts are about as reliable as those about Bigfoot or Elvis in the weeklies sold at supermarket checkout counters.

Another common kind of book, found especially in Christian bookstores, disputes the teachings of new religious groups on theological grounds. For example, some books provide Christians with arguments to use when confronting missionaries from the Jehovah's Witnesses, Mormons, and Hindu groups. It is entirely appropriate for people to disagree about religion, and anyone has every right to denounce another's doctrines as false, unscriptural, illogical, or otherwise intellectually wanting.

Many other books adopt the perspective of the officials who judged Jesus. Their purpose is to warn readers against the "threat" of cults, and many propose means to suppress these deviant religious movements. These books do not focus on incorrect doctrines but specialize in lurid and fanciful stories about how the cults victimize their members financially, sexually, and psychologically; plan to subvert our religious lives; or seek to overthrow democratic government. Having raised sufficient alarm, the authors conclude that the cults must be stopped, usually by government repression. No one would deny that some religious groups at times victimize their members, for such groups come in an immense variety, as do secular organizations. Not all of them are respectable; some are led by disreputable people. But these groups are rare, and most of the "revelations" about cults are not true. It is curious that the most alarmist claims in the books that intend to protect Judaism or Christianity from cults are by secular writers who regard all religions as dangerous cults and who believe all sincerely religious people are brainwashed fanatics. A common suggestion by these anti-cult authors is that we enact laws restricting religious conversion—for example, by requiring a waiting period of many years and providing for the legal restraint of persons who do not obey. These laws, which have nearly passed in several states, would not simply prevent people from joining new religious movements but would keep them from joining any religion: not only the Hare Krishnas but also the Roman Catholics, Reform Jews, or Episcopalians (but it would remain legal for a person of religious background to join an antireligious group). What is one to make of "religious" writers who rely on such allies for their views?

This brings us back to the qualifications of Irving Hexham and Karla Poewe to write this book. Not only are they highly respected social scientists, they are themselves active Christians. Thus they do not write about cults because they find them entertaining or because they are attracted to their messages or lifestyles. They write about them because they think the topic of new religious movements is important. And because they think Pontius Pilate was wrong.

# Preface

*T*his book is designed to help students and anyone interested in religion understand contemporary religions from an interdisciplinary and global perspective. Writing the book was difficult because we recognized that many readers probably lack a background in both the social sciences and religious studies. We develop our argument, therefore, by taking the reader from popular examples to ones from the social sciences in an effort to lay bare the framework of contemporary religions. This framework consists of globality, primal experiences, new mythologies, aspects of the great Yogic and Abramic traditions, and the impact of modernity.

Anyone who wishes to talk to members of new and contemporary religious movements needs to recognize that understanding must precede criticism. We believe that many of the arguments found in secular books and the press, as well as in a vast array of "Christian" books, lack substance. They fail to provide real insight into the lifestyles and beliefs of movements and their adherents. In practice such arguments, even many found in secular sources, are based on theological assumptions and prejudices that tend to do more harm than good.

Our aim is to develop an understanding of contemporary religions and the people who join them because we see this as the first step toward enabling members of contemporary religions and outsiders to communicate with one another. Only when the people involved in and concerned about contemporary religions can find a common ground of discussion can they seriously consider such issues as truth claims and arguments about the possible "harm" certain groups may do.

We believe that most new and contemporary religions are legitimate expressions of spirituality that can best be understood from an interdisciplinary perspective grounded in a theory of global culture. Although we reject the argument that *all* contemporary religions are dangerous cults, we do recognize that some new religions cause harm. This is why scholars like Margaret Singer need to be taken seriously. Singer and others express a legitimate concern when they worry about the adverse influence of some groups (Singer 1995). Nevertheless, we argue that *most* contemporary religions do not fall into the "dangerous" category and that labeling them in this way prevents people from understanding why others are attracted to them.

At the end of each chapter, we provide a Key Terms section. In the text these terms appear in **bold** the first time we use them.

We would like to thank the many people who helped us with our research—particularly the members of numerous contemporary religions who detailed their lives for us. We also thank the Social Sciences and Humanities Research Council of Canada and the University of Calgary for their generous financial assistance and encouragement.

*Irving Hexham*
*Karla Poewe*

## ❊ 1 ❊

# The Great Anti-cult Crusade

*Today, the kingdom of the cults stretches throughout the world.*

*Walter Martin (1976:15)*

*In the past twenty years, the destructive cult phenomenon has mushroomed into a problem of tremendous social and political importance.*

*Steven Hassan (1990:36)*

*T*hroughout the world numerous news reports reflect public concern about "**cults.**" These reports give rise to sometimes puzzling questions: Why do people join cults? Are people brainwashed, or do they make free choices? Are cults sinister groups? How should responsible people respond to cult members? Is it possible to carry on a meaningful discussion with cult members, or must we resort to coercive deprogramming?

Most of us have at one time or another met someone who has joined a new religion. Often it seems impossible to have a reasonable conversation with that person. Faced with probing questions, **Jehovah's Witnesses**, members of **Sun Myung Moon**'s **Unification Church** (popularly known as **Moonies**), and converts to many other groups seem to give stock answers and don't appear to take seriously questions that are important to outsiders. Cult members may use in-group jargon unintelligible to the rest of us, and when they speak plain English they don't seem to use our language in quite the same way we do.

In this chapter we examine the creation of the public image of contemporary religious movements as "dangerous cults." We expose the poor scholarship and exaggerated claims that have prevented a balanced understanding of such movements. Finally, we caution that although most contemporary religious move-

1

ments are genuinely harmless, it is unwise to underestimate either the influence or the potential danger of seemingly insignificant groups.

## *"Heigh-ho! Heigh-ho!*
## *A-Crusading We Will Go!"*

This book deals with cults or, more accurately, contemporary religious movements. By "contemporary religious movements," we mean religions that have gained notoriety during the past twenty-five years. Many of these groups have long historical roots; others emerged in the nineteenth century. Some are genuinely **new religions**. Many more are **revitalization movements** that seek to breathe life into ancient traditions. Although their critics label them "cults," scholars usually call them "new religious movements."

As we shall see, the names used to identify various types of religious movements are not very satisfactory and need to be redefined. In Chapter 2 we discuss the origins of terms like "church," "sect," and "cult," enabling us to provide working definitions. Later, in Chapters 8 and 9, we discuss the uniqueness of genuinely new religious movements. But before we continue, we need to understand why the word "cult" has such negative connotations.

There can be little doubt that one of the main sources for negative images of contemporary movements is the abundance of books that supposedly expose cults. We must therefore examine some popular anti-cult literature and recognize the existence of what some writers call "the anti-cult movement" (Shupe and Bromley 1980, 1981; Bromley and Richardson 1983).

Since the 1970s a seemingly endless torrent of personal testimonies claiming to expose life in cults has poured forth from numerous presses. These books, which range from enlightening accounts of personal growth to sensational claims about human sacrifice and bestiality, have added an immediacy to what might otherwise be dull polemics. The sheer volume of popular anti-cult literature is an important factor in shaping public attitudes to contemporary religions in **secular** society.

## *The Importance of van Baalen*

One of the first popular writers to use the term "cult" was Jan Karel van Baalen in his best-selling text *The Chaos of the Cults* (1938). A graduate of Princeton Theological Seminary and an ordained minister in the Christian Reformed Church, van Baalen was a traditional **Calvinist** pastor with an excellent education in theology and church history. As a result, he approached the topic of contemporary religions, which he called "cults," from the perspective of Christian **orthodoxy** as defined by the historic Calvinist **creeds**.

Although van Baalen was devastating in his theological criticism of various groups, he made an effort to be scrupulously fair. His objections were doctrinal, not personal or vindictive. For him, cult membership was an issue of theology and biblical exposition. Thus even though he totally rejected the beliefs of numerous groups, he began his book by telling readers, "We can learn from cultists, not only noting what not to believe, but also bearing in mind that 'the cults are the unpaid bills of the Church'" (van Baalen 1956:14).

Using this idea of cults as "the unpaid bills of the Church," van Baalen sought to explain the rise of new religions in terms of the failure of established churches. In doing so he warned his readers, "Above all, never . . . suspect the cultist of dishonesty or mercenary motives" (van Baalen 1956:366). After making these and a number of related points, he concluded his advice by saying, "Combating cults is not a dunce's task" (van Baalen 1956:369). This reasoned approach is very different from what followed.

## Walter Martin's Ad Hominem Arguments

More than anyone else, Walter R. Martin shaped modern attitudes to contemporary religions. His early books dealt with specific groups such as the **Seventh-Day Adventists**, whom he defended, and the Jehovah's Witnesses and **Mormons**, whom he attacked. In 1965 Martin published his most successful book, *The Kingdom of the Cults*, which sold millions of copies.

What makes this book different from van Baalen's, on which it seems to have been modeled, is the emphasis on the personal failings of cult leaders and their use of "deception" to attract converts. Martin begins reasonably enough by paying lip service to van Baalen's maxim that "cults are the unpaid bills of the Church." But he quickly adds, "They are this and more" (Martin 1976:13). With this "more," Martin departs from van Baalen's intellectual critique.

To prove his point, Martin devotes a chapter to what he calls "the psychological structure of cultism" (Martin 1976:24–33). In the remainder of his book, Martin outlines the history and beliefs of such groups as the Jehovah's Witnesses, Mormons, and **Christian Scientists**. He concludes his work with a chapter significantly entitled "The Road to Recovery" (Martin 1976:352–359), in which he outlines his plans for research, propaganda, and the mobilization of Christian resources to counter cults. In many ways he met these aims by establishing the Christian Research Institute.

A good example of Martin's technique can be seen in his discussion of the Jehovah's Witnesses. Instead of concentrating on theological differences between the Witnesses and traditional Christianity, Martin makes a concerted effort to prove that the founders of the movement were "hypocrites" and rogues. This allows him to argue that no one knowingly follows a hypocrite or rogue (Martin 1976:35–42). Central to his case against the Witnesses are his claims that the founder, **Charles Taze Russell**, was divorced, that he called himself a "pastor" though he wasn't ordained by an established church, and that he claimed to be better educated than he actually was (Martin 1976:35, 39–40).

The irony is that Martin himself was divorced not once but twice. He was charged with "cruelty" in his first divorce and with "extreme mental and physical cruelty" in the second divorce (Brown and Brown 1986:5, 196). And Martin's own ordination was highly questionable: After his first remarriage in 1953, his ordination was revoked and does not seem to have been renewed by another church despite his insistence that it had (Brown and Brown 1986:7–18). Further, he claimed to hold a doctorate at least ten years before he obtained a rather dubious degree from an unaccredited correspondence school. It is also true that he consistently misled his readers about his academic qualifications (Brown and Brown 1986:31–53).

What Martin's personal history shows is that people who live in glass houses should not throw stones. We need to be very careful before accepting charges against new religions by people who earn their living denouncing such groups. Even if everything Martin said about the personal lives of some founders of contemporary religions were true, this would not prove their teachings wrong. He indulged in what philosophers call **ad hominem** arguments, which are directed against the person rather than the person's ideas.

## *The New Age Crusade*[1]

The next step in the development of public attitudes toward new religions can be traced to the publications of Constance Cumbey (1983) and Dave Hunt (Hunt and McMahon 1983), who "awoke" people to the existence of the **New Age movement,** arguing that a vast conspiracy existed to create a new world religion. Following the success of these works, an entire anti-cult literature arose. But few of these books really add to our knowledge of new religions or why people are attracted to them. If we review such works, several serious shortcomings become clear:

First, there is a tendency among anti-cult writers to misuse footnotes. Many authors use quotations from prominent experts to lend authority rather than to convey information. Such usage of authorities is fallacious. But the abuse goes even further: A surprising number of writers seem to think that footnotes in and of themselves make a work scholarly, when of course it is the quality of the footnotes that really matters. Notes are intended to direct readers to the sources of an author's argument so that readers can check the truth of the author's interpretation for themselves.

For instance, it is common practice for authors of anti-cult books simply to cite a secondary source rather than the primary source. Thus in *What Is the New Age? A Detailed Candid Look at This Fast Growing Movement,* instead of quoting directly from the *Confessions of Saint Augustine,* Michael Cole cites **Saint Augustine of Hippo** "as quoted" in *The History of Christianity* (Cole et al. 1990:29; 199, n. 1). Other contributors to that book repeatedly indulge in the same technique (e.g., Cole et al. 1990:44; 45, n. 10; 200, n. 4). It never seems to occur to these writers that the secondary sources they are using may have misquoted the authorities. Such lack of care makes their work of dubious value.

Second, many authors accept the fantastic claims of New Age advocates far too easily. Thus Gary North is prepared to believe in the reality of phenomena such as **Kirlian photography,** which claims to capture the "**human aura**" on film (North 1988:98–101). He is equally credulous about "spontaneous human combustion" (North 1988:52–56) and a whole range of other occult phenomena that ought to be treated with the utmost skepticism. In other words, North wants to be critical of New Age religions yet uncritically accepts many of their more fantastic claims. Arleen J. Watkins and William S. Bickel show Kirlian photography to be a natural and nonoccult phenomenon (Watkins and Bickel 1986). Joe Nickell and John F. Fischer examine and dismiss a number of cases of so-called human combustion (Nickell and Fischer 1987). Yet most anti-cult writers never discuss such works, which they seem to regard as potentially damaging to their own religious beliefs.

Third, many authors create guilt by association. Dave Hunt and T. A. McMahon, for example, say, "Since **reincarnation** is a belief basic to **witchcraft**, it is not surprising that it is *amoral*" (Hunt and McMahon 1988:213). Belief in reincarnation may be faulted for many reasons, but it is not necessarily "amoral" or linked to witchcraft. Nor should witchcraft automatically be associated with **sorcery** and evil.

## Anti-cult Literature:
### A Critique of the Critiques

Another major problem with critiques of new religions is a strong tendency toward reductionism. For example, Douglas Groothuis explains New Age thought under the headings

1. All is One
2. All is God
3. Humanity is God
4. A Change in Consciousness
5. All Religions Are One
6. Cosmic Evolutionary Optimism (Groothuis 1986:18–31).

These ideas, which boil down to **monism, pantheism, relativism,** and evolutionary philosophy, are central to many critiques (Hoyt 1987:248–255; Miller 1989:17) of New Age thought. Yet despite the importance these authors place on the concepts they use to identify various ideas, few take the time to adequately define their terms.

Monism, for example, is loosely used as a bogey word. No one seems to realize that even Christianity can be seen as a form of monism because it claims all things are created by one being: God. The orthodox Calvinist Gordon H. Clark wrote "actually Christianity is more successfully monistic than **Neoplatonism** was. God alone is the eternal substance, the independent principle; apart from the creation of the world nothing exists besides him" (Clark 1957:231).

Thus, in taking a strong stand against the use of certain words, anti-cult writers do not seem to recognize that many of the alternatives they prefer are equally problematic. This is a particular difficulty for orthodox Christian writers. In rejecting monism, for example, many writers identify Christianity with **pluralism**. In doing so, they fail to recognize that Bertrand Russell promoted pluralism in his rejection of Christianity, embracing pluralism because "the universe is all spots and jumps, without unity, without continuity, without coherence or orderliness" (Russell 1931:98). Is this what Christians mean by "pluralism"?

Finally, along with a tendency to intellectual reductionism goes the desire to force opponents into a preconceived theoretical framework. This is most clearly seen in Clark and Geisler's *Apologetics in the New Age* (1990). In the book's introduction, the reader is told, "We will explore the basic world view of pantheism, examining the views of its greatest defenders. . . . Pantheism is a multiform world view that needs to be understood and evaluated. This is especially true in its New Age manifestations" (Clark and Geisler 1990:14). The authors then devote five chapters to the works of **D. T. Suzuki, Śankara, Radhakrishnan, Plotinus,** and **Baruch Spinoza,** who, Clark and Geisler claim, contributed to the creation of New Age thought. The problem is that with the exception of Spinoza it is highly debatable whether any of these thinkers was a pantheist.

Clark and Geisler are correct when they see pantheism as a central tenet of much popular New Age thinking. Where they go wrong is in projecting an essentially modern view onto writers of the past and in identifying pantheism with religious traditions that contain pantheistic elements but are not necessarily pantheistic. The central teachings of these thinkers, other than Spinoza, certainly do not fit Clark and Geisler's definition of "pantheism." Surprisingly, the authors do not mention such figures as **Marcus Aurelius, Johannes Scotus Erigena, Giordano Bruno, Jakob Böhme, Johann Wolfgang von Goethe, Gotthold Ephraim Lessing, Johann Gottlieb Fichte,** and **Georg Wilhelm Friedrich Hegel,** who *can* plausibly be represented as pantheists.

Since these are works written for readers with college educations and since they claim to be serious scholarly critiques of new religions, we must evaluate them as such. And when they are critically examined, they are inevitably found wanting.

## Charismatics as the New Enemy

Anti-cult crusaders bear a striking resemblance to medieval crusaders. Like those who fought the Crusades, they began by defending "Christianity" against the external threat of loss of membership to rival religious movements. Soon, however, they took the offensive and started to criticize any religious movement they deemed heretical. Later, as in the sacking of Acre and Jerusalem, these attacks turned into orgies of destruction. Then as public interest in cults waned, the target began to change.

Just as soldiers in the Fourth Crusade in 1204 found it more profitable to sack Constantinople than to engage a powerful enemy in the Holy Land, so, too, some Christian anti-cult writers began to attack fellow Christians who were part of the **charismatic movement**. Central to their denunciation of charismatics is the claim that the charismatic movement is a new religion that deviates from historic Christianity. As we shall see in Chapter 6, this claim is false. More important, it distorts our ability to identify clearly the essence of new religions.

The growing tension between cult "experts" and charismatics was spearheaded by the publication of Hunt and McMahon's best-selling *Seduction of Christianity* (1985), a blistering attack on charismatics from a **fundamentalist** Christian perspective that set the stage for numerous other attacks (McConnell 1988; Hannegraff 1993). Although Hunt and McMahon's work gave rise to several responses, none of these tackled the central problem of *Seduction* because they all concentrated on theological issues and questions about spirituality (cf. Reid et al. 1986; Wise et al. 1986).

In fact the basic problem with Hunt and McMahon's work is its lack of academic rigor. Even though they sometimes have interesting insights, neither Hunt nor McMahon is an academic researcher, as can be seen from a close examination of their footnotes and citations. Hunt and McMahon argue that "cults are only part of a much larger and more seductive deception known as the New Age movement"; this they define as "the 'great delusion' that the Bible warns will sweep the world in the 'last days' and cause humanity to worship the **Antichrist**" (Hunt and McMahon 1985:7). They go on to "quote from the books and sermons as well as radio, television, and seminar talks of a number of influential Christian leaders," whom they describe as "the *victims*" of the deception they have identified (Hunt and McMahon 1985:9).

After acknowledging the sincerity of many of the people whom they propose to attack and admitting that those people are not the only ones at fault, they justify their assault on the basis of their "deep conviction, based upon years of research" (Hunt and McMahon 1985:9). With this introduction Hunt and McMahon find "New Age influences" behind many successful Christian ministries they dislike. Their treatment of Korean church leader Paul Yonggi Cho provides a good example of their technique—and shows how *not* to quote people (Hunt and McMahon 1985:101–102). To prove that Yonggi Cho is influenced by New Age teachings that "mislead" sincere Christians, Hunt and McMahon claim Cho says "that *anyone*, including **occultists**, can . . . perform **miracles**." They follow up this statement by telling their readers that "Cho commends the Japanese **Buddhist** occultists, the **Soka Gakkai**, for performing 'miracles'" and "scolds Christians for not doing likewise" (Hunt and McMahon 1985:101–102, citing

Cho 1979:64). They also say that Cho invokes the authority of the Holy Spirit to support these claims (Hunt and McMahon 1985:102, citing Cho 1979:36–43).

To ordinary American Christians in conservative evangelical churches, such charges are serious indeed. The problem is that this is *not* what Cho does or says when his words are read in context. What Cho actually says is, "Sokagakkai . . . has performed miracles; but in Christianity there is only talk about theology and faith" (Cho 1979:64). It is clear that Cho is chiding Christians for failing to take God seriously by comparing Christians to members of Soka Gakkai. But this does not mean that he "commends" anyone. In fact Cho warns, "Do not be deceived by the talk of mind expansion, yoga, transcendental meditation, or Sokagakkai. They are only developing the human fourth dimension, and in these cases are not in the good, but rather the evil, fourth dimension" (Cho 1979:65–66). This is hardly a commendation.

To understand Cho's point, we must realize that earlier in his book he wrote, "In the Orient I have real trouble preaching about the miraculous power of God, for in Buddhism monks also have performed fantastic miracles. In Korea . . . when attending meetings of the Japanese Sokagakkai, many are healed—some of stomach ulcers. . . . So naturally we Christians . . . have real difficulty in explaining these occurrences" (Cho 1979:36–37).

After outlining the problem of preaching Christianity in an Oriental culture, Cho explains his understanding of non-Christian miracles. Emphasizing the uniqueness of the Christian God, who created the universe, he writes, "The **Holy Spirit** said to me, 'Look at the Sokagakkai. They belong to Satan.' . . . It was in this manner that the **magicians in Egypt** carried out dominion" (Cho 1979:37, 40). To say that members of Soka Gakkai "belong to Satan" hardly shows sympathy for them. Cho takes a strong position against such groups. In fact his arguments are similar to those Hunt and McMahon themselves use. It is unclear whether Hunt and McMahon deliberately distort their evidence or consistently misread the texts they claim to expound.

This example illustrates how some Christian arguments against new religions and other religious traditions quickly degenerated from the type of intellectual argument van Baalen used to misguided polemics by one group of Christians against another. It is obvious that this type of argument simply creates prejudice and prevents anyone from understanding the appeal of contemporary religions. Yet the works of writers like Hunt are extremely popular and are frequently used as though they were academic works by scholars who had devoted their lives to the study of religions.

## Brainwashing

The arguments we have presented so far have largely concerned anti-cult criticisms of contemporary religious movements. Understanding the weaknesses in such critiques is important in order to understand the far weightier charge that cults are abusive social groups that brainwash their members. Without propaganda against the cults, it is doubtful that many people would seriously consider charges of spiritual abuse and brainwashing.

In North America and Europe, many newspapers have told bizarre stories about life in new religions, depicting cult members as mindless zombies. Supporting this view, ex-members appear on TV and radio talk shows to tell tales of being trapped in cults through sleep deprivation, protein-deficient diets, and isolation from family and friends. The media spotlights parents who describe tragic stories about misled children they have attempted to rescue from "evil cults." Best-selling books like Josh Freed's *Moonwebs* (1980), which became a TV movie, and Barbara and Betty Underwood's *Hostage to Heaven* (1979) set the tone for scores of other similarly graphic accounts of "mind control."

Such stories create a strong impression that people join contemporary religions only because cult leaders are in some mysterious way able to control the minds of their converts. This "control" is usually called "brainwashing" and is associated with psychological manipulation and emotional blackmail. To begin to answer the question whether it is really possible to control someone's mind, we must consider the history of brainwashing as a theory of religious conversion. The British psychiatrist William Sargant first used the term "brainwashing" in his *Battle for the Mind* in 1957. This book is the main source of the term as it is used today.

Sargant believed that evangelical conversions from **Saint Paul** to **Billy Graham** could be explained in terms of psychological processes akin to what was called **shell shock** during World War I. Shell shock produces personality changes in soldiers under fire. Sargant claimed that similar effects can be deliberately produced without the trauma of a real battle through a process of "brainwashing," the psychological mechanism that leads to religious conversion. By equating religious conversion with shell shock, Sargant was intentionally associating the conversion process with a severe and undesirable medical condition.

In developing his theory, Sargant argued that the conversions observed at Billy Graham crusades were similar to those reported by early Methodists. Both types of conversion, he said, were based on a belief in the Bible as the Word of God and the reality of a "new birth" through the work of the Holy Spirit. He considered such beliefs irrational and antiscientific:

> This is no longer the eighteenth century. Then it did not seem to matter what the common people believed because they exercised no political power and were supposed only to work, not think; and because they read no books or papers. But religious conversion to fundamentalism seems out of date now; . . . the brain should not be abused by having forced upon it any religious or political mystique that stunts reason. (Sargant 1959:214)

Sargant regarded fundamentalists—by whom he meant evangelicals—as dangerous, saying that they mentally abused people and gained followers by brainwashing. In his *Conversions: Psychological and Spiritual* (1959), the eminent medical specialist and evangelical preacher D. Martyn Lloyd-Jones challenged Sargant's argument, but among secular thinkers it was widely accepted.

Since Sargant wrote *Battle for the Mind*, evangelical Christians in Britain and America have grown in numbers. As their ranks have increased, so has their political and social influence, and criticism of them has subsided. New religions, however, continue to stand accused of brainwashing and mind abuse—and, ironically, Christians are among the first to make such accusations. As early as 1965, Walter Martin wrote "The Psychological Structure of Cultism." Later books, like Ron Enroth's *Youth Brainwashing and Extremist Cults* (1978), applied the theory of brainwashing to new religions generally.

Flo Conway and Jim Siegelman produced a variation of the brainwashing thesis in their book *Snapping* (1978). They argued that groups like the Unification Church use conversion techniques that place people under psychological pressure until they snap. Thus personality change among converts was possible. When it was first published, many Christians welcomed Conway and Siegelman's book because it presented a direct attack upon the Moonies and their leader. But these readers completely ignored a short statement on page 46 that equates the conversion practices of the Moonies with those of evangelical Christians. Later, in *Holy Terror* (1984), Conway and Siegelman press their attack upon evangelicals directly, insisting that all conversions—not only among would-be new religionists but also among would-be evangelical Christians—are a form of snapping or brainwashing.

We reject the brainwashing thesis because it is based on a mechanistic view of the human being that denies choice and responsibility. The notion of brainwashing is both anti-Christian and opposed to the entire Western tradition of philosophical, political, and social thought, which has always been grounded in the assumption that individuals are responsible for their actions. Once we allow that under certain circumstances individuals can be brainwashed, the basis for our entire justice system crumbles, making a mockery of such institutions as the Nuremberg war crimes tribunal. If brainwashing exists, then war criminals in Bosnia-Herzegovina, Rwanda, or anywhere else could win acquittal simply by claiming that they were not responsible for their actions because they were brainwashed. Seen in this light, the brainwashing thesis is an attack on all religions and human decency in general.

Equally important is the considerable evidence that people join new religions of their own free will. We have four main sources of information about recruitment to cults. First, there are testimonies by ex–cult members who have totally repudiated the beliefs of the cult but strongly deny that they were trapped by techniques of mind control. Second, there are many parents, relatives, and friends of cult members and former members who seem to understand that the person they knew freely chose to join the cult. Third, there are many studies by social scientists indicating that individuals have different conversion careers, which would suggest that the conversion process is voluntary. Finally, accounts of the cult members themselves often indicate that their decision to become members in new religions followed a long search not only for meaning but also for the resolution of major life crises (see Barker 1984; Levine 1984; H. Richardson 1980; Bromley and Richardson 1983).

## The Question of Deprogramming

Those who assume that members of new religions are in fact brainwashed sometimes attempt to undo the brainwashing by means of a process called "deprogramming." Deprogrammers claim to "rescue" people from cults by using a variety of techniques to coerce them into renouncing their former allegiances. In the past deprogramming always involved kidnapping and forceable detention. But more recently such clearly illegal activities have given way to milder forms of persuasion known as "exit counseling" (Hassan 1990).

Nevertheless, we have many questions about both the premise and the effectiveness of deprogramming. For deprogramming to work, subjects must be convinced that they joined a religious group against their will. They must, therefore, renounce all responsibility for their conversion and accept the idea that in some mysterious way their minds were controlled by others. But this idea has some very unsettling implications. If one has lost control of one's mind once, why can't it happen again? What is to prevent another person or group from gaining a similar influence? How can deprogrammed people ever be certain that they are really doing what they want to do? By its very nature, deprogramming destroys a person's identity and is likely to create permanent anxiety about freedom of choice. In other words, deprogramming returns subjects to a state of perpetual childhood where they are forever dependent on the advice and judgment of others.

Instead of encouraging people to accept that they chose to join a religion or to realize that they made a mistake, deprogramming allows people to deny their actions and blame others: It robs people of their sense of responsibility. Western morality, the legal tradition, and social norms are built upon the assumption of responsibility. This emphasis comes from both the Greek **Socratic tradition** and the Bible. Socrates and the majority of Greek and Roman philosophers after him repeatedly argued that humans are responsible for their actions. Likewise, the Bible emphasizes human accountability and calls humans to choose between good and evil. Yet deprogramming denies humans' responsibility to make such choices.

Saul Levine, a professor of psychiatry in Toronto, writes that although there are many reports of individuals having been successfully deprogrammed, he has himself seen only one such case. To make his case, he defines a "successful deprogramming" as one that results in "the avoidance of the religious group for longer than a year after deprogramming, and the maintenance of a 'normal' symptom-free life outside the cult" (Levine 1979:600).

Levine presents numerous examples that suggest that for many young people cult membership can be understood as part of the process of growing up. That is not to say that Levine endorses new religious movements. Rather, he believes that fears about the supposed harm they do are grossly overstated and that in most cases the cure is worse than the temporary problems that membership in a new religion may create (Levine 1984:194).

The importance of Levine's work is that he shows scientifically that popular claims about brainwashing as an explanation for why some people join contemporary religious movements are false. He also provides an alternative way of viewing conversion that makes more sense of the data than crude arguments about psychological manipulation. Before we can accept his case and develop our own views using a framework that rejects the brainwashing thesis, however, we must examine some popular evidence that is often presented to "prove" that contemporary religions are dangerous cults.

## Jonestown and the Case Against New Religions

The strongest arguments against new religious movements are emotional ones based on lurid press reports about cult suicides and other bizarre events. The most famous of these events is the **Jonestown** tragedy of 18 November 1978, when over 800 people appear to have committed suicide in the jungles of Guyana (see *Newsweek,* 4 December 1978).

It is not surprising that the People's Temple, with its utopian community in Jonestown, Guyana, has been the subject of intense debate and academic study (J. Richardson, 1980). Steve Rose's readable *Jesus and Jim Jones* (1979), which contains a transcript of Jones's last tape-recorded message to his followers, shows clearly that the events in Jonestown do not fit the image propagated by anti-cult crusaders.

John Hall (1989) provides ample evidence that **Jim Jones** was a social malcontent from early childhood who as a teenager and college student embraced a crude form of Marxism. He saw religion as one way of "**exploiting the contradictions**" in American society and used religion to gain a following for his communist agenda. Faking faith healings, repudiating Christian dogma, and mimicking Christian experiences, Jones built a solid group of followers devoted to the apocalyptic message he openly identified with communism. David Chidester (1988) attempts to understand the inner logic of the group in a sympathetic and provocative manner. Unfortunately, the results of investigations like these, which contradict the image of Jonestown as a mass suicide based on fanatical religious commitments, are not generally reported in the press.

Reviewing the vast literature on Jonestown, we find several points we need to take into consideration if we want to understand new religions. First, as we will see in later chapters, far from fitting the usual profile of a contemporary religious movement, the People's Temple is more accurately described as a bizarre leftist political movement led by a failed social reformer.

Second, although its leader, the Reverend Jim Jones, was an ordained minister, he was not a Bible-thumping fundamentalist who became a cult leader. Jones was a minister in a mainstream, respectable American denomination, the **Disciples of Christ**. After gaining his first degree from Indiana University in Bloomington, Jones did graduate work at Butler University in Indianapolis. He was active in numerous left-wing causes and was widely respected for his social work; he despised fundamentalism and ridiculed anyone who took the Bible seriously.

Third, the social profile of People's Temple members was far different from that of most other contemporary religious movements. At that time such groups tended to attract well-educated young professionals. But most members of the People's Temple were poor, semiliterate welfare recipients.

Given these differences, it is difficult to argue that the People's Temple is in any way typical of new or contemporary religions. Even more significant is the startling evidence that although many members may have unwittingly committed suicide, they did not realize that they had drunk poison until it was too late. Others who seem to have seen their comrades dying appear to have attempted to escape, only to be shot dead by Jones and his closest companions. Thus the evidence suggests that the majority of the people who died at Jonestown did not commit suicide because they were brainwashed into obeying whatever Jones told them to do. Rather, they were murdered by a leader and inner circle of confidants who had gone insane (Richardson 1980).

## The Waco Tragedy

Even if the public has misunderstood the significance of Jonestown, vivid TV images of the last hours of **David Koresh** and the **Branch Davidians** at their compound in Waco, Texas, on 19 April 1993 reinforce the view that cults are dangerous. Add to this highly publicized event the deaths associated with the **Solar Temple** in Canada and Switzerland as well as the **Aum cult**'s gas attack on commuters in the Tokyo underground and a scary picture emerges.

Once again we have to be careful in the way we understand media reports. What is certain is that Koresh and his followers died in a fiery hell. What is uncertain is how the fire started. Conspiracy theorists blame the U.S. government in general and the Bureau of Alcohol, Tobacco, and Firearms in particular, but arguments that attempt to exonerate Koresh completely seem unfounded.

We can see the depth of feeling on both sides of this issue by comparing David Leppard's *Fire and Blood: The True Story of David Koresh and the Waco Siege* (1993) with Dick J. Reavis's *Ashes of Waco* (1995). The dust jacket of Leppard's book boldly proclaims that Koresh was a "seriously disturbed paedophile and murderer" who practiced "child abuse and sexual ritual." In contrast Reavis and defenders of Koresh accuse the U.S. government of a cover-up, and some suggest criminal acts on the part of government agencies (for an evenhanded treatment, see *The World and I*, June 1994).

The commonsense view is that neither the government nor Koresh was totally innocent in this tragic affair. It is clear that government agents made some big blunders. But even tragic mistakes are no proof of a deliberate murder plot. The wilder accusations against Koresh and his group, such as ritual abuse, seem equally invalid. Koresh and his followers held beliefs that outsiders misunderstood. As a result of a custody battle, accusations of sexual misconduct were made that government agencies were forced to take seriously, and after that things got out of control.

It seems plausible that neither Koresh nor his followers started the fire but that it began by accident and quickly spread through a building that was tinder dry. This being the case, the tragedy may not have been suicide at all. Some people counter by saying that some of Koresh's followers had been shot and that this surely proves either a planned suicide or murder. This is not necessarily so. An accidental fire may have trapped a large number of people who chose to kill themselves rather than die in the flames.

Then, too, it is quite possible that Koresh and his followers did commit suicide. All we can say is that the few survivors claimed the fire was accidental and that there was no suicide plan. Of course they may have lied or have been deceived by Koresh. We simply do not know the truth.

## The Solar Temple and Terror in Tokyo

Anti-cult groups also cite the murders associated with the Solar Temple and Japanese Aum movement as proof that cults represent a threat to society. On the morning of 4 October 1994, police were called to fires at properties owned by the Solar Temple, a New Age movement, in Canada and Switzerland. At least twenty-three people had died in what appeared to be a murder-suicide. From police reports, it now seems quite certain that the majority of the people who died were murdered (*Alberta Report*, 24 October 1994). As at Jonestown, the leaders seem to have decided to carry out the murders. In this case it may be that they planned to commit suicide and take their followers with them.

But there are disturbing indications that perhaps a more banal criminal motive led to the deaths. The Swiss and other police, for example, found evidence of links to money laundering and the drug trade (*Stern*, 13 October 1994). It is possible, therefore, that everyone was murdered. To date all that can be said for certain is that members of the group died under suspicious circumstances. Of course saying that people may have been murdered rather than having committed suicide is little comfort to their families. But the differences between murder and suicide become important when politicians and lawmakers consider their social implications and decide on steps society can take to prevent a repeat of such happenings.

The poison gas attack on the Tokyo underground on 20 March 1995 is a completely different sort of atrocity. Members of a new religious movement, Aum

Shinrikyo, deliberately plotted and executed an act of unspeakable barbarism against innocent civilians. Over 5,000 people fell victim to the attack; ten died and more than fifty were seriously injured. Quick action by the Japanese police led to rapid arrests and the trial of the movement's leaders (*Time*, 3 April 1995). The difference between this event and earlier cult-related deaths is that for the first time uninvolved outsiders were the target of violence.

## Cause for Concern?

In all of these cases, people were murdered apparently at the instigation of the leaders of religious groups. But to draw the conclusion that these examples prove that *all* contemporary religions are harmful is to commit the fallacy of logic called composition, that is, to use a property or part of a whole as though it were the same thing as the whole. Although a few contemporary religious movements may be dangerous, this fact does not make all of them dangerous cults (Singer and Lalich 1995).

The question we must face is, Do new religious movements as a whole represent a threat to society? Here it is important to recognize that however destructive some religious groups may be, they represent a small minority of religious groups in the world. Compared to the number of deaths from automobile accidents, airplane crashes, and gang killings in major U.S. cities like Los Angeles, the number of people whose deaths can be connected with new religions is negligible.

Once again, telling the relative of a victim of a cult-related death that the person who died was statistically more likely to have been killed by a gang member or to have died in a car accident is no comfort. But for legislators and concerned individuals who are seeking to create a viable society, it is important data. The problem is that any legislation specifically aimed at cults inevitably affects all religions, including contemporary religious movements that offer their members genuine religious experiences. Therefore, instead of passing laws that identify cults as a problem, it is always safer to rely on more general laws against fraud and so on. As we will see in the next section, legislation against new religions is often inspired by the self-interest of established religions, which, like any business, resent competition and the loss of their market share.

## Judgment in Berlin

The global significance of what we have called the great anti-cult crusade and the threat to civil liberties when governments regulate religion can be seen by examining an obscure 1995 court case in Berlin. In the wake of the Waco tragedy, German social agencies and lawmakers developed a renewed interest in "dangerous cults." As a result, in October 1994 the Youth Department of the Berlin senate published a short booklet on "new religious and ideological movements and so-called psycho groups" (Schipmann 1994). This 143-page publication identified thirty religious groups as potential dangers and warned individuals to avoid them. These groups included the International Society for Krishna Consciousness (ISKCON), better known as the **Hare Krishna movement; transcendental meditation** (TM); the Unification Church; **scientology;** and a fast-growing, American-style charismatic church called the **Church on the Way** (Gemeinde auf dem Weg).

Realizing that official recognition as a potentially dangerous cult would affect its ability to obtain planning permission to construct a new church building, the Church on the Way launched an appeal. The first step was to seek a court injunction against the distribution of the booklet, which government agencies were giving away free of charge. Instead of agreeing with the church that the booklet represented a gross infringement on religious and civil liberties, the Berlin high court upheld the right of the state to publish such literature. The judges reasoned that as long as a "suspicion of danger" existed about any religious group, the state had a right, indeed a duty, to warn citizens about such groups.

In reaching their decision, the judges accepted testimony from people who claimed the church was manipulative and had harmed them psychologically. This testimony by witnesses who were never cross-examined was supported by hearsay evidence and the opinions of various German theologians who called themselves cult experts. But no valid scientific evidence based on sociological or psychological studies was presented. The court ignored North American and even German sociological studies that disagreed with the findings of the theologians.

Countertestimony by people who had found the church helpful and the views of expert witnesses who had carried out participant observation in the congregation were dismissed with the comment: "The fact that such psychical derogations are not noticed by active church members and other persons . . . contradicts neither the credibility of the informants of the opposing petitioner nor the actual existence of group-manipulative elements in the worship services" (Twenty-seventh Chamber of the Administrative Court of Berlin 1995).

The case of the Church on the Way is of great interest to anyone studying new religious movements because it highlights the ease with which theological judgments can be translated into legal realities. We must recognize that what may be presented to the public as a religious issue may be rooted in economic and other concerns. The Church on the Way is a charismatic church alien to many Germans. Like all American churches, its ministers are supported by freewill donations from the congregation. By contrast, ministers in Germany's state churches are paid out of funds raised by the government in the form of a church tax. They are highly educated civil servants with all the rights, privileges, status, and lifelong security that make a job in the German civil service such a desirable achievement. Many German pastors in the state churches thus consider churches financed through freewill offerings as a direct threat to their own economic well-being. They fear that someday an ambitious politician might decide that German churches ought to be privatized rather than having the government support them through a complex tax system.

To pay for German reunification, the German government raised taxes and created a series of new taxes. Many people responded by going through the complicated procedures required to exempt themselves from paying church tax. As a result, German state churches saw a dramatic decline in their incomes (*Der Spiegel* 25, 46, 15 June 1992; 10, 49, 6 March 1995). In the newly formed diocese of Berlin-Brandenburg, for example, around 5,000 people a month were withdrawing from the church tax scheme in late 1994 (*Berliner Zeitung*, 30 January 1995). Such a massive loss of support made deep inroads into church finances throughout Germany, increasing the anxiety of the clergy.

At the same time, in sharp contrast to the state churches, many free evangelical and charismatic churches, like the Church on the Way, were experiencing rapid growth (Johannes Institut 1991:xix–xxiv; Daiber 1995:134–137). These churches are typical of many growing churches found throughout North America and increasingly in Europe. On any Sunday morning their large congregations attend lively worship services that feature understandable sermons. These congregations typically include a large number of non-Germans, mainly refugees from Eastern Europe but also a surprising number of English-speaking members, who are provided with instantaneous translations.

In North America churches like these are seen as success stories. In Germany they are definitely outside the norm and so are easily labeled cults. Of course we must recall that the virulent cult activities in the 1920s and 1930s helped usher in national socialism (Mosse 1981). This history has made Germans cautious.

## The Anti-cult Network

In Germany criticism of cults serves to bolster the authority of the state churches and provides a basis for seeking legislation to hinder the development of rival religious organizations that might create a free market, offering a wide range of religious choice (Stark 1996; *Charisma,* November 1995:18–19). But there is more at stake. German cult experts are actively lobbying various European governments to enact laws that will limit evangelical activity by religious groups.[2] For example, the Protestant Church's cult expert for Berlin-Brandenburg, the Reverend Thomas Gandow, has taken an active role in criticizing the charismatic churches and new religions (*Stern,* 4 May 1995:37–40). At the same time, he has helped to establish an international anti-cult organization and attended a meeting to advise Russian legislators about the need to limit religious freedom in Russia. He makes no secret of his hope that eventually the European Community will adopt legislation to limit the activities of new religions and American-style evangelical or independent churches. Once this happens, he told us in March 1995, he hopes the U.S. Congress will act to "regularize" religious organizations.

German cult experts exchange information with anti-cult groups in America and other parts of the world (*Berliner Dialog* 1, Easter 1995; Lange 1993). At the same time, German theologians such as Friedrich-Wilhelm Haack add academic weight to American anti-cult propaganda such as the film *Gods of the New Age*.

It is thus no exaggeration to talk about a global anti-cult network. David Bromley and Anson Shupe have documented the growth of a well-organized and complex anti-cult movement in America (Bromley and Shupe 1981; Shupe and Bromley 1980). More recently, they have drawn attention to cross-cultural aspects of the anti-cult movement (Shupe and Bromley 1994). As do religious movements in America, the anti-cult movement draws together concerned individuals. But in Europe, especially in Germany, the anti-cult movement is part of the church establishment and as such is supported by government-raised church taxes. The German anti-cultists thus have far more resources available to them than do their North American counterparts (Haack 1994:70–80).

## How Many People Are Cult Members?

In 1965 Martin believed that there were 10 million cult members worldwide. To arrive at this figure, he estimated the number of people who belonged to groups like the Christian Scientists, the Church of Jesus Christ of Latter-Day Saints, and Jehovah's Witnesses. Twenty-five years later, Hassan claimed that more than 3 million Americans were involved with "destructive cults." Nowhere in his book does he explain how he reached this figure. Bromley and Shupe argued that contrary to popular opinion, which put cult membership in the millions, we simply do not know how many new religions exist in North America or how many people they attract. Nevertheless, they did estimate that the total membership of six better-known groups was relatively small (Bromley and Shupe 1981:24–56). Another observer has estimated that there are about 600 new religions in the United States, with a total membership of no more than between 150,000 and 200,000 (Miller 1995:4–5). It is clear that these are not large movements.

Taking a very different approach, based on complex statistical analysis of multiple sources, Rodney Stark and William Bainbridge estimate that in 1985 there were 417 sects and 501 cult movements in the United States. According to their figures, around 7 million Americans, or 3 percent of the U.S. population, may be involved with new religions (Stark and Bainbridge 1985:130–131). Their numbers seem to be confirmed by the Gallup Organization's finding that in 1987 2 percent of Americans identified themselves with "other" religions. Significantly, however, this figure went up to 5 percent among young people (Gallup and Castelli 1989:25). Similar figures are available for Canada, Great Britain, and Germany (Bibby 1993:45–57, 1995:129–130; Barker 1989:145–155; Daiber 1995:136–138, 148, 151).

It is no wonder, then, that the attention of cult experts turned to the so-called New Age movement and conservative Christian groups in the 1980s. Yet in 1990 Gordon Melton expressed his belief that the New Age movement had managed to attract no more than a few "hundreds of thousands of individuals," and as a result he foresaw a "bright" but strictly limited future for the movement (Melton,

Clark, and Kelly 1990:xxv). Stark and Roger Finke, using a survey by Barry Kosmin, estimated a much lower figure of "religious preference" for New Age beliefs—a mere 20,000 Americans (Finke and Stark 1992:245).

Such estimates could easily lead to the conclusion that new religions are unimportant. Pronouncements about the death of the New Age movement were made at least a decade before Melton, Stark, and Finke, yet it is clear that it continued to grow (Ferguson 1992). And it is impossible to deny New Age influences on medicine and education (Rankin-Box 1995).

The problem is the difficulty in estimating influence and membership using indirect means. For example, Finke and Stark argue that because the *New Age Journal* has a circulation of "fewer than 150,000," the "audience" for New Age ideas "is probably not all that large" (Finke and Stark 1992:245). But this logic is obviously false. The circulation of *Christianity Today*, the flagship magazine for American evangelicals, is around 250,000. Yet no one disputes that around 50 million Americans identify themselves as evangelicals. Circulation figures can be misleading.

Predicting future events is risky. With few exceptions most observers completely failed to recognize the decline of the Soviet Union and were completely taken by surprise by the fall of the Berlin Wall. If the large and well-financed U.S. Department of Defense has a hard time predicting political developments, should we expect a few academics with minuscule resources to fare any better in forecasting developments in religious and social life? In 1990 British sociologist Steve Bruce published a well-researched book proclaiming the demise of the Christian right in American politics (Bruce 1990). Yet only a short time later the Christian Coalition emerged as a major force (*Time*, 15 May 1995). Social scientists have an excellent track record for getting things wrong.

## Conclusion

We have argued against exaggerating the size, influence, and danger represented by contemporary religious movements. We have also attempted to show how the public was led to believe that cults represent a major threat to society. Nevertheless, we disagree with many of our academic colleagues in dismissing contemporary religions as either unimportant or totally benign. Many contemporary religions are simply revitalization movements. Others are genuinely new religions that lack strong social ties and thus can develop dangerous tendencies.

The fears of German cult experts like Gandow are not unfounded: A cultlike movement led by **General Erich von Ludendorff** and his trance-channeling wife, Mathilde von Kemnitz (Ludendorff 1937), played an important role in the destruction of the Weimar Republic. In many respects the early Nazi movement can be seen as a cult movement (Rhodes 1980; Laqueur 1962). Like today's cults, it was so small and clearly on the fringe that few educated Germans took it seriously. As late as the 1928 election, National Socialists were able to attract only 3 percent of the vote; by 1930 this had risen to 18 percent, and by the time of the last free election in March 1933 it was 44 percent (Gordon 1984:31).

Of course social unrest and the distress caused by the Great Depression were primarily responsible for the Nazi victory (Kershaw 1990). Nevertheless, that their share of the vote rose by a phenomenal 41 percent in five years ought to warn us that with the right combination of social and economic factors, seemingly insignificant groups can seize power with relative ease. No wonder many Europeans are scared by *any* movement that demands commitment from its members.

On the one hand, there are good reasons some people are afraid of new religions. On the other hand, exaggerated claims and unnecessary panic have led many people to fear and attack genuine religious movements. Since the mid-1960s new religious movements have regularly made headlines. Consequently, many people, including legislators in the United States, Britain, and Germany, have a deep distrust of unfamiliar religious movements.

At the end of June 1996, many Americans were shocked by the comments of the newly appointed security adviser to Russian president Boris Yeltsin, Alexander Lebed, who wanted to restrict the actions of Mormons and American evangelists in Russia. Yet Lebed was simply reflecting the views of American and German cult experts. Lebed and many other Russians regard evangelical movements as dangerous cults. But what is a cult? To answer this question, we must consider the issue of definition and the identification of different types of religious organization. We do this in Chapter 2.

## KEY TERMS

**Ad hominem:** Latin for "to the man." This classic fallacy of logic may be abusive, involving an appeal to passions or prejudices rather than the intellect, or circumstantial, pointing to a supposed or real relationship between people's circumstances and their contentions.

**Antichrist:** Used by the author of the Johannine epistles for those who deny Christ (I John 2:18–22; II John 7). The New Testament implies that at the end of human history the Antichrist will wage war on the Church. This belief has fueled many millenarian movements.

**Apologetics:** The reasoned defense of the Christian religion against intellectual objections; attempts to establish certain elements of Christianity as true or at least not demonstrably untrue.

**Augustine of Hippo, Saint** (354–430): The greatest of the Latin Christian fathers and African theologians and one of the outstanding thinkers of all time; author of *Confessions*, a spiritual classic and the first real Christian autobiography.

**Aum cult:** A fanatical Japanese new religion that blends shamanistic practices, New Age beliefs, and meditation and has been accused of carrying out a gas attack on the Tokyo subway on 20 March 1995.

**Aurelius, Marcus** (121–180): Emperor of Rome and a Stoic philosopher famous for his *Meditations*.

**Böhme, Jakob** (1575–1624): German Lutheran mystic who speculated about God and his relationship to creation and was accused of being both a pantheist and a dualist. His work influenced pietism, romanticism, and New Age movements.

**Branch Davidians:** A very small religious movement that originated in 1934 and claimed secret knowledge about the impending end of the world. The movement came to a fiery end in a confrontation with U.S. government forces in Waco, Texas, in April 1993.

**Bruno, Giordano** (1548–1600): Italian Dominican priest and theologian who developed a pantheistic view of the universe based on the Copernican theory. He was burned at the stake for heresy.

**Buddhist:** The Western name for a follower of the teachings of Gautama (563–483 B.C.?), an Indian prince who claimed to have attained spiritual enlightenment and is known as the Buddha.

**Calvinist:** Someone who accepts the teaching of Calvinism, which originated with the reformer John Calvin's interpretation and exposition of Scripture in his *Institutes of the Christian Religion* (1536).

**Charismatic movement:** A religious revival movement within the historic Christian tradition that started in the 1950s and took form in the early 1960s, spreading Pentecostal-like experiences to mainline denominations.

**Christian Scientists:** The Church of Christ Scientist founded by Mary Baker Eddy (1821–1910), who dedicated her life to promoting a form of healing based on ideas taken from Christianity, Hinduism, and Buddhism.

**Church on the Way:** A large charismatic Christian church in Berlin, Germany.

**Creeds:** From the Latin *credo,* "I believe"; an intellectual statement of belief that is a distinctive feature of Christianity.

**Cults:** Deviant religious organizations with novel beliefs and practices.

**Disciples of Christ:** A mainline American religious movement that began to develop in 1811 out of Presbyterianism through the work of Alexander Campbell. Associated churches vest organizational power, including the appointment of ministers, in the local congregation. Thus they reject the more centralized Presbyterian system that places an area presbytery, or ministerial association, over the local congregation.

**Erigena, Johannes Scotus** (815?–877): Irish philosopher who translated the works of Dionysius (A.D. 500?) from Greek. These works encouraged the growth of medieval theology and Christian mysticism and promoted a form of Christian pantheism.

**Exploiting the contradictions:** A popular term in Marxist theory. According to Marx, capitalist society is riddled with contradictions that can lead to revolution. The task of the revolutionary is to increase popular awareness of social contradictions to provoke a revolution.

**Fichte, Johann Gottlieb** (1762–1814): German philosopher who promoted his own version of Kantian thought. His *Address to the German Nation* (1808–1809) is one of the foundation documents of modern nationalism.

**Fundamentalist:** A conservative theological movement that arose in American Protestantism in the 1920s in opposition to theological "modernism." Fundamentalism should be understood primarily as an attempt to protect the essential doctrines, or "fundamentals," of the Christian faith from the eroding effects of modern thought. The term has recently been applied to Muslims and members of other faiths who wish to retain their traditional beliefs.

**Goethe, Johann Wolfgang von** (1749–1832): Arguably the greatest German poet, philosopher, and man of letters.

**Graham, William** ("Billy") (1918–): Evangelist and Southern Baptist preacher whose work did much to revive evangelical religion in America.

**Hare Krishna movement**: The International Society for Krishna Consciousness (ISKCON), founded on his arrival in the United States in 1965 by Swami A. C. Bhaktivedanta Prabhupāda.

**Hegel, Georg Wilhelm Friedrich** (1770–1831): German idealist philosopher whose work strongly influenced Karl Marx and many other nineteenth-century thinkers.

**Holy Spirit**: The Third Person in the Christian godhead, or Trinity, believed by Christians to indwell believers and guide the Church. In the twentieth century, the theology of the Holy Spirit has become a central issue in the charismatic movement.

**Human aura**: The occult belief that each human has a spiritual body that occupies and envelops the physical body.

**Jehovah's Witnesses**: A highly rationalist, pacifist sect founded by Charles Taze Russell in the late nineteenth century. It originally mixed a blend of interpretation of biblical prophecy with pyramidology.

**Jones, Jim** (1931–1978): Minister of the mainstream Christian denomination the Disciples of Christ and founder of the People's Temple, whose followers may have committed mass suicide at Jonestown, Guyana, in 1978.

**Jonestown**: The small utopian communal settlement in the jungle of Guyana founded by Jim Jones that became the site of a mass murder or suicide that claimed the lives of over 700 people.

**Kirlian photography**: A photographic technique that shows a pattern of colors around the subject, which occultists say is the human aura. Scientists offer a different explanation.

**Koresh, David** (1959–1993): Leader of the Branch Davidians, whose life ended when he and his followers died in a fire in April 1993 after a long siege by U.S. agents.

**Lessing, Gotthold Ephraim** (1729–1781): German Enlightenment philosopher, publicist, playwright, critic, and art theorist who worked for the free and democratic development of the German people and their culture and was highly critical of the possibility of historical knowledge, especially of religious events.

**Ludendorff, Erich von** (1865–1937): German supreme commander during World War I who refused to accept responsibility for the German defeat and blamed Jews and socialists for the Allied victory.

**Magicians in Egypt**: A reference to the biblical story of the contest between Moses and the magicians of the Egyptian pharaoh in Exodus 7–10.

**Miracles**: Unusual events seen as the significant intervention in human affairs of the divine. They are believed to confirm the spiritual power and authority of a teacher or religious leader. The idea of miracles came under strong attack in the eighteenth century, when a miracle was defined as an event that broke the law of nature and was by definition impossible.

**Monism**: The metaphysical theory that there is one fundamental reality of which all other beings are attributes, or modes, if they are real at all.

**Moon, Sun Myung** (1920–): Korean founder and prophetic leader of the Unification Church.

**Moonies**: The name given to followers of Sun Myung Moon and members of the Unification Church, who prefer to be called Unificationists.

**Mormons**: The name given to members of the Church of Jesus Christ of Latter-Day Saints, founded by Joseph Smith in 1830.

**Moses** (12th–13th century B.C.): The great lawgiver of the Jews and the founder of the Jewish nation. He is traditionally credited with writing the Pentateuch.

**Neoplatonism:** A religious and philosophical movement that emerged in Greco-Roman society as a blend of essentially Platonic, Pythagorean, Stoic, and Aristotelian elements; its chief exponent was Plotinus. The philosophy had a strong mystical inclination and was easily adapted to the needs of Christian thinkers seeking to reconcile Christian and pagan thought.

**New Age movement:** A loosely linked set of religious movements that began as a self-conscious entity with the publication of the *East-West Journal* in 1971 and found its most forceful advocate in the writings of actress Shirley MacLaine. It promotes a mystical occultism based on a synthesis of Yogic and Abramic religions and philosophies.

**New religions:** Religious movements, cults, and sects that have developed in the past 200 years as a reaction to modernity. Although they embrace the new and reject a single, ongoing tradition, they borrow their ideas, doctrines, and practices from older religious traditions.

**Occultist:** A modern term used to describe someone who holds a wide spectrum of beliefs and practices that involve ritual magic and the practice of various forms of spiritualism. In recent years many occult ideas have merged in the so-called New Age movement.

**Orthodoxy:** A religious system that claims to be the true or right belief. It contrasts itself with heresy, the deviation from the historical tradition of a particular faith.

**Pantheism:** The doctrine that all things and beings are attributes or appearances of one single unified spiritual reality or being—hence nature and God are believed to be identical. Although the term is often incorrectly applied to Hinduism and various other Yogic religions, it appears to describe many new religious movements and the views of most New Age thinkers.

**Paul, Saint** (1st century A.D.): The second most important figure in Christianity, whose letters form an important part of the New Testament.

**Plotinus** (A.D. 205–270): The last great Neoplatonist philosopher in the Greco-Roman world.

**Pluralism:** Any philosophical system that emphasizes diversity and rejects monism. Many modern societies use the term to refer to social systems in which different religious communities live together in one nation.

**Radhakrishnan** (1888–1975): Major Indian philosopher, educator, and statesman who promoted interreligious dialogue based on a revitalized Hindu tradition in accord with scientific thought and the Vedas, ancient sacred texts of the Hindus.

**Reductionism:** To reduce a complex argument or state of affairs to a single or few simple concepts in such a way as to distort reality.

**Reincarnation:** A technical term in Hindu and Buddhist thought associated with the doctrine of karma, implying the continuation of consciousness after physical death but not necessarily the rebirth of a soul. In the West, however, it is usually confused with ideas of transmigration of the soul or rebirth through many lifetimes and is promoted by claims that people "remember" their "past lives."

**Relativism:** Recognizing the importance of the social environment in determining the content of beliefs. Relativism maintains that there are no universal standards of good or bad, right or wrong, truth or error.

**Revitalization movements:** Religious movements that seek to revive, or revitalize, an ancient religious tradition.

**Russell, Charles Taze** (1852–1916): Known as "Pastor Russell," he preached that the return of Christ had occurred invisibly in 1874 and predicted the end of the world would come in 1914. His followers became known as Russellites and formed the International Bible Students' Association, which later split into a number of groups, the best-known being the Jehovah's Witnesses.

**Śankara** (788–838): Indian philosopher and advocate of Vedānta who founded a number of monasteries in India and seems to have regarded Siva and Vishnu as equal manifestations of the universal spirit. He taught the illusory nature of the separate existence of the spirits of humans and Brahman (the universe as a spiritual entity) and emphasized that māyā existed from all eternity as the only material or substantial cause of the external world.

**Scientology:** A controversial therapy based on a new religious movement founded by L. Ron Hubbard (1911–1976), who in many respects was a modern shaman.

**Secular:** The profane, worldly, civil, or nonreligious as distinguished from the religious or the sacred.

**Seventh-Day Adventists:** The name adopted in 1861 by a dynamic revitalization movement that expects the imminent return of Christ. Now a fast-growing denomination with extensive missionary programs, the members emphasize education and have an impressive record for medical work.

**Shell shock:** A term that originated during World War I, when many soldiers became mental wrecks as a result of continuous artillery bombardment in the trenches.

**Socratic tradition:** The Western philosophic tradition of questioning attributed to the method used by the Greek philosopher Socrates.

**Soka Gakkai:** A Japanese new religious movement dating back to 1930 but formally founded in 1937 by Tsunesaburo Makiguchi and Jōsei Toda as a lay association of Buddhists.

**Solar Temple:** A New Age occult group whose members were involved in a murder/suicide on 4 October 1994.

**Sorcery:** The exercise of ritual magic used with evil intent and often involving the use of physical objects, spells, potions, and poisons.

**Spinoza, Baruch** (or Benedict) (1632–1677): Dutch materialist philosopher who was excommunicated for his free thought by the Jewish community of Amsterdam. He believed that mastery over nature and the perfection of humans was the purpose of knowledge.

**Suzuki, Daisetsu Teitaro** (1870–1966): Japanese scholar who popularized Buddhism in the West through his writings on Zen.

**Transcendental meditation** (TM): The first really successful new religious movement of the 1960s, which emerged from the Hindu tradition as a kind of therapy offering psychological well-being. The founder, Maharishi Mahesh Yogi (1913–), denies that TM is a religion. After receiving U.S. government funding as a form of therapy, the movement's leaders were taken to court in 1978, and TM was found to be a religion under the terms of U.S. law.

**Unification Church:** A new religious movement founded by the Korean spiritual leader Sun Myung Moon in 1954. The aim of the movement is to unite all Christian churches and, later, other religions.

**Witchcraft:** A system of beliefs and practices involving supernatural power and agencies thought to influence human affairs. It is generally distinguished from sorcery and takes many forms in different cultures. Since the Enlightenment it has been usual to regard witchcraft as an irrational system of beliefs belonging to a primitive past. In the West popular belief in witchcraft died out during the seventeenth and eighteenth centuries to be revived in the late nineteenth century by various occultists as a form of ritual magic; it continues today with groups such as Wiccans.

## NOTES

1. A fuller discussion of this issue is to be found in Irving Hexham, "The Evangelical Response to the New Age Movement," in Lewis and Melton 1992:152–163.

2. Information from Olga Polykosvskaya, former special adviser on religious education to the Russian minister of education; David Goodenough, the Berlin-based Eastern European representative of the Church Missionary Society (CMS); and Per Borgaard, editor of the Danish magazine *Ikon*.

## 2

# From Cults to New Religions and Global Culture

*By religion I mean Christianity; by Christianity I mean Protestantism; by Protestantism I mean the Church of England as established by law.*

*Henry Fielding,* Tom Jones, *book 3, chap. 3*

Clearly defining the term "cult" is difficult. In popular usage the word has come to be equated with brainwashing and sinister manipulation. Many scholars therefore prefer to speak about "new religious movements." In this chapter we begin by surveying various uses of "cult." We then look at terms like "**church**" and "**sect**," which often involve a built-in theological bias. This discovery leads to a redefinition of our terms. We conclude the chapter with a discussion of contemporary and new religions.

## Defining Cults

In addition to adopting a **theological** definition of "cult," Walter Martin introduced various social indicators such as "terminological deception" and "closed mindedness" (Martin 1976:19, 24). Later social indicators like those Martin used became the basis for secular definitions of cults. For example, in his book *Combatting Cult Mind Control*, Steven Hassan says a "destructive cult . . . is a group which violates the rights of its members and damages them through the abusive techniques of unethical mind control" (Hassan 1990:37).

The problem with definitions like this is that they raise more problems than they solve. Before we can decide whether a group is a cult or not, we must first define "rights," "abusive techniques," and "mind control." Hassan attempts to do this, but his explanations are not very helpful. According to Hassan, the three key indicators of a cult are "leadership, doctrine and membership" (Hassan 1990:97). But as soon as he tries to explain how these indicators work, he runs into trouble. Under the heading "leadership," for example, he asks his readers to consider the life histories and qualifications of religious leaders. Then he provides examples of a car salesman, a truck driver, and a science fiction writer, all of whom founded successful religious movements. The problem, of course, is that before becoming a religious teacher **Jesus** was a carpenter, **Muhammed** was a camel driver, and the **Buddha** lived by begging. Occupation clearly has little to do with religious insight. Nor does education, because at one time or another Jesus, Muhammed, and the Buddha were all accused by their critics of lacking suitable education.

Hassan's second criterion of a cult is that it goes against the premise that "a group's beliefs should be freely disclosed to any person who wants to join it" (Hassan 1990:99). There are two problems with this criterion. First, what does Hassan mean by "disclosed"? A common criticism of groups such as the Unification Church is that they overwhelm members and potential converts with "silly but engaging lectures on their beliefs" (Freed 1980:28, 51). Yet Hassan, who is an ex-Unificationist, complains that cults (and he clearly has the Unification Church in mind) provide too little information to converts. How much information does someone need, then, in order to be allowed to join a religious movement?

If Buddhists convert to Christianity, should they be required to spend years studying **doctrine** before they are baptized? In other words, does Hassan's "disclosed" mean "available to anyone who takes the time to study a group's beliefs" or "ensuring that potential converts completely understand all aspects of a movement's doctrines before they are allowed to join"?

The second problem is equally difficult. Many groups, for example, the Church of Jesus Christ of Latter-Day Saints (or Mormons), have "secret" beliefs and rituals that are disclosed only to the initiated. Does their secrecy make them "dangerous"? Once again, Hassan's criterion does not seem a terribly helpful guide for identifying "dangerous cults."

Hassan's final criterion breaks down to "recruitment, group maintenance and freedom to leave." According to Hassan, the "basic feature of most cult *recruitment is deception*" (Hassan 1990:99; italics in the original). But deception is a common human practice, not something unique to religions. We agree that if a religious group is truly deceptive, something is wrong. We are still left with the problem of knowing, as in the case of the Berlin Church on the Way, whether we are being told the truth or whether the group is being slandered by malicious rivals.

Second, Hassan maintains that cults deliberately "undermine the new member's relationship with family and friends" (Hassan 1990:101). This is a common claim by ex-members of numerous groups, but it doesn't really stand up to scrutiny (Barker 1984). In practice most religious groups grow by recruiting friends and family members of converts (Stark and Bainbridge 1985:307–345). In fact it is often a new convert's attempt to recruit family and friends that leads to conflict. It was Jesus, not some modern messiah, who said, "I have come to set a man against his father, and a daughter against her mother. . . . He who loves father or mother more than me is not worthy of me" (Matthew 11:35–37).

Finally, Hassan says that "cults plant phobias into members' minds so that they fear ever leaving the group." Therefore, he claims, a lack of "freedom to leave" is a key indicator of a cult (Hassan 1990:104). This trait is as problematic as the rest. What constitutes freedom? Does the traditional Buddhist belief in karma create a phobia that restricts individual freedom because it says that anyone who does not follow the Buddha is condemned to eternal rebirth? Are books like C. S. Lewis's classic *Screwtape Letters* indications of cult activity because Lewis uses imagery involving Satan, which could create a phobia, to encourage people to remain Christians?

All these questions show how difficult it is to apply Hassan's criteria. Those who doubt this should try applying them to a religious group they consider legitimate. Good examples that easily yield to the charge that they are cults are the **Salvation Army** and Roman Catholic monastic orders. The Salvation Army specializes in "converting" alcoholics. But do alcoholics on drinking binges really want to change their lifestyles? Roman Catholic priests take vows of celibacy and accept the authority of their superiors. Do they know what they are doing? Bromley and Shupe addressed this issue in their provocative article "The Tnevnoc Cult" (Bromley and Shupe 1980), which showed how easily socially acceptable practices can become anathema through a name change ("tnevnoc" is "convent" spelled backwards).

## Theology and Prejudice

Henry Fielding's comment, at the head of this chapter, illustrates the problem of defining cults by making a joke about religious prejudice. He draws attention to the ease with which people define religion in terms of their own beliefs and practices. No doubt if we substituted the Roman Catholic Church or the Berlin-Brandenburg **Landeskirche** for "the **Church of England**," many Irish Catholics and German Protestants could easily adopt Fielding's view as their own. By identifying "religion" with one particular tradition, we exclude all others. Yet when people begin to talk about "cults," they often use definitions that are no better than Fielding's.

The case of Salman Rushdie, whose book *The Satanic Verses* led to a sentence of death by the fundamentalist Islamic government of Iran, illustrates how dangerous this can be. Westerners reject the claim that Islamic governments have the right to pass the death penalty on anyone on purely theological grounds (*Observer*, 19 February 1989). But when we come to cults, we find that the very people who are appalled by the judgment on Rushdie are quite prepared to argue that Western governments ought to accept milder but nonetheless theological judgments on cults as a basis for legislation.

## *Theological Definitions of "Cult"*

The word "cult" has a long history of different meanings. During the nineteenth century, various theologians used the term to describe **ritual** practices associated with religious centers. Starting with the German scholars Hermann Gunkel and Hugo Gressmann around the turn of the century, a concerted attempt was made to identify **liturgical** texts, such as the **Psalms**, and place them in the context of cultic rituals (Harrison 1969:46–66).

Using the notion of cults as a means to understand the development of Israelite religion is common in many modern studies such as John Bright's now classic *History of Israel* (Bright 1962). In this influential work, Bright argues that in the Bible "the cult of the patriarchs is depicted as exceedingly simple." It was, he tells the reader, "never a local one, but always the cult of the ancestral deity of the clan" (Bright 1962:92). With this introduction to his usage of "cult," Bright develops the idea that the "symbols of that early cult were symbols of . . . kingship" (Bright 1962:135). He goes on to show how the idea of kingship and the Kingdom of God, which he sees as central to the Old Testament, became the full-blown theology of the royal cult centered on the Davidic kingdom (Bright 1962:204–207).

A similar use of the term appears in the work of some New Testament scholars who locate the origins of Christianity in a prophetic rebellion against the deadening rituals associated with the **Temple** cult located in Jerusalem. These scholars, too, identify liturgical performances and religious rituals as cult practices. This is how the **phenomenologist** and historian of religion Joachim Wach used the word "cult" in his *Sociology of Religion* ([1931] 1944).

The towering figure of the German philosopher Hegel gave great impetus to the development of critical studies of the Bible. Hegel's students, including **Bruno Baur** (1809–1882) and **D. F. Strauss** (1808–1874), forged the tools that made possible the analysis of the Bible as a secular text. At the root of Hegel's influence in this sense were his early theological writings (1793–1800), where he displayed an undisguised disgust for **Judaism** (Hegel 1961:68–69, 182–205). Hegel believed the Germans made a fundamental mistake when they converted to Christianity (Hegel 1961:145–151). True, he admitted, Jesus was an unusual Jew; nevertheless, Hegel clearly lamented the "servile" and essentially life-denying influence of the Jews on German society (Hegel 1961:68–70, 177–179).

The implicit and often explicit anti-Semitism of Hegel is an important factor in our understanding of the development of biblical criticism. Behind many critical theories, there seems to be an unacknowledged desire to distance Christianity from Judaism. The great German Old Testament scholar **Julius Wellhausen** was openly anti-Semitic (Silberman 1983:75–79; Reventlow and Farmer 1995:15–49, 132–148), and even widely accepted theories like **Markan priority** in New Testament studies seem tinged with anti-Semitism, the intent of some early exponents being to distance Christianity from the "Jewish influences" of the Gospel of Matthew.

Consequently, the word "cult" came into general and theological usage loaded with negative connotations. It came to represent a form of "dead" religion or "formal ritualism" that was contrasted with the vigor of prophetic movements and the spontaneity of faith. In attacking their theological opponents, Christian apologists like van Baalen naturally chose the word "cult" to designate groups they believed represented false religions. Van Baalen defined a cult as "any religion regarded as unorthodox or even spurious" (van Baalen 1956:363). He went on to carefully define orthodoxy in terms of traditional Christianity (van Baalen 1956:385–392). Martin followed suit by defining a cult as "a group of people gathered about a specific person or person's interpretation of the Bible," adding that "from a theological viewpoint, the cults contain not a few major deviations from historic Christianity" (Martin 1976:11).

For most people today, such narrow definitions are unacceptable, and many therefore turn to definitions that involve a description of cult activities. As a result, sociological definitions of the term "cult" have gained popularity.

## Academic Definitions: Weber and Troeltsch

Academic discussions about the classification of religious organizations are strongly influenced by the works of **Max Weber** and his friend and colleague **Ernst Troeltsch**, who categorized organizations according to the notion of the ideal type, an approximation that expresses the essence of an organization in its pure form (Burger 1976:115–140).

Using this methodology, Weber and Troeltsch developed the classic sociological formulation of "church" and "sect." To these basic categories Troeltsch added a third type, mystical groups, along with some general references to cults. Later, H. Richard Niebuhr (1894–1962), the brother of Reinhold Niebuhr, contributed the idea of the denomination (Niebuhr 1957). Finally, in the 1970s social scientists began seriously to discuss cults and new religious movements (McGuire 1981:107–144).

Many introductory texts describe Troeltsch as Weber's student or disciple (Macionis, Clarke, and Gerber 1994:468; Hill 1973:51; Samuelsson 1957:20). This is incorrect and misleading. One reason for the neglect of Troeltsch may be that Talcott Parsons (1902–1979), who dominated American sociology for many years, devotes an entire volume of his *Structure of Social Action* (Parsons [1937] 1968) to Weber while relegating Troeltsch to four short footnotes. In fact, Weber moved to the University of Heidelberg in 1896, two years after Troeltsch had been appointed to the chair of theology. Both men were already working on similar topics, as were a group of like-minded friends (Liebersohn 1988:52–62; Mommsen 1987:215–233). In 1904 Troeltsch and Weber spent "five weeks or so" together on a trip to America, and for a number of years their families shared the same house (Mommsen 1987:217).

Weber's essay *The Protestant Ethic and the Spirit of Capitalism* appeared *after* the American trip. In this work Weber introduced the distinction between "church" and "sect." As a result, many writers attribute this terminology to Weber (McGuire 1981:107; Bendix 1962:314). But other writers attribute it to Troeltsch (Yinger 1970:252; O'Dea 1966:68). It would probably be impossible to discover whether the terminology originated with Weber or Troeltsch. What is clear is that the two men owed a great deal to each other (Mommsen 1987:223–224), and their relationship had a significant influence on subsequent scholarship.

If, as most texts wrongly state, Troeltsch was Weber's student, then anyone reading their works would assume that Weber taught Troeltsch to think in socio-logical terms. But if Weber was in any sense a student of Troeltsch, we need to re-think our understanding of the "scientific" nature of Weber's concepts. Commenting on this possibility, Friedrich Graf argues that Weber's reliance on Troeltsch is established by a careful examination of Weber's footnotes to *The Protestant Ethic* (Mommsen 1987:222). He then suggests that in fact a study of Weber's work and its sources would reveal a far greater reliance on Troeltsch's the-ological judgments than is usually recognized, illuminating the negative conno-tations of "sect" found in both Weber's and Troeltsch's work. Rather than a set of completely disinterested observations, their concept of sect is subtly influenced by preconceived theological judgments.

Contrary to popular opinion, the research of neither Weber nor Troeltsch was motivated by abstract intellectualism. Behind them lay a passionate commitment. Both men recognized that Germany and German Christianity faced grave dan-gers. Thus Troeltsch argued that on the one hand the old "system of *absolute es-tablishment*," which created a monopoly situation through the close union of church and state, was dead. On the other hand, Troeltsch considered an American or French style of "disestablishment" un-German. This left a "system of *mixed es-tablishment*" as the only viable option (Troeltsch [1906] 1991:109–117).

In particular Troeltsch hated American-style free churches, which he saw as "based on **Baptist** and **Puritan** ideas . . . and on an enlightened relativism," creat-ing "a democracy that is as individualistic as it is egalitarian" (Troeltsch [1906] 1991:111). First, Troeltsch didn't think it was possible to transplant American ideas to Germany. Second, it worried him that under the American system "or-thodox" groups, which he argued were always strong among the laity, dominated churches. In his view this orthodoxy was dangerous because it rejected "scientific education," by which he seems to have meant German higher criticism of the Bible (Troeltsch [1906] 1991:112).

To counter this tendency, Troeltsch believed it was essential that the state select a small number of churches that would be granted "corporate privileges grounded in public law." These churches would be chosen because of their "con-tribution to public life." In return for "a considerable degree of state control," they would be provided with "the material base of support" (Troeltsch [1906] 1991:109). Thus in Troeltsch's view, "The separation of church and state can be no separation of state from Christianity" (Troeltsch [1906] 1991:115). Rather, the "concept of revelation" represented a holistic fusion of life and history in a manner worthy of **Immanuel Kant** (1724–1804) and Goethe. This reality forever set Germany apart from France and the United States (Troeltsch [1906] 1991:116).

Because he had such a philosophy and political agenda, it is no surprise that Troeltsch's comments on sects were less than enthusiastic. To be fair, he saw the problems with established churches and understood the appeal of sectarian movements. But behind his apparent scientific spirit is an apologetic thrust that shapes his conclusions.

Weber appears to have been more sympathetic to the American model than was Troeltsch. It seems to have intrigued him. In his view sects gave "American democracy its own flexible structure and its individualistic stamp" (Weber [1906] 1985:10). Like Troeltsch, however, he believed that German religion and society had developed in their own unique way, which meant that it was both impossible and undesirable for American-style sects to develop in Germany. With Troeltsch, Weber agreed that by definition sects were anti-intellectual (Weber [1906] 1985:11). Although he recognized the piety and commitment of sects, Weber believed that the only viable option for an educated person was church membership, not commitment to a sect, which, he implied, was intellectually narrow and thus inferior (Weber [1906] 1985:12).

The sociological definitions of both "church" and "sect" promoted by the work of Weber and Troeltsch clearly show the influence of Troeltsch's ideological concerns and dislike of American religion. The two scholars use "church" to refer to any religious organization that is universal in its scope and inclusive in membership. That is, a church is a religious body that counts as its members anyone living within a certain geographic area.

This definition uses as one basis for identifying a religious group as a church the indiscriminate baptism of infants or some similar rite that secures membership. Consequently, the **Orthodox Church, Roman Catholicism,** and many older forms of **Protestantism** (often called mainstream forms) that arose during the **Reformation,** including almost all **Lutheran** and German Landeskirchen and many **Episcopalian, Presbyterian,** and **Congregational** churches, may be easily recognized as churches. In contrast, almost all **evangelical** groups that preach conversion, be they **Anglican,** Lutheran, Presbyterian, Pentecostal, or independent charismatic churches, fall outside this definition. This is because, according to Weber and Troeltsch, they display sectarian characteristics.

A sect, as Weber and Troeltsch defined it, is characterized by the exclusive nature of its membership. That is, not everyone can become a member of a sect. Some form of conversion experience is needed to secure membership. According to Weber and Troeltsch, this insistence on conversion creates a tension with the surrounding society because some people are excluded from certain sect activities. In the words of British sociologist Bryan Wilson, "Sects are movements of religious protest" (Wilson 1970b:2).

According to Weberian thought, any evangelical Christian group is *by definition* a sect, or sectarian movement. Thus the early Methodists in England are a classic example of a sectarian movement. Other groups that proponents of Weberian thought define as sects include the Puritans, German **Pietists**, the **Plymouth Brethren**, Baptists, and so on. If we use this definition, it becomes clear why in modern Germany independent churches like the Church on the Way in Berlin are regarded as sects. So, too, following Weber and Troeltsch, would be many Episcopalian congregations—for example, All Souls Langham Place in London, Southern Baptist congregations in the United States, and all **African indigenous or independent churches**. In sociological terms these churches are sects because their ministers preach the necessity of conversion. In this sense Wolfhard Margies, who founded the Church on the Way; Billy Graham; George Carey, archbishop of Canterbury; and even Desmond Tutu are all sectarian leaders.

## From Sect to Denomination

Because it is clear that in terms of the Weber-Troeltsch typology some religious groups have characteristics of both church and sect, H. Richard Niebuhr, who wrote his doctoral thesis on Troeltsch, began using the term "denomination." Denomination is a term derived from the Latin word meaning "to name." Niebuhr uses it to distinguish religious organizations that are not churches in Weber and Troeltsch's sense. Denominations are organizations that do not encompass everyone in a given geographical area. Yet they are not sects because they lack exclusivistic tendencies and do not demand a profession of faith or acceptance of particular teachings before granting membership.

Many denominations, however, began as new religious movements displaying sectlike qualities that faded over time. Some writers therefore describe a denomination as a sect on the way to becoming a church. For example, **Methodism** emerged in the eighteenth century through the work of **John** and **Charles Wesley**. It grew to be a major Christian revitalization movement that made a significant impact on the nineteenth-century missionary movement and Christian enterprise throughout the world. It did this by emphasizing that true Christians must be "born again." In the twentieth century, however, Methodism has tended to encourage liberal theology and has moved away from its revivalist roots to become a respectable religious movement that rarely regards a declaration of conversion as a prerequisite for church membership.

## Sociological Definitions of "Cult"

Finally we come to the sociological definition of "cult." Again, one of the first attempts to define the concept of cult in sociological terms is found in the work of

Max Weber (1956). Weber followed the theological usage, which he expanded to embrace ancient and non-Christian religions. More important, Weber associated the notion of cult not with ritualism, as did the theologians, but with an antirational and mystical form of religion (Weber 1956:10–11, 93, 152–153).

At about the same time that Weber developed his theories of religion, his friend Troeltsch developed his own (Troeltsch 1931). The latter used a church-sect typology almost identical to that of Weber. To these basic categories he added a third type, which he identified as "Protestant **mysticism**" (Troeltsch 1931:691–808). The English translation of Troeltsch's work does not use the word "cult" in relation to this form of religious expression. In the original German, it falls under the heading *Sekten,* which can be translated as either "sect" or "cult." Nevertheless, it is fair to argue that in fact Troeltsch's "mystical" groups conform to the ideal type that Weber recognizes as a "cult."

Building on Troeltsch's work, Leopold von Wiese explicitly developed the notion of cult (von Wiese [1932] 1974). His understanding of cult was taken up by William E. Mann in his pioneering *Sect, Cult and Church in Alberta* (Mann 1955:6). To Mann, "Sects emphasize recovery of primitive, first-century Christian doctrine." By contrast, "Cults blend alien religious or psychological notions with Christian doctrine" in order to obtain "a more adequate, or modern faith" (Mann 1955:6). The big problem with these definitions is that they are too closely tied to the Christian tradition. Since the mid-1960s many new religions have openly rejected Christianity. Therefore we need to find a more satisfactory approach to the whole issue.

## Stark and Bainbridge's Criticism of Ideal Types

Rodney Stark and William Bainbridge criticize the way sociologists identify church, sect, and cult using the Weberian methodology of ideal types (Stark and Bainbridge 1985:19–24). According to Stark and Bainbridge, ideal types have an intuitive rightness even though they are very imprecise tools. Their intuitive nature, however, makes it easy to engage in endless arguments about whether a particular group should be identified as a church, sect, or cult—in the meantime ignoring theory and empirical evidence.

Stark and Bainbridge also blame the use of ideal types for having misled generations of sociologists by confusing rather than clarifying issues. In their words, ideal types "serve as tautological substitutes for real theories" and "often use *correlates* in their definitions of concepts. But it is *attributes*, not correlates, that belong in a definition" (Stark and Bainbridge 1985:20). They propose replacing ideal types with clear definitions. For our analysis of religious movements, we follow their suggestions.

## Redefining "Church," "Sect," and "Cult"

Stark and Bainbridge use the work of sociologist Benton Johnson (1963) to construct a more reliable guide to religious organizations. They define three key terms as follows:

1. A *church* is a conventional religious organization.
2. A *sect* is a deviant religious organization with traditional beliefs and practices.
3. A *cult* is a deviant religious organization with novel beliefs and practices (Stark and Bainbridge 1987:124).

These definitions are precise and for the most part avoid value judgments on the worth of each movement. They also allow for change over time so that what may be a novelty today can become a tradition tomorrow and convention in a hundred years' time. Another advantage is that they clearly distinguish religious from non-religious organizations. After all, not everything is a religious phenomenon.

According to Stark and Bainbridge, a **religion** must be based on some "**supernatural** assumptions" to distinguish it from secular thought. In short, they see religions as "systems of general compensators based on supernatural assumptions" (Stark and Bainbridge 1987:39). By "compensators" they mean whatever people regard as rewards, whether or not they are immediately apparent (Stark and Bainbridge 1987:36).

Finally, the groups Stark and Bainbridge identify as sects and cults are revitalization movements (Stark and Bainbridge 1987:188). Revitalization movements attempt to revive religious traditions through practical innovations and new expressions of traditional piety. They do not, however, seek to fundamentally change a tradition or incorporate radically new beliefs. Consequently, revitalization movements do not produce new religions; rather, they reaffirm old traditions.

## Contemporary and New Religious Movements

Despite the wonderfully concise meaning that Stark and Bainbridge assign it, the word "cult" remains an emotionally loaded term burdened with negative imagery. For this reason, many writers have adopted the convention of employing the term "new religious movements" or simply "new religions." Unfortunately, redefining cults as new religions only confuses the issue. Cults grow out of established traditions to which they remain attached. New religions, in contrast, break with existing traditions to create something that did not previously exist.

To identify the whole range of modern religious movements, we use the terms "contemporary religions" and "contemporary religious movements." Then, as a first approximation, we define new religious movements as cults and sects that are directly related to modernity (see Chapter 8). Implied is a love for the new and a dislike of a single ongoing tradition.

Historically, groups defined as either cults or sects developed against the background of common assumptions based in a shared tradition. Since the advent of industrialism, these traditional assumptions have been fundamentally challenged by modernity. By "modernity" we do not mean the spread of industrialization, which has yet to reach some societies. Rather, we mean the changes brought about by an awareness of industrial goods, science, and technology. "Modernity" implies a distinction between that which is new as opposed to that which is ancient, or that which is innovative as opposed to that which is traditional. It usually involves an explicit and self-conscious commitment to be "modern" in intellectual, cultural, and religious affairs.

New religions that arise in response to modernity involve modernization, or a program committed to remaking society, the political order, and/or religious beliefs in terms of what is understood as "the new." All religious traditions have experienced the effects of modernity, but their response has rarely been enthusiastically to embrace the new. Christianity, for example, often associates modernity with rationalism and the new with the loss of Christian values, thus threatening its continued existence.

In the past it was assumed that "cult," because it is most similar to a conception of "new religion," could be used interchangeably with that term. But new religions, or at least their leaders, are now so adept at mixing bits and pieces of various distinct traditions and disseminating these "new" recombinations across the world that it is better to regard new religions as distinct global phenomena. Therefore we must consider the meaning of global culture. We do that in the next chapter.

## KEY TERMS

**African indigenous or independent churches:** The thousands of new religious movements that have developed in Africa since the late nineteenth century, many of which claim to be Christian, though they reject traditional missionary churches and attempt to incorporate African beliefs and practices.

**Anglican:** *See* **Episcopalian.**

**Baptist:** A major religious movement that grew out of Puritanism in the seventeenth century. Baptists believe that the baptism of professed believers is the accepted mark of church membership.

**Baur, Bruno** (1809–1882): Adopted a position even more extreme than that of D. F. Strauss in 1839, saying the story told in the gospel came from the imagination of the Christian community and was based on Greco-Roman philosophy.

**Buddha:** A title denoting an enlightened being. Just as the title "Christ" has become a name for Jesus, so the title "Buddha" has become associated with Gautama (563–483 B.C.?), the historic founder of Buddhism whose deeds are recorded in various manuscripts, such as the Lotus Sutra.

**Church**: According to Weber and Troeltsch, any religious organization that is universal in its scope and inclusive in membership. That is, a church is a religious body that counts as its members anyone living within a certain geographic area. We prefer Stark and Bainbridge's definition of a church as a conventional religious organization.

**Church of England**: The Anglican or Episcopalian Church in England.

**Congregational**: A church belonging to that Protestant tradition which places the authority for church government in the local congregation.

**Doctrine**: The teachings or official beliefs of a religious group; a set or principles, creeds, or theory of a religious, social, or political movement.

**Episcopalian**: A church governed by bishops. The Episcopalian Church in America belongs to the Anglican tradition stemming from the Church of England.

**Establishment**: When a church is "established," it is the official religion of a country and is supported by law, given special privileges in exchange for varying amounts of government control. "Disestablishment" means the state's removal of special status from a church. Many European churches are established churches; American churches are free, or disestablished.

**Evangelical**: Any religious group that seeks to make converts by the proclamation of its message or, in Christian terms, the gospel.

**Jesus** (5 B.C.–A.D. 33): The historic founder of Christianity whose works are recorded in the New Testament.

**Judaism**: The religion of Jews based on the Hebrew Bible interpreted through the Talmud.

**Kant, Immanuel** (1724–1804): Prussian thinker whose *Critique of Pure Reason* (1781) created a revolution in academic thought and has given rise to his reputation as the father of modern philosophy. Kant argued that we can know only the appearance (phenomena) of things, not the things-in-themselves (noumena). Consequently, we can neither prove nor disprove the existence of God. Belief in God is a matter of faith.

**Landeskirche**: The state or established church in Germany that stems from the Protestant Reformation and was strongly influenced by Lutheranism.

**Liturgical**: From "liturgy," the term used to describe the order or structure of worship in a religious service.

**Lutheran**: A Protestant Church in the tradition of Martin Luther (1483–1546), German theologian and biblical scholar and one of the most important figures in Western Christianity. He reluctantly launched the Protestant Reformation by posting his *Ninety-five Theses* in October 1517. He taught justification by faith, the priesthood of all believers, and that Scripture alone is the source of authority for the Church.

**Markan priority**: The generally accepted theory that Mark's was the first written gospel, which was used as one source for the writings of Matthew and Luke.

**Methodism**: A religious movement founded by John and Charles Wesley in the eighteenth century that grew to be a major Christian revitalization movement in the nineteenth century.

**Muhammed** (A.D. 571–632): The founder of Islam, who claimed to be the last in a long line of prophets. His message was that there is one God, named Allah, who is revealed in the Qur'ān. Muhammed's deeds were recorded by his followers in the Haddith.

**Mysticism**: The immediate experience of a sacred-human relationship, in particular the experience of oneness with a divine or transdivine being or state. This type of religion centers on the spiritual experiences of the believer, which are often said to be indescribable in ordinary language.

**Orthodox Church:** Those belonging to the Greek Orthodox tradition, one of the oldest Christian traditions, usually recognized by its use of icons in worship.

**Phenomenologist:** Someone who practices phenomenology, developed in the philosophy of Edmund Husserl (1859–1938), who tried to establish the basic structure of consciousness and conditions for all possible experience. More recently, "phenomenology" has come to designate a method of investigating fundamental human activities, such as religion.

**Pietists:** Adherents of any religious movement that promotes religious devotion or piety. Pietism originated as a reaction to the Enlightenment in eighteenth-century Germany and profoundly influenced the English-speaking world through Methodism and the evangelical movement.

**Plymouth Brethren:** One of the most influential new religious movements to emerge in the 1830s, closely associated with the Irish preacher John Nelson Darby (1800–1882). They have had an immense influence on American Christianity through their emphasis on the imminent return of Christ. They also helped popularize both premillennialism and dispensationalism and the idea of "faith missions."

**Presbyterian:** A church governed by elders, or presbyters, stemming from the Scottish Protestant tradition.

**Protestantism:** The Christian revitalization movement that grew out of the sixteenth-century Reformation, which sought to reform the church on the basis of the authority of the Bible.

**Psalms:** A book of the Bible containing poetry, most of which was traditionally ascribed to King David.

**Puritans:** Members of a much-maligned dynamic religious movement that arose in the sixteenth century as a Calvinist party within the Church of England. They emphasized preaching, pastoral care, and the reformation of the church in terms of biblical norms, democratic government, and, eventually, republicanism. They were bitterly persecuted before and after the English Civil War, causing many to flee to America. As a result of aristocratic propaganda, the name "Puritan" came to be falsely identified with dour killjoys. Puritanism is important to the work of Weber and Troeltsch.

**Rationalism:** Any theological or philosophical position that values reason as the ultimate arbiter and judge of all statements and therefore rejects revelation. It is a form of secular humanism.

**Reformation:** Any religious movement that reforms a preexisting tradition to restore its primitive purity or orthodoxy. It is more specifically associated with the religious movement that began in 1517 with the protest of Martin Luther against abuses in the Roman Catholic Church in Germany, including the sale of indulgences as a means of obtaining salvation. This led to the creation of independent churches that renounced the claims of the pope and sought to return to a form of Christianity based on the Bible.

**Religion:** A set of institutionalized rituals identified with a tradition that together express and evoke sacral sentiments directed at a supernatural, divine, or transdivine focus seen in the context of the human phenomenological environment. Rituals, tradition, and sentiments are at least partially described by myths or doctrines and offer general rewards to practitioners.

**Ritual:** Sacred custom or any form of repetitive behavior fixed by tradition.

**Roman Catholicism:** Along with Greek Orthodoxy and Coptic and Syriac Christianity, one of the oldest Christian traditions. It acknowledges the supremacy of the bishop of Rome, the pope, as the head of the Church and teaches that salvation is based on faith and works.

**Salvation Army:** An evangelical Christian movement founded in Britain in the nineteenth century by William ("General") Booth to work among the poor and oppressed. It took a strong but nonmoralistic stance against alcohol and other forms of drug abuse as well as providing homes for the homeless and meeting other chronic needs.

**Sect:** According to Weber and Troeltsch, a sect is characterized by the exclusive nature of its membership. We prefer Stark and Bainbridge's definition of a sect as a deviant religious organization with traditional beliefs and practices.

**Strauss, D. F.** (David Friedrich) (1808–1874): A radical German theologian and one of the founders of biblical criticism. His book *The Life of Jesus* (1835) caused a storm of controversy because of its denial of the supernatural and his use of myth, which he defined as a story contrary to the laws of nature.

**Supernatural:** A realm beyond nature that can affect this reality; a spiritual dimension invisible to the everyday world of the senses.

**Temple:** A holy building used for ritual sacrifice and worship. The Temple in Jerusalem was the center of Jewish worship and was destroyed by the Romans in A.D. 70.

**Theological:** Having to do with theology, from the Greek words *theos*, meaning "God," and *logos,* or "discourse." It means the study of God, the sacred, or divine and includes the relationship of humans to God.

**Troeltsch, Ernst** (1865–1923): Liberal German theologian and sociologist who devoted his energies to the problems raised for religion by the scientific method as applied to history. His most famous work is *The Social Teaching of the Christian Churches* (1911).

**Weber, Max** (1864–1920): German sociologist whose influential works, including *The Protestant Ethic and the Spirit of Capitalism* (1920), did much to promote the sociology of religion.

**Wellhausen, Julius** (1844–1918): The most important German biblical critic of the nineteenth century. His work did much to win acceptance for higher criticism and the documentary hypothesis to explain the origins of the Hebrew Bible.

**Wesley, Charles** (1707–1788): John Wesley's younger brother, called a "Methodist" by fellow students because of his methodical habits of study and fanatical zeal for regularity of living. He is best remembered as the author of over 5,500 hymns, including the Christmas carol "Hark! the Herald Angels Sing."

**Wesley, John** (1703–1791): English founder of Methodism who was influenced by German Pietists. He experienced a dramatic conversion at a prayer meeting in London in 1738 that inspired him to practice controversial open-air preaching. His work led to the creation of the Methodist Church in 1791.

❀ **3** ❀

# New Religions as Global Cultures

*Folk ideas . . . constantly recur and are open to constant rearrangement by and in each culture.*

Adolf Bastian *(Koepping 1983:172)*

*T*his chapter explores the concept of global culture and its relationship to new religions. We begin by defining global culture and showing how our understanding of both it and new religions grew out of empirical research. We then discuss a popular misrepresentation of the globality of new religions that sees them as an expression of U.S. capitalism. This leads us to examine tradition-linked global cultures before we move on to new religions that selectively combine aspects of many traditions to create new cultures. We outline the European origins, North American development, Asian response, and African reaction to new religions. Finally, the chapter closes with a section on spiritual experience and iconic leadership in new religions.

## Global Cultures and Religious Traditions

In 1994 Karla Poewe published her study of charismatic Christianity as a global culture. It was easy to pinpoint the global cultural aspect of this religion. To begin with, Poewe could trace empirically how the renewal aspect—the Pentecost story—of the Judeo-Christian **tradition** traveled the world with awakened or renewed missionaries who related their experience of the Pentecost to diverse local peoples. Reworked in accordance with these peoples' own cultural predilections, the story became a living reality. One could say that a global culture is a tradition that travels the world and takes on local color. It has both a global, or metacultural, and a local, or situationally distinct, cultural dimension.

New religions complicate this picture. The global aspect of new religions is there for all to see. For example, a Hindu idea is popularized by a charismatic

Indian philosopher named Rajneesh, who finds for his idea an audience in Germany, the United States, Japan, Brazil, and South Africa. This globality, however, differs from charismatic Christianity in very important ways. The idea that travels is a fragment of a tradition intent, first, on fragmenting other traditions and then on uniting with these fragments to bear new fruit in the soil of a distinct **folk religion**. Like charismatic Christianity, it, too, has global and local aspects. The recombination of fragments makes such a religion global; rooting this recombination in a local folk religion makes it authentic and local.

One could simplify the above distinction as follows. To be a global culture, charismatic Christianity, despite its numerous local adaptations, must remain true to one world tradition. By contrast, new religions, despite their globality, must fragment existing traditions, recombine with others in new ways, and yet remain true to a very old and very local folk religion. The nineteenth-century German anthropologist **Adolf Bastian** (1826–1905) said that folk religions arise everywhere from the deep yearnings of people. We are in the presence of just this phenomenon, for new religions, authenticated by specific local folk religions, are a response to urban sophisticates' deep yearnings for global folk religions. Their broad perspective and their novelty make any one new religion a global culture.

## The Empirical Roots of a Theory

Our understanding of the global nature of new religions came about as a result of empirical research in Africa. While living in the black township of Katatura, Namibia, in 1981, Poewe observed that black religious movements prided themselves in having global links that they saw as a source of inspiration. At the same time, Irving Hexham was working in South African archives on the **Afrikaner** visionary **Johanna Brandt** (1876–1964). In *The Millenium* (1918) and *The Paraclete, or Coming World Mother* (1936), Brandt talked about such things as the coming Age of Aquarius and feminist spirituality. Like the African prophets Poewe interviewed, Brandt treasured her global vision and contacts with the United States and Germany through theosophical organizations. We thus became aware of the role of global visions for individuals intent on creating their own new religions.

Later, in 1987, we began to develop our own theory of global cultures while researching new religions and charismatic movements in South Africa. This research led Poewe to organize a conference on global culture at the University of Calgary in 1991. At the same time, and quite independently, other scholars, primarily Roland Robertson, were developing their own theories of globalization and global culture (Featherstone 1990).

There is also a school of thought, popular in Europe and the Third World, that sees new religions as an expression of U.S. capitalism. According to the authors of this theory, new religions are promoted by both the U.S. Central Intelligence Agency (CIA) and various capitalist fronts to undermine liberation movements and socialist governments. Ridiculous as this theory may sound, it has received academic support and sometimes appears in American publications (Gifford 1988:29, 73–82).

One aspect of this theory that makes it plausible is the global nature of new religions. Anyone who wants to prove that a particular movement has ties to the United States can readily find evidence. By showing links to America or Americans, proponents of this theory can argue that these ties are manipulated by the CIA. It is also fairly easy to show that new religions have financial interests. The next step is to suggest that fundraising and business interests prove a capitalist orientation. Since the United States is a capitalist country, new religions must be part of a capitalist plot to control the world.

Of course the above argument is wrong. It is based on jumps of logic and the misuse of fragments of empirical evidence. Yet like so many conspiracy theories, it is based on a germ of truth. Most new religions have American interests because America is seen as a vast mission field. Leaders of new religions need money to establish themselves and finance their projects. Of necessity, they engage in fundraising and creating businesses to support their spiritual goals. Critics use these facts against new religions. In the process they blur the image of new religions, making it difficult for many people to see the significance of global culture.

## The Global Dynamics of Religious Cultures

Far from taking the conspiratorial view, we concentrate on the cultural give-and-take of new religions. But before discussing the global nature of new religions, we need a general sense of what a global culture might be. It is best to think of a global culture as a transnational or transsocietal network of cosmopolitan people who self-consciously cultivate "an intellectual and aesthetic stance of openness toward divergent cultural experiences" (Featherstone 1990:1, 239). As Ulf Hannerz points out, rather than being territorially defined, global cultures "are carried as collective structures of meaning by networks" that are transnational (Featherstone 1990:239). People who belong to new religions, for example, may be "somewhat footloose": They are as ready to move on as they are to stay in order to immerse themselves temporarily within other cultures and religions (Featherstone 1990:240, 241).

Buddhism, Christianity, and Islam have always been global cultures. The ideal of these religions, however, was to spread a religious **metaculture** that was perfectly capable of remaining identifiable while being absorbed by local cultures. A metaculture consists of a bare minimum of elements (of a faith) "that are reasonably consistent and uniform" and are recognizable even when the metaculture is absorbed into cultures to become movements, denominations, or cultic processes (Burridge 1991:xiv, 36).

For example, in A.D. 601, Roman Catholic missionaries from Italy asked **Pope Gregory** (540–604) for advice in their efforts to convert the heathen English. Gregory's reply was recorded by **the Venerable Bede** (673–735) in his *Ecclesiastical*

*History of the English People* (Bede 1965:86–87). Put simply, the pope advised his missionaries to find points of common ground with the English that would allow them to absorb pagan celebrations into Christian festivals. The aim, however, was not to create a new synthesis of Catholic and pagan thought. Rather, the goal was to accommodate the uncompromised metaculture of a world religion and cosmopolitan culture to the folk religion of a local culture. As those who have researched renewal aspects of world religions know, the accommodation was in fact mutual. Not infrequently, indigenous and non-Western spiritual practices were the spark that rekindled the embers of tradition or threw new light on old interpretations of ancient religious texts.

## Charismatic Christianity as a Global Culture

Because Poewe has detailed the idea of charismatic Christianity in another book (Poewe 1994), we describe here but a few examples that highlight the intercultural dynamic involved in this global culture. We do so by discussing a few Christians whose true Christianity—a Christianity lived with anyone anywhere on this earth—emerged through the influence of people from other cultures. For example, **David du Plessis** (1905–1987) is usually called the father of the charismatic movement (Quebedeaux 1983:110–114). Two things are particularly interesting about du Plessis. First, he was not an American but an Afrikaner who had "responded to a **prophecy**" that the Englishman Smith Wigglesworth (1859–1947) spoke over him in South Africa in 1936. Second, du Plessis was deeply affected by the spirituality of black South African Christians, for whom healing, **tongues**, dreams, and visions were both African and Christian. The experiences of South African blacks threw new light on the mention of dreams, visions, and tongues in the Old and New Testament. This gave du Plessis the courage to assert not only that speaking in tongues and having premonitory dreams was perfectly natural but that such spiritual phenomena were perfectly scriptural. Du Plessis's work and that of the American black William J. Seymour (1870–1922) refute the claim that charismatic Christianity is solely a middle-class, white American product that subverts religious expressions across the world (cf. Gifford 1988; for a balanced view, see Stoll 1990).

Other mainline Christians who had great influence on religious renewal in American and European mainline churches were **Agnes Sanford** (1897–1982) and **Edith Schaeffer** (1914–). The former spent her youth in China. The latter, who with her husband founded the L'Abri Fellowship, was born in China. Sanford directly affected the charismatic movement through her teachings on healing, Schaeffer indirectly through her books about Christian living. Both women were profoundly influenced by the religious practices and beliefs of Chinese, which gave them a living faith that revived the faith of others (Burgess, McGee, and Alexander 1988:767; Schaeffer 1981).

Many American **megachurches**—Earl Paulk's Chapel Hill Harvester in Atlanta, Georgia, for example—function much like international corporations. Their literature, tapes, and videos are exported to Latin American, African, Asian, and European markets. The business ethos of these churches can easily give casual observers the impression that they are essentially American movements intent on Americanizing the world.

Such a superficial analysis overlooks the other aspect of these institutions. Just as American religion is exported throughout the world, so large religious organizations abroad export their products to North America. The network links of international fellowships play a vital role because they host international conference programs that maintain the sense that charismatic Christianity is a dynamic worldwide movement. Fellowship networks exist in most countries and across the globe. We have observed several in South Africa, Germany, Britain, and Canada. Because their structures are relatively loose and ever changing, we mention here only a few examples to illustrate the way they work.

The International Communion of Charismatic Churches was led by a ministry team including Bishops John Meares and Earl Paulk of the United States, Bishop McAlister of Brazil, Bishop Idahosa of Nigeria, as well as a bishop from the Caribbean. This network and its affiliated churches are international and interracial. Furthermore, both Paulk and Meares claim to have been inspired by South Africa's **Nicolas Bhengu** (1909–1986), whom they knew personally (interviews by the authors, Decatur, Georgia, 1989). Bengt Sundkler also mentions Bhengu's work in his books on African independent churches (Sundkler 1961, 1976; Dubb 1976).

Similarly, students from the Third World who attended **Fuller Theological Seminary** in Pasadena, California, initially inspired John Wimber to abandon his Western rationalism and embrace a more spiritual outlook. His healing sessions with a large student group that included many overseas visitors led to the establishment of the **Vineyard movement**. Wimber's example inspired Canadian churches and led to the so-called **Toronto Blessing,** which quickly spread around the world (Beverley 1995; Roberts 1994).

In South Africa the New Covenant Ministries fellowship network was founded in 1983 by Dudley Daniel, a former Kenyan who had lived in Zimbabwe. Inspired by the British Ichthyus Fellowship and the experience of Chinese Christians like Watchman Nee and Nora Lam, the network spread to Australia, East Germany, Hong Kong, the Soviet Union, and most recently Los Angeles (Jenkins n.d.; Lam 1980).

Thus it is not the case that American networks force themselves on the rest of the world. In fact during our research in South Africa, we learned that some leaders of fellowships discouraged ties with American Christians. According to these people, Americans came to take rather than to give. But it is often the case that networks that rise spontaneously in various other countries actively seek contact with America because they regard Americans as generous. In other words, one simply cannot generalize.

## New Religions and Global Culture

As indicated earlier, the global nature of new religions is significantly different from that of charismatic Christianity. The strict accommodation between a local religious culture and the metaculture of a world tradition is absent in new religions. Instead, new religionists revel in diversity itself, so that cultures coexist "in the individual experience" (Featherstone 1990:239). This results in the sense of having created a new world culture that is more than a recombination of fragments and experiences from numerous great and small traditions. Furthermore, their success depends on finding the proper mix between spiritualizing science and scientizing the exotic. It depends on finding a new buzzword, such as "**trance channeling**," for an old practice like spirit possession.

In practice and theory, the creators of new religions selectively extract and combine elements they find significant from numerous local cultures. Although one great tradition, such as Christianity, Hinduism, or even the scientific tradition, may predominate, all new religions incorporate, often indiscriminately, insights from other cultures and traditions. They also use the idea of lost civilizations and relics from ancient cultures that no longer exist to create their claim to authenticity. People living anywhere can be incorporated into this type of global culture. But not everyone is necessarily allowed to participate.

New religions, as we observed already, are the product of modernity. They emerged since the eighteenth century as one response to technological innovations that shrank the world: Mind-boggling innovations in communications and travel allowed people to mine traditions in order to produce shining ideas for a growing religious market. Only recently native Americans began to complain that their traditions are being strip-mined. A kind of protectionism or ecology of tradition is emerging. It is unlikely, however, that such moves will change the stance of openness of those who practice new religions. How can one expunge the sense that cultures coexist in individual experience? And how can one prove, not to say stop, the appropriation of ideas in a computer-linked world?

It is the vision of creating a radically *new* world culture that energizes new religions. To succeed in today's religious market, new religions attempt to convince their followers that they offer a global vision. From this description it might be thought that all new religions are catholic in the sense of including everyone. But as our comments on charismatic Christianity made clear, this is not so. Including all people anywhere within one distinct tradition is a Christian practice. Including people for whom the coexistence of ideas from diverse cultures, traditions, and practices is an inner experience is new religionist. In other words, creating a new religion does not prevent people from adopting **hierarchical** forms of organization or restricting membership. Absolute tolerance is a chimera.

To be catholic means to be inclusive; a catholic movement is universal in scope and membership. For this reason, the early Christian creeds incorporated the expression "the holy catholic church" to convey the belief that, like Buddhism and

Islam, Christianity is open to all people regardless of race, class, or gender. Many new religions share this vision. Others are deliberately exclusive. Such groups draw from numerous world traditions but purposely exclude certain people.

## The European Origins of New Religions

Europe was the home of industrialism. It took root in Britain in the eighteenth century and spread to Germany and America. Only later did the rest of the world feel its impact (Laslett 1984; North and Thomas 1980; Marshall 1973). During the nineteenth century, the growth of new religious movements coincided with the spread of Christian missions that exported the gospel and modernity and imported other religious texts and exotica (Porter 1985).

In Europe there is a long history of religious revitalization movements stretching back to Roman times. The Reformation, for example, began as a cult movement proclaiming a novel interpretation of Scripture. It quickly developed into a sect and then, throughout most of northern Europe, became a church. Similarly, the Puritan movement and Lutheran Pietism developed as sects within Protestant churches. All of these movements sought to revive the Christian tradition through spiritual awakenings.

Only in the late eighteenth century did self-consciously modern religious movements emerge. These movements no longer sought to revive the Christian tradition but to create new traditions that merged old Christian themes with exotic elements from other sources. In these movements we find the origins of today's new religions.

By far the most important influence on the growth of new religions in the nineteenth century was **Emanuel Swedenborg** (1688–1772). After an excellent education and extensive travel, he embarked on a brilliant career as a natural philosopher, or in modern terms a scientist. In this capacity he became inspector of mines for the whole of Sweden. After publishing a series of scientific books on various subjects, including medical topics, he turned to the spiritual in 1749. At first these writings appeared anonymously, but later he published under his own name (Block 1968:3–18).

Swedenborg's spiritual writings, which stretch over twenty years, purport to be expositions of the Bible and descriptions of spiritual truths that he learned through dreams, visions, and communication with spirits. Although cast in a semi-Christian mold, they nevertheless repudiate most beliefs of traditional Christianity. They launched a massive spiritual movement throughout Europe.

Behind his work lay the conviction that science and the growth of rational thought had created a religious crisis. It was this crisis that he sought to overcome through direct revelations from God. We know little about the roots of Swedenborg's theories. Although he never left Europe, he took a keen interest in Africa and China and was an avid reader of mythology, both ancient and modern (Sigstedt 1952:166, 182–183, 119; Block 1968:54–55, 427).

Swedenborg appears to have had contact with Swedish or Finnish shamans—a fact not brought out by his biographers but mentioned in a footnote in Gloria Flaherty's book on **shamanism** (1992). Flaherty points out that at least one eighteenth-century writer of religion who set out to debunk shamanism specifically mentioned Swedenborg's work on the topic (Flaherty 1992:97–113; 227, n. 2). If this is so, it is an important link between Swedenborg and later spiritual figures, for although Swedenborg did not found a new religion, his followers did. On 5 December 1783 the first meeting of a group of devotees took place in London. From this group was born the New Church, originally called the Theosophical Society (long before Helena Blavatsky adopted the name in 1875). Swedenborgian societies quickly spread through Britain, and in 1784 the first missionary arrived in America, where the new faith took root quickly (Block 1968:62–111).

The impact of Swedenborg's teachings was immense. In America the popular folk hero John Chapman (1774–1845), better known as Johnny Appleseed, was a Swedenborgian preacher who spread religious tracks far and wide (Block 1968:115–117). **Joseph Smith** (1805–1844), the founder of Mormonism, was strongly influenced by Swedenborgian teachings, as was **Mary Baker Eddy** (1821–1910), the founder of Christian Science and the entire New Thought and "mind cure" movement (Parker 1973; Washington 1993:17–18).

Even more intriguing is the finding that at least one African independent church in South Africa's Transkei openly admitted its dependence on Swedenborg's writings (Pretorius 1985:54–55). Further afield, Sun Myung Moon, the founder of the Unification Church, was also influenced by Swedenborgian ideas (Kim 1980:58–59). Finally, many terms used in new religions, such as "New Age" and "theosophy," as well as doctrines like celestial marriage were first popularized by Swedenborg and his followers (Beaman [1881] 1971; Bochinger 1994: 282–293).

The psychologist **Carl Gustav Jung** (1875–1967), who had a major impact on the New Age movement, adapted many ideas from Swedenborg (Wehr 1987:62; Noll 1994:186, 297). Later, **Gerald Gardner** (1884–1964), who is generally acknowledged as one of the founders of modern witchcraft, or **Wicca**, was influenced by Swedenborg and the nineteenth-century occult revival. He moved to Sri Lanka in 1900 and worked in Malaya as a colonial civil servant, traveling throughout Asia. After developing an interest in Malay folk religion and occult practices, he returned to England in 1938, where he joined a theosophical group run by the daughter of the famous theosophist Annie Besant. Through this group Gardner met Dorothy Clutterbuch, who encouraged his interest in witchcraft and initiated him into ritual magic. His books *Witchcraft Today* (1954) and *The Meaning of Witchcraft* (1959) laid the foundation for the contemporary witchcraft revival (Adler 1986:46, 56, 60–66; Luhrmann 1989:42–54).

From this brief overview, we see that a well-established tradition of occult writings, originating with Swedenborg, gave birth to numerous new religions. Now we need to examine the way this tradition developed and expanded in America.

## America's Contribution

Throughout the nineteenth century, America was a hotbed of new religions. Swedenborgianism, mind cures, and various forms of New Thought created a climate for the growth of spiritualism. Theosophy eventually emerged out of this rich occult mix. Before it did, the most successful of all new religions was Mormonism.

It will surprise some readers that we classify the Church of Jesus Christ of Latter-Day Saints as a new religion. Surely, some will argue, the Mormons are a Christian sect. In fact, as their early literature shows, this is not true. Jehovah's Witnesses, Christadelphians, and similar groups are sects because they remain part of the Christian tradition, however heretical their views. By contrast, Joseph Smith made it quite clear that his movement represented a complete break with the Christian tradition. Of course he maintained that he was "restoring" the original teachings of Christ. But unlike Charles Taze Russell of the Jehovah's Witnesses, he did not do this on the basis of biblical exposition. Rather, Joseph Smith's "restoration" was based on new revelations he claimed to have found in *The Book of Mormon* (1830) and, even more important, *The Doctrine and Covenants* (1835).

Early Mormon theologians such as **Parley P. Pratt** (1805–1859) understood the revolutionary nature of Smith's revelations. In his *Key to the Science of Theology* (1855), Pratt argued that the original knowledge of God and the gift of prophecy was lost among the Jews in the fall of Jerusalem. After reappearing and flourishing for a brief period, it was lost again among other nations. Therefore, from the time of the early Church to the revelations of Smith, true religion did not exist (Pratt [1855] 1973:19–33, 166–167).

Smith ushered in a new era with teachings that were completely different from those of the historic Christian churches. Included in the "new" or "restored" doctrine was the idea that the earth was created by a "Grand Council" of gods and that evolution, what Pratt called "endless progression," is the basic law of the universe (Pratt [1855] 1973:61, 53). Accordingly, "Gods, angels and men are all of one species, one race, one great family" (Pratt [1855] 1973:40–41), and all humans originally existed as spirit beings before being given bodies on earth. Finally, the ultimate goal of humans is to govern other planets, which will be populated by their own gods. This theology is totally different from anything found in traditional Christianity. It incorporates ideas (preexistent souls, for example) that are taken from many traditions. They are bound together by a science fiction vision of the universe that reflects nineteenth-century ideas of modernity. Lest we begin to think that Pratt was eccentric, we should note that he merely expounded ideas found in *The Doctrine and Covenants*. These ideas have been reaffirmed by Mormon theologians ever since (Talmage 1962:392).

If Mormonism is the most successful new religion that originated in America, then theosophy must be regarded as the most creative. Like Mormonism, theosophy grew out of the Swedenborgian revival. Its founder, **Helena Blavatsky**, was an extraordinary Russian who in 1875 cooperated with an American, Henry Olcott (1832–1887), to found the Theosophical Society. The extent to which Blavatsky drew on Swedenborg is unclear. What has now been proved beyond reasonable doubt, however, is that Blavatsky based her first major work, *Isis Unveiled* (1877), on the novels of Robert Bulwer-Lytton, whose writing was clearly influenced by Swedenborg (Liljegren 1957; Campbell 1980:14, 56). Later, Blavatsky and Olcott traveled to India, where they imbibed the religious ethos of Hindu society (Meade 1980:111–189; 206–210).

Blavatsky's sojourn in India had a major impact on her thought. It led to the publication of *The Secret Doctrine* (1888), which includes claims about telepathic contact with spiritual teachers, known as mahatmas, who dwelt in Tibet. Blavatsky said these enlightened beings were part of a hierarchy of teachers who were leading humankind to a new age of **enlightenment** (Meade 1980:217–260).

One of Blavatsky's most prominent converts was the English freethinker and political activist **Annie Besant** (1847–1933). The latter became a theosophist in 1889 (Dinnage 1986). More than any other European, she encouraged the growth of Hindu revitalization movements and political nationalism through her tireless efforts to spread theosophy in India. Because of Besant and like-minded individuals, theosophy—which might otherwise have remained an insignificant new religion—played a major role in modern intellectual history (Dinnage 1986: 109–114; Nethercott 1963:213–304, 413–422, 468–469).

The teachings of theosophy are a strange mix of occult wisdom, late Victorian fiction, and bits of doctrine culled from the great world religions. Buddhist and Hindu ideas eventually predominated, although at the beginning of her career Blavatsky seemed drawn to Egyptian themes (Campbell 1980:31–74). As a movement, the Theosophical Society proper never succeeded in attracting more than a few thousand members (Campbell 1980:175). But then the importance of theosophy is not evident in the growth rates of the society's membership. Rather, its significance is found in the spread of theosophical ideas that stimulated both Buddhist and Hindu revitalization movements and numerous new religions (Wessinger 1988:323–344; Washington 1993; Singer 1972:29).

## New Religions in Asia

The nineteenth century saw a religious renaissance in Asia that arose in reaction to the outreach of Christian missions and gave birth to hundreds of new religious movements (Neil 1979:261–280, 255–366; Thomas 1969). Ram Mohun Roy (1772–1833), the founder of the Brahmo Samajin in 1828, and **Maharishi Dayananda Sarswati** (1824–1883), who founded the Arya Samaj fifty years later, bitterly attacked the Hindu tradition. Both men set out to create a new religious synthesis incorporating elements from Christianity and Islam within a scientific framework (Saxena 1989:53; Vable 1983:9).

Some of their successors cooperated with British and American **Unitarians** in the hope of creating a new global religion (Saxena 1989:16–25, 54–63; Baird 1981:2–6, 20–23). Many others were attracted to the political vision of Roy and Sarswati and freely admitted the intellectual debt they owed them yet retained a deep commitment to Hinduism. Attempts to create new religions were thus quickly superseded by numerous revitalization movements that swept through nineteenth-century Indian society. The founders of many of these movements sought to revive the Hindu tradition. Probably the most important of all such figures was Sri Ramakrishna, whose Ramakrishna Path and Mission began in 1880.

It was Ramakrishna's disciple, Vivekananda (1863–1902), however, who successfully blended traditional Hindu religious teachings and practices with modern Western ideas (Romain [1931] 1965; Baird 1981:197–198, 209–221). Vivekananda's greatest triumph came when he spoke at the World's Congress of Religions in 1894. In his speech he argued that the Hindu tradition was a dynamic one that valued "being and becoming" over dogma. This, he believed, made the ancient scriptures of India far more relevant to the modern world than the Christian Bible. Hindu scriptures, he argued, were in harmony with modern science (Hanson 1895:366–376).

Following Vivekananda's example, many gurus have tried to bring traditional forms of Hindu religion to the West. The best known of these today is Sri Prabhupada, the founder of the International Society for Krishna Consciousness, also known as the Hare Krishna movement (Goswami 1983). It is very important to note, however, that these expressions of Hindu religion are revitalization movements and not new religions (Judah 1974; Williams 1992). Other movements, like that of **Bhagwan Shree Rajneesh**, are truly new religions (Joshi 1982; Thompson and Heelas 1986). So, too, is transcendental meditation (Kroll 1974; Forem 1973). But by comparison with Hindu revival movements both in India and the West, these movements are small indeed.

The new religions of Korea also developed in response to modernity and Christian teachings that entered Korea in the second half of the nineteenth century (Palmer 1967b; Grayson 1989:187–193, 234–254). The first major new religion there, founded in 1860, was the Religion of the Heavenly Way, or Ch'ondogyo, named after its founder, Ch'oe Che-u, who received "heavenly manifestations" calling upon him to restore true spirituality (Palmer 1967:92–100; Weems 1964:7–13, 21–35). Other new religions combined ancestral practices with elements of traditional shamanism, **Confucianism,** Buddhism, and Christianity in the name of science and progress (Palmer 1967b; Grayson 1989:234–239).

The best known of these Korean groups in Western society is of course the Unification Church of the Reverend Sun Myung Moon. Identified as one of the more dangerous cults by its enemies, the Unification Church is a self-consciously global religion that blends Korean traditions with Christianity and science in a manner that raises many important questions for the student of religion (Chull et al. 1981; Chryssides 1991:46–107).

Sun Myung Moon was originally influenced by Southern Baptist missionaries in Korea (Chryssides 1991:70–80). He received an excellent scientific education in Japan, enabling him to become an engineer. Exposure to communism as the result of the Korean War led him to study Marxist works (Chull et al. 1981:67–75). His teachings about the nature of religion thus reflect a complex interaction among Korean religious traditions, Christianity, science, and secular philosophies (Barker 1984:74–93).

Moon created a religion that not only cultivated a global consciousness but made it an integral part of its theology. The basic text of the Unification Church is *The Divine Principle* (Moon 1973), which most church members regard as a new revelation (Quebedeaux and Sawatsky 1978:248). In this work providence is the power of management that makes possible the comfortable coexistence of shamanism, Confucianism, Judaism, and Christianity in individual experience (Kim 1980:241–255).

Following the end of World War II in 1945, new religions mushroomed in Asia. Many observers seek the origins of these movements in the shock of Japan's military defeat and the impact of the atomic bomb, interpreting the new religions in terms of **deprivation theory**, as pseudopolitical reactions (McFarland 1970: 11–13, 37–70; Mullins 1991:4–11). Others view them as interesting but superficial movements (Offner and van Straelen 1963:268–275). Finally, certain studies show that the roots of these movements are far deeper than generally thought and are genuinely religious in nature (Reader 1991).

Nevertheless, all agree that the rapid growth of new religions from the middle of the nineteenth century followed Western intrusions that began to disrupt the Tokagawan shogunate from 1571 to 1867, a time when outside influences were discouraged and Christianity was persecuted. During the Meiji restoration, the return of imperial rule to Japan and a period of rapid Westernization from 1868 to 1910, science, technology, and Christian missionaries flooded into Japan (Ooms 1993; Ichirō et al. 1972:24–27, 89–104). New religions, such as Sikai Kyuseikyo, the Teaching of World Salvation, founded by Mokichi Okada in 1882 (Offner and van Straelen 1963:76–82), flourished. Other new religions, such as Sukyo Mahikari, the True-Light Super Religious Organization, founded by **Yoshikazu Okada** in 1960 (Davis 1980), appeared later. Movements such as Rissho Koseikai, the Association of Truth and Fellowship, founded by Myoko Naganuma (1899–1957) and Nikkyo Niwano (1906–) in 1938, and Soka Gakkai, the Value Creation Society of Tsunesaburo Makiguchi, founded in 1937, are genuine revitalization movements within Japanese Buddhism (Offner and van Straelen 1963:95–109; cf. Clarke and Somers 1994).

## Africa's New Religions

New religious movements abound in Africa where they are usually called African indigenous, or independent, churches. As John Buchan's classic novel *Prester John* shows, African new religions were initially seen as dangerous political movements opposed to white rule. A modified version of this view, which is popular among scholars, is that African new religions began as a reaction to colonialism. It is often said that the first independent church of any consequence, the Thembu Church led by Nehemiah Tile, was born in the Transkei around 1883 (Saunders 1970).

This analysis was recently shown to be false: In fact new religions are part of African life and must be interpreted as genuine expressions of African spirituality, not simply as a negative reaction to Europeans. In South Africa, for example, the earliest reported mass religious movement among blacks was that of the prophet Ntsikana in the early nineteenth century (Hodgson 1980). He combined elements of traditional religion with a form of Christianity to develop a new religion suitable for a rapidly changing society. Other recent research makes it clear that although racism may have played a role in the development of African independent churches, the drive to create genuine religious innovation had its source in African dreams and visions (Poewe 1996).

For many Africans, Ethiopia became the symbol of liberation because it was never under colonial control. Various secessions from mission churches led to an Ethiopian independent church movement and later a Zionist movement. By 1913 there were 32 new religions in South Africa. This number had grown to 800 by 1949, 2,000 in 1960, 3,270 in 1980, and 6,000 by 1993. Of these 6,000 groups, about 90 percent have between twenty-five and sixty members. In other words, some 35 percent of South African blacks, or 8 million people, belong to the independent churches, which have more members than the largest mission churches, the Roman Catholics and Methodists, combined.

The oldest and arguably best known of the larger new religions is the ama-Nazarite movement of the "prophet" **Isaiah Shembe**. Founded in 1912, this movement has around three quarters of a million followers who are mainly **Zulu**. Anyone who has seen the BBC film *Zulu Zion* or read Sundkler's books knows that Shembe's religion preserves the essence of traditional Zulu culture. Nevertheless, in one scene of the BBC film, Zulu dancers are wearing Scottish kilts and pith helmets. Shembe was acutely aware of the need to integrate tradition and modernity. To do this, he reached out to Europeans and Indians, encouraged education, and used a combination of traditional, modern, and biblical ideas to prepare for a new world (Daneel 1987:35–67; Hexham 1996; Vilakazi, Mthethwa, and Mpanza 1986:85–94, 101–112).

The perplexing question is whether the ama-Nazarites form a new religion or a Christian sect. Deciding whether particular African independent churches are Christian sects or new religions is both complicated and academically dangerous. Many scholars who identified African groups as new religions were perceived to do so simply to dismiss them as unworthy of serious consideration, and critics of independent churches were often labeled as explicit or implicit racists. In 1976, when G. C. Oosthuizen presented evidence that the ama-Nazarites should be regarded as a new religion, he was torn apart by academic colleagues (Sundkler 1976:190–192; Vilakazi, Mthethwa, and Mpanza 1986:88–110).

It has since become clear that Oosthuizen was probably correct in his analysis (Hexham 1994:xix; Hexham 1996). Yet this does not solve the issue. Londa Shembe, who was brutally assassinated in 1989, believed that his grandfather had deliberately created a new religion with roots in Christianity, Judaism, and even Hinduism (interview with the authors, Ekuphakameni, South Africa, August 1987). But Isaiah's son Amos Shembe, who led a rival branch of the church, believed that although Oosthuizen's interpretation was essentially right, the ama-Nazarites were becoming increasingly Christian. So we are left with a puzzle that applies not only to the ama-Nazarites but to many similar movements in Africa.

## Global Religions and Spiritual Experiences

In the beginning people tend to become members of new religions as a direct consequence of a religious conversion or **proleptic experience**, a happening that so shatters an individual's basic assumptions as to bring about a paradigm shift, for example, from agnosticism to faith in the reality of the sacred. That these experiences later become rituals does not detract from their transformative power.

A religious experience establishes such a strong link between the individual and the sacred that beyond this specific link the individual revels in diversity, new insights, and openness to the world of diverse cultures. All members of new religions whom we interviewed mentioned having a direct and certain relationship with the sacred, whatever its shape. They took their receptivity to spiritual realities to be the source of their power to function comfortably in a plural world.

At times spiritual awakenings can lead to major changes in social and political outlooks. For example, one South African convert who was brought up in a tight-knit ethnic and language community had a strong spiritual experience and a vision confirming a new direction in his life. Although he had attended an ethnic church up to that time, he moved to a nondenominational new religious movement. As he said, "We are Afrikaners. The new church was 70 to 80 percent English-speaking and perhaps 10 percent black. But when we visited there, we sensed love. . . . So first we gave up our Afrikaans language and then our inculcated racism" (interview with the authors, Pretoria, 1987).

This process of "giving up racism" was also reported by a South African member of the Unification Church. His acceptance of a Korean **messiah** led him to reject his racist upbringing and embrace blacks as brothers and sisters. In both cases the process was one of moving from experience to experience along a dialectical exchange whereby an experience illuminated doctrine and doctrine illuminated new experiences. It is this dialectic, or **"reciprocal illumination"** (Mühlmann 1984:44), that accounts for the "revelatory" aspect of the experience.

It is perhaps not surprising that it was a devout French Jesuit missionary, Joseph François Lafitau (1670–1740), who is regarded as the founder of modern comparative ethnology. According to W. E. Mühlmann, Lafitau developed the comparative method based on reciprocal illumination, by which Lafitau meant specifically that Iroquois customs and institutions illuminated antiquity just as the customs and institutions of antiquity illuminated contemporary indigenous culture. This process is vividly recreated in the 1991 Canadian film *Black Robe,* which dramatized the encounter between the Jesuits and native Canadians.

## Iconic Leadership

**Iconic leadership** is of major importance in African-initiated churches and other new religions, yet few academics have commented upon it. People we interviewed, whether Zulu, Europeans, or North Americans, recognized the power of iconic leadership, expressing a clear sense that exceptional leaders awakened in their listeners powers of perception and insight of which they had until then been unaware.

In Christian contexts these powers are understood to be in effect anointed upon the leader by Jesus Christ. Traditional Zulus believe ancestors endow individuals with gifts of power. In both Zulu and Western society, these spiritual gifts change the existential reality of those who come to the leader to share in their anointing. Thus the spirit of the ancestors or, in the charismatic case, the Holy Spirit is said to use the imagination and senses of receptive individuals, enabling them to perceive what they formerly missed (Daneel 1988:108; Poewe 1994:234).

Inus Daneel says that in African independent churches an "iconic leader is a reflection and concretization of Christ without necessarily usurping Christ's place" (Daneel 1988:108). In a more general sense, an iconic leader is understood to be a living manifestation of a religious figure. Thus Prabhupada, the founder of the Hare Krishna movement, was clearly an iconic leader of great power. Numerous stories are told about such leaders by their followers. For many converts, it is the encounter with the iconic person that leads them to accept a group's teachings and way of life. Through such life-changing encounters, people feel that they have participated in the divine. When followers proclaim the deeds of such a leader, they wittingly or unwittingly prepare others for a similar encounter that makes the sacred a living reality.

In secular terms, an iconic leader has the ability to stimulate formerly repressed sensory perceptions. The iconic leader opposes the Enlightenment mind-set that censored experience of the transcendent (Roszak 1981:58). An iconic leader does not have to be a **magician** or brainwasher but simply sanctions the use of otherwise neglected powers of perception.

New religions are undoing what Peter Berger (1969:111–112) called the "shrinkage" of the sacred. They are putting back precisely that which the Enlightenment removed, namely, the sense of the **numinous**. Genuine experiences of the numinous are so rare, real, and powerful that people preserve them in stories and myths passed on from generation to generation.

## KEY TERMS

**Afrikaner:** White South African of Dutch descent who speaks Afrikaans. Prior to 1875 Afrikaners were known as Boers.

**Bastian, Adolf** (1826–1905): German anthropologist who profoundly influenced Bronislaw Malinowski through his emphasis on the importance of fieldwork.

**Bede, the Venerable** (673–735): Called the father of English history, a Christian monk who devoted himself to scholarship and the preservation of traditions. He is best remembered for his classic work *The Ecclesiastical History of the English People.*

**Besant, Annie** (1847–1933): English freethinker and radical who converted to theosophy and did much to popularize its teachings.

**Bhengu, Nicolas** (1909–1986): Black South African evangelist who had a major influence on the worldwide charismatic movement.

**Blavatsky, Helena** (1831–1891): A spiritualist in New York in the 1870s. Born and educated in Russia, she claimed to have visited Tibet and India and in 1875 founded the Theosophical Society, which has influenced many new religions. Her most important books are *Isis Unveiled* (1877) and *The Secret Doctrine* (1888).

*The Book of Mormon*: A collection of writings published by Joseph Smith in 1830 and regarded by Mormons as scripture. Essentially a Christian novel, the book claims to tell the religious history of native Americans.

**Brandt, Johanna** (1876–1964): Afrikaner mystic who discussed the coming Age of Aquarius and feminist theology in *The Millenium* (1918) and *The Paraclete, or Coming World Mother* (1936).

**Confucianism:** The traditional religious or, more correctly, philosophical practices that underpin Chinese society. The system is based on the teachings of Kung Fu Tzu (551–479 B.C.), who believed that he had a mission to bring peace and good government to China. It is distinguished by ethical rather than religious teachings, loyalty, and the cultivation of humanity.

**Deprivation theory:** The popular sociological theory, inspired by Marxism, that religious movements can be explained in terms of the poverty, or deprivation, of their members.

*The Doctrine and Covenants*: A series of revelations published by Joseph Smith in 1835. In these Smith claimed to be a prophet with a unique message from God, his theology radically departing from traditional Christianity. Mormons regard the book as scripture.

**du Plessis, David** (1905–1987): Often called the father of the charismatic movement, a South African Pentecostal whose experiences with black religion and world travel led him to develop a deep ecumenical spirituality.

**Eddy, Mary Baker** (1821–1910): Founder of Christian Science and author of *Science and Health with Key to the Scriptures* (1875).

**Enlightenment:** In Yogic religions the attainment of a state of spiritual knowledge, awareness, or bliss; in Buddhism the revelatory experience of the Buddha and attaining nirvāna. This use of the word "enlightenment" should not be confused with "the Enlightenment," a movement characterized as the beginning of the modern period of European culture. Kant defined "the Enlightenment" in his book *Religion Within the Limits of Reason* (1793) as humans' emergence from a self-inflicted state of minority.

**Folk religion:** A local religious tradition preserved by oral transmission.

**Fuller Theological Seminary:** Probably the leading Evangelical seminary in North America.

**Gardner, Gerald** (1884–1964): One of the key figures in the modern revival of witch-craft through his books *Witchcraft Today* (1954) and *The Meaning of Witchcraft* (1959).

**Global culture:** The tapestry of culture that expresses global dimensions interwoven to form a lively pattern. Global cultures transcend national, international, ethnic, racial, and class boundaries to create a new whole. They are then, in effect, local cultures because they always grow out of and incorporate local beliefs and practices, their participants self-consciously cultivating an openness to diverse cultures. Global cultures are therefore meaning networks or transnational webs of culture.

**Gregory, Pope** (540–604): Known as "the Great," he did much to preserve learning and culture in Western Europe after the collapse of the Roman Empire in the West.

**Hierarchical:** An organization arranged in ordered ranks with recognized leaders and followers.

**Iconic leadership:** Someone who is perceived as a concrete representation or revelation of the holy.

**Jung, Carl Gustav** (1875–1961): Swiss psychiatrist and early disciple of Sigmund Freud who developed his own system of psychology with strong religious and even occult over-tones. Drawing upon alchemy, Yogic religions, and various esoteric traditions, he proposed a theory of archetypes that verges on pseudoscience.

**Magician:** Someone who practices magic to produce effects in the world by means of invisible or supernatural causation.

**Malinowski, Bronislaw** (1884–1942): Polish-born English anthropologist normally credited with developing participant observation.

**Megachurch:** A church with a congregation of over 2,000 members.

**Messiah:** A Hebrew word meaning "anointed" that is applied to a man sent by God to restore the fortunes of the people of Israel. Christians believe that Jesus of Nazareth is the expected Messiah.

**Metaculture:** A bare minimum of essentially consistent and homogeneous elements of a specific faith. These elements remain recognizable even when the metaculture is absorbed into specific cultures to become movements, denominations, or cultic processes.

**Numinous:** A term coined by Rudolf Otto (1869–1937) to evoke the feeling or sense of the holy, which he viewed as fascinating, fearful, and beyond rational analysis.

**Okada, Yoshikazu** (1901–1974): Also known as Okada Kotama; the founder of the Japanese new religion Sukyo Mahikari.

**Pratt, Parley P.** (1805–1859): Mormon apostle and author of *The Key to the Science of Theology* (1855).

**Proleptic experience:** A life-changing, revelatory experience that profoundly affects the individual and is ascribed to the work of God or a spiritual being or supernatural force.

**Prophecy:** In general the foretelling of future events or the deep insight into a condition. Prophesying is common in charismatic churches, where it is often linked with giving people "words of knowledge" to encourage them in their life's work.

**Rajneesh, Bhagwan Shree** (1931–1991): Founder of a highly successful new religious movement that claimed to have no roots in previous religions. His followers are called Rajneeshies.

**Reciprocal illumination:** The act of knowledge whereby one person is able to communicate insight to another through a mutual interchange of feelings and ideas.

**Roy, Ram Mohun** (1774–1833): Indian political reformer and religious leader who founded the Brahmo Samajin in 1828 to revitalize Hindu society.

**Sanford, Agnes** (1897–1982): A leading figure in the charismatic movement who emphasized the gifts of healing. She was born in China of missionary parents.

**Sarswati, Maharishi Dayananda** (1824–1883): Founded the Arya Samaj in 1875 as a social, political, and religious reform movement in Indian society.

**Schaeffer, Edith** (1914–): Daughter of missionaries to China and cofounder of the L'Abri Fellowship in Switzerland. Her many books emphasize "living by faith," by which she means trusting God for all one's needs.

**Shamanism:** The indigenous religion of northern Eurasia, featuring trance and the control of spirits by exceptional individuals, or shamans, who negotiate between this world and the spirit world.

**Shembe, Isaiah** (1867–1935): Zulu religious leader, healer, and founder of the ama-Nazarites, the largest independent religious movement among the Zulus. Regarded as God by many of his own people, Shembe is usually spoken of as a prophet by Europeans. His writings and sayings were the first scriptures of a new religious movement in Africa to appear in English (Hexham 1994).

**Smith, Joseph** (1805–1844): The founder of the Church of Jesus Christ of Latter-Day Saints, probably the most successful of all new religions.

**Swedenborg, Emanuel** (1688–1772): Swedish mystic whose writings led to the development of many new religions.

**Tongues:** Glossolalia, literally "speaking in tongues." It refers to an ecstatic spiritual state that manifests itself in utterances that sound like a foreign language.

**Toronto Blessing:** An ecstatic religious experience that broke out in late 1994 at the Vineyard Church located near Toronto Airport. Initially it was associated with uncontrolled laughing. The phenomenon quickly drew visitors from many countries and spread through the world.

**Tradition:** A distinct and integral body of knowledge or belief that sits on identifiable faith assumptions and is passed on from the past to the present in recognizable form despite numerous interpretations and reinterpretations. The basic assumptions of one tradition guarantee its distinctiveness from other traditions, much like basic rules of grammar keep languages distinct despite the borrowing of words and expressions.

**Trance channeling:** A modern version of spiritualist mediumship.

**Unitarians:** A diverse religious movement that emerged in the early nineteenth century simultaneously in America, England, and other parts of the world. Unitarians deny the deity of Christ and Christian teachings about the godhead in terms of the Holy Trinity.

**Vineyard movement:** A Christian revitalization movement founded by John Wimber that grew out of his classes at Fuller Theological Seminary in the 1970s. It is often described as the "third wave" of the charismatic movement.

**Wicca:** The name adopted by practitioners of a vigorous new religion that claims to practice "witchcraft." Members of Wicca claim that the traditional perception of witchcraft as something evil is wrong, that they practice ancient healing arts and a pre-Christian religion.

**Zulu:** One of the best known of all African nations, numbering around 7 million people who live along the southeastern coast of South Africa near the port city of Durban.

## ❀ 4 ❀

# New Religions and
# Primal Experiences

*Shembe was overwhelmed by a deep drowsiness and fell asleep. In his dream,
he saw himself flying in the firmament. Also his chest opened and his spirit
went out to meet the spirit. And a Voice spoke to him.*

Petros Dhlomo (Hexham 1996:17–18)

*I*n this chapter we look at the nature and common occurrence of primal experiences, examining their relationship to various shamanic religions, possession
practices, and new religions. Rather than focusing on psychological explanations
of primal phenomena, we describe their dynamic function in mythmaking and
look briefly at three mythmakers.

## Primal Experiences and the Global

At the heart of many religious movements, particularly new religions, lie **primal
experiences**—unexpected vivid encounters that are considered to be other than
normal. Such experiences take many forms. Above all, they not only shock those
who experience them but also bring about a change in their attitude toward the
material world. Social scientists like Stark and Bainbridge recognize the importance of such experiences but concentrate on quantifiable sociological aspects of
conversion (Stark and Bainbridge 1985:85–89).

Likewise, Eileen Barker's truly excellent *Making of a Moonie* (1984) provides a
mass of information about the sociological dynamics of conversion to the
Unification Church. Yet in this pioneering book Barker makes no mention of individual conversion accounts involving primal experiences. It is our argument
that contemporary religious conversion, whether it is to a church, sect, cult, or

new religion, cannot be understood without taking into account the central role of primal experiences.

On the basis of numerous interviews and published accounts, we believe that primal experiences play a crucial role in the creation of new religions, in the conversion of members to new religions, and in their religious lives thereafter. Naturally, people join new religions for many reasons, for example, peer pressure or to escape unhappy home situations. But the core group of converts always reports vivid proleptic experiences that compel them to see the world and their lives in a new way and to make practical changes accordingly.

Primal experiences involve such things as dreams, visions, voices, tongues, spiritual healing, a sense of presence, notions of destiny, fate, sightings of ghosts, inexplicable spiritual phenomena, and other occult events. Primal experiences are important for new religious movements because they affirm the reality of an unseen world. In other words, they bring an individual face to face with the supernatural. Indeed Hotoshi Miyake (Reader 1991:23) has argued that contemporary religions are effective in Japan precisely because they are but a minor variation of the concern for ancestors, spirits, and magical healing that has dominated folk religion for centuries. Reader develops this theme by showing the way Japanese new religions blend with folk traditions and practices (Reader 1991:194–233). Similarly, in *Dojo* Winston Davis provides an extended example of the way Japanese folk traditions enter a new religion (Davis 1980).

Primal experiences are usually enough out of the ordinary that secular society tends to deny that they are real. Alternatively, because they are unusual, our medical and psychiatric establishments identify them as abnormal. Consequently, people who report such experiences may be classified as disturbed or mentally ill (Kakar 1982). Since no one likes to be labeled in this fashion of course, even people whose lives are fundamentally changed by primal experiences become reluctant to talk about them or talk about them only with like-minded individuals.

There is another problem concerning the nature of religious experiences. Students have often asked us how people of different religions can have similar religious experiences. For example, because speaking in tongues is the defining experience of Pentecostals, these believers have great difficulty when they are told that Buddhists may also speak in tongues. Can religious experiences be meaningful for followers of one religion when they are also common among adherents of another religion?

We can answer the above questions simply and positively by using analogies. Just as people speak different languages using the same speaking tools (lips, tongue, brain, and so on), so people of different religions have uniquely meaningful experiences using the same faculties (the receptive imagination, trance sounds, meditation, rhetorical figures, and so on). A somewhat different analogy brings out another aspect of this phenomenon. Just as the hearing impaired read gestures as signs, so believers read **happenings** as signs. And just as the gestures are part of a specific sign language that the hearing impaired must know in order to interpret the gestures, so happenings are part of a specific experiential language, a doctrine, for example, that the believers must know in order to interpret happenings. Since most religious doctrines postulate that certain happenings are caused by supernatural beings, believers tend to interpret happenings as telling them that the supernatural, whatever it may be, is working in their lives.

Expanding on the argument of Sudhir Kakar, who contrasts what he calls superficial idiomatic differences with underlying universals, we might simply argue for the universality of primal experiences that are interpreted differently by different idioms or frameworks. We in the West have tended to feel most comfortable using a psychological framework; others may use a "demonological framework" (Kakar 1982:24), a mystical framework, and so on.

In line with the major theme of our book, we want to alert the reader to one other aspect of religious experiences. Primal experiences, too, have local and global aspects and are part of local and global religious cultures. Thus a global phenomenon like speaking in tongues has very specific meanings in specific local religious cultures. Alternatively, some experiential phenomena, meditation, for example, may be closely linked to a global tradition like Catholicism or Buddhism. Finally, as we mentioned in Chapter 3, a very local, almost forgotten religious experience like **possession** (Bourguignon 1976) may be taken up by new religions, given a new name like "trance channeling" (MacLaine 1983; Heinze 1991:8), and used to communicate seemingly new and globally relevant messages.

An example of the transformation of a premodern primal experience, like possession by ancestors, into a postmodern primal experience, like trance channeling from guiding spirits, is found in Japan. Ryuho Okawa, the young founder of the Science of Happiness Association (Kofuku no Kagaku), claims to receive messages from such luminaries as the Buddha, Jesus Christ, **Edgar Cayce**, Swedenborg, Isaac Newton, and Pablo Picasso. One cannot be much more global than that. He has turned these messages, or "spirit revelations," into 150 "spirit world" books within four years (Mullins 1990:14).

## Frequency of Primal Experiences

As it turns out, primal experiences are remarkably common. David Hay became interested in the phenomenon when some postgraduate students surveyed at the University of Nottingham, England, admitted that they had primal experiences that profoundly affected their outlooks (Hay 1975). The majority of these students said that they had no adequate explanation for their experience and would welcome one. Following this initial survey, Hay and Ann Morisy arranged a statistically valid national survey of the British population. In this more qualified survey, they found that 36.4 percent of those included in the random sample reported having had primal experiences. Significantly, 45 percent of those who had these experiences had no real contact with churches or organized religions (Hay and Morisy 1978).

In a national survey in the United States, some 30 percent of Americans responded positively to questions about having primal experiences. Robert Wuthnow obtained a much higher figure in his survey of the San Francisco Bay area, where the positive response rate went up to 50 percent (Wuthnow 1978). In Canada Reginald Bibby found that 60 percent of Canadians reported positively when asked about primal experiences. According to Bibby, all of this evidence suggests a "pool of religiosity" that is largely untapped by established religions (Bibby 1985; cf. Hardy 1979).

Similar findings are reported in other industrial nations (Mullins 1990; Davis 1980), Africa (Lee 1954; Oosthuizen 1992:1–3), and other parts of the world (Kakar 1982). In his study of hundreds of Zulu in South Africa, for example, S. G. Lee reports that before individuals would become diviners in divining cults, they would have a variety of primal experiences, including numerous visual and auditory communications (Lee 1954). Fifteen percent reported a history of minor possession that involved fugue states, hallucinations, dreaming, and so on. Seventeen percent reported diseases that they attributed to sorcery. The difference between those who merely consulted diviners and those who actually became diviners was largely a matter of the severity of their condition. Chronic or severe sufferers went through rigorous six-month-long initiations and converted from client to diviner to have their "ways cleared" (Lee 1954; Beattie and Middleton 1969:28–55).

## Primal Experiences and Shamanism

As Hahm Pyong-choon says, "Nothing in human life can be totally new, having no connection whatever with the old and existent. Thus, a continuum exists which links the new and the old" (Yu and Guisso 1988:75). These words apply particularly to new religions. The latter draw some of their ideas, those that authenticate them, from an existing font of local folk religions. Most of these ancient but persistent folk religions are shamanic. Few if any of them occur in pure form. For example, in Korea and Japan the interaction between shamanism and what might be called the four world religions—Buddhism, Confucianism, Taoism, and Christianity—has been "prolonged and intensive" (Yu and Guisso 1988:60).

Shamanistic folk religions are revived again and again. This is particularly noticeable when we look at founders of both contemporary and new religions. The latter have functioned essentially as traditional shamans (Mullins 1990:18; Heinze 1991; Hori 1968). This being the case, we first take a closer look at the nature of non-Western shamanic religions. Second, we consider the nature and role of primal experiences in shamanic and new religions. And third, we compare the psychological state of members of shamanic religions with that of members of new religions.

Shamanistic religions are ecstatic, or trance-based, religions (I. M. Lewis 1971, 1986). A central feature of such religions is the drama of a person's being seized by the divine—a transcendental experience that is typically referred to as a trance or state of possession (Lewis 1986:81). Adherents of shamanistic religions believe that while mystics or shamans are in the trance state they have direct experiential knowledge of the divine and can serve as channels of communication between the human community and the supernatural. In Japan shamans are understood to perceive God's will either through glossolalia (speaking in tongues) or as "new" revelations or inspirations (Mullins 1990; Goodman 1972, 1988). In non-Western societies shamans are usually inspired prophets and healers who have "the power to control the spirits, usually by incarnating them" (Lewis 1986:88).

The primal experiences reported by shamans include such things as visual and auditory communications, waking visions, revelatory dreams, out-of-body experiences, and spirit possession. These ecstatic experiences, especially spirit possession, may be either spontaneous or self-induced (Lewis 1986:86). Japanese and Korean shamans use strenuous bodily exercise or repetitious dance to induce trances (Yu and Guisso 1988:86). Similar states are achieved by American Zen Buddhists through meditation and by Hare Krishnas through chanting and dancing. Simple, repetitive tasks; physical exhaustion that leads to hypoglycemia; drugs; and other methods can all be used to bring on trancelike states.

Primal experiences in shamanistic religions are much the same as primal experiences in new religions. In the modern Western context, trance states and experiences of spirit possession are popularly referred to as trance channeling, altered states of consciousness, and paranormal experiences. They include such things as prophetic dreams, out-of-body experiences, encounters with the dead, seemingly miraculous healings, and supernatural knowledge. In both cultural contexts (ancient and new), such experiences serve a similar purpose: They cause many people to join religious communities because these groups offer explanations of what are otherwise inexplicable experiences. Alternatively, they cause many such people to stay in their adopted religion because the community encourages them to continue having these experiences. Whatever we may think of the nature of these experiences, it is clear that many of the people who have them are convinced that they constitute evidence of the existence of a spiritual realm.

## The Issue of Mental Health

One of the most important issues for us as we consider these phenomena is the question of the mental health of those who report having had primal experiences. Members of new religions *rightly* resent that the psychiatric profession sees them as having psychological problems. Nevertheless, old and new studies from many parts of the world report that would-be shamans suffered from psychological disorders referred to as **hysteria** (Kakar 1982:75–81; Davis 1980:139; Langless 1965:56; Caudill and Lin 1969) and psychogenic diseases like psychosis and schizophrenia (Yu and Guisso 1988:141–142). In other parts of the world, such individuals have histories of consistent failure and social maladjustment. In many cases these individuals overcame their own problems and helped others with theirs. Even shamans had proleptic experiences that transformed them from sufferers to spiritual healers.

In our view religious experiences are common phenomena in a pre- and post-Enlightenment world. They involve the use of faculties such as the **receptive imagination** that are sanctioned by religions. They simply point to the recognition that the sole use of reason and logic is not enough to live full lives. It made sense to use razor sharp reason to cut through dead traditions of the seventeenth and eighteenth centuries. But the world recent generations have inherited is fragmented, so that we observe once more the yearnings of people for wholeness and the willingness to "quell a natural scepticism" (Luhrmann 1989:286). As André Droogers observes, this globality, a sense of wholeness, was understood to be integral to primal experiences from time immemorial (Poewe 1994:39–49). Therefore when we invoke psychological terminology in the following sections, it must be understood as part of the history of thought and not misinterpreted as a way to dismiss the experiences of members of new religions. Furthermore, we must remember that in much of the world primal experiences are closely associated with healing and therapy (Wallace 1966; Ichirō et al. 1972; Davis 1980; Kakar 1982; Laderman and Roseman 1996).

## Okinawan Shamans

Shamans and diviners universally report primal experiences. Looking closely at some examples of shamanism in the non-Western world should help us understand not only these spiritual experiences themselves but also their status in terms of the standards of traditional psychology. As a first example, we consider the account of Okinawan shamans as described by William Lepra (Caudill and Lin 1969:216–222).

According to Okinawan beliefs, shamans (usually women) are different from birth. They are said to be born with and possessed by a *kami,* or divine, spirit, although they may not recognize this for some time. An individual typically becomes a shaman following notification from her or his own *kami* spirit. These notifications initially take the form of strange occurrences, such as visual and auditory hallucinations. If the individual ignores these experiences, the *kami* sends a sickness that can't be diagnosed or cured by either modern or traditional doctors. After all else fails, the only cure that remains is for the individual to seek out and accept the special guardian spirit. Individuals who are thus cured are considered shamans; individuals who are not cured at this point are considered insane. Shamans subsequently learn which specific *kami* spirit possesses them through dreams.

We would stress that before individuals are recognized as shamans, they often are considered—and consider themselves to be—mentally disturbed. After they become shamans, their condition is reinterpreted: They are instead held to be endowed with the capacity for spirit possession and the ability to see the past and the future. As we will see later, such a change in perception is reminiscent of that made by Anton Boisen concerning the patients in an American mental hospital (Boisen [1936] 1971).

When would-be Okinawan shamans recognize their potential to become shamans and yet refuse to accept the role, they are often regarded as continuing to suffer from behavioral disorders inflicted by their *kami.* Note that failure to accept the office of shaman is regarded as a symptom of a pathological condition, an indication that an individual is or is becoming insane. Once such people assume the office, their past behavior is reinterpreted as having been deviant in a divinely inspired fashion. Individuals who assume the office of shaman and then fail to carry out the duties of the office or behave too extravagantly are once more considered to be insane.

It is part of Okinawan belief that hopeless mental pathologies begin at birth and are punishment inflicted by the supernatural. People who suffer from such pathologies may try to find a cure. When they are unsuccessful, their affliction is ascribed to some irreparable wrong committed by ancestors. Less serious mental pathologies and simple behavioral disorders that arise later in life are held to be symptomatic of impaired relations with the supernatural. It is assumed that once the situation is accurately recognized and put right, the victims will be cured.

Okinawan shamans cure their maladjustment by realizing their special status through a process of self-discovery and self-enlightenment with supernatural assistance. Two points should be emphasized. First, it is assumed that the supernatural may offer a cure when all else fails. And second, however their behavior or condition may have been perceived and described before, once individuals assume the role of shaman, their problem comes to be regarded as *religious* rather than psychological in nature. Problems that a shaman experienced early in life are reinterpreted as an indication of having been chosen.

## Primal Experiences and Religious Leaders

We find similar patterns in the lives of the leaders of many contemporary and new religions. The threat of failure, illness, catastrophe, and a sense of messianic consciousness are recurrent themes in the biographies of such individuals as Yoshikazu Okada, the founder of Sukyo Mahikari (Davis 1980); Mormon prophet Joseph Smith; John Humphrey Noyes of the **Oneida Community**; and the messianic figure of the **Shaker community, Ann Lee.** With small variations in the details, similar descriptions apply to the Reverend Sun Myung Moon, the Bhagwan Shree Rajneesh, Jim Jones of the ill-fated People's Temple in Guyana, and other leaders of recent new religions.

We wish to emphasize the relative frequency of "failure" and the sense of being an outsider in the lives of those who later become shamans or charismatic figures—and the kind of knowledge that is required to overcome such shortfalls. We agree with the assertion John Calvin makes at the beginning of his *Institutes* that the form of knowledge that is most essential to living a full life is self-knowledge. It is regrettable that self-knowledge (and the means by which it is obtained—namely, self-discovery) is the form of knowledge that is most ignored in modern Western systems of formal education. Those who go through the educational system acquire self-knowledge at best by means of nonverbal, unacknowledged, and unrewarded processes that are almost wholly incidental to the processes by which they acquire the formal thinking tools and skills to function in the larger world. In order to know themselves and to feel whole, even sophisticated people turn to new religions, revived witchcraft, and generally small groups that dabble in magic, the **esoteric**, and the "multifarious occult" (Luhrmann 1989:6, 10).

## The Significance of Failure and the Uniformity of Experience

With this in mind, we should turn once more to Lepra's study of shamanism in Okinawa (Caudill and Lin 1969). He notes that the life histories of shamans reveal long records of discord in interpersonal relations. Their early lives are characterized by frail health and time spent alone doing unusual things, slighted by their parents. Their relations with kin tend to be strained and distant, their marital lives marked by sexual incompatibility, frequent divorce, and bickering. Their ability to perform work and meet responsibilities is consistently poor. In short, the best way to describe their early lives is as failure—in home, school, occupation, sex, marriage. Most important, however, is their failure in interpersonal relationships and general achievement.

Poewe (1985) noted much the same phenomenon among the Herero of Namibia, especially among those who became "prophets" in African independent churches. These individuals might be described as Christianized shamans. The major spirit that possesses them is no longer an ancestor but the Holy Spirit. The Bible, fortuitously opened and inspiringly interpreted, leads them to their revelations.

Okinawa shamans, like Herero prophets, describe long bouts of illness that set them off from others. They recall these periods of illness as times of extreme anxiety, misery, and helplessness that were, however, overcome to benefit the larger community. In Namibia most black women, but especially Herero women, also suffer from unrelieved anxiety and a sense of helplessness. Those who do not themselves become "prophets" seek them out to be healed. In these situations religious experiences have very practical functions: They make individuals whole or transform them. They reconnect them to their community, the cosmos, and, in the case of Herero prophets, to the international world of African independent churches in South Africa or to the world of Pentecostals everywhere.

Finally, we see in these lives, and in others we discuss later, something larger than the merely personal and local. As shamans, diviners, and founders of new religions tell their stories, we become aware of a common mythological pattern, a structure that once again has both local and global aspects. When the personal story is projected outward to embrace a people, the story assumes the structure of a life-changing myth. It proceeds from a major catastrophe to a sense of death and rebirth, to revelations that have a cosmic importance, followed finally by a sense of mission.

This pattern is easily observed, for example, among the ama-Nazarites of South Africa. The Zulu suffered devastating defeats by the Boers and British. The displacement and loss of land constituted a social death. Their sense of rebirth was awakened through Isaiah Shembe, an iconic leader who stood for and indicated the presence of God. According to his grandson, Londa Shembe, God caused Isaiah to happen. Emphasizing the meaning of iconic leadership, Londa Shembe told us, "Isaiah made God real for us" (interview with the authors, Ekuphakameni, South Africa, August 1987; Poewe 1994:28–29, 243). He connected the Zulu of the ama-Nazarites to the cosmos and gave them a new sense of mission.

## Shamans and Spirit Possession

I. M. Lewis characterizes the shaman as "an inspired prophet and healer, a charismatic religious figure with the power to control the spirits, usually by incarnating them. If spirits speak through him, he is also likely to have the capacity to engage in mystical flight and other 'out of the body experiences'" (Lewis 1986:88). Shamanism usually involves a trance induced at will. When a shamanic tradition exists in a society, shamanism may be a vocation like any other. In most situations becoming a shaman requires rigorous training. In Japan this training is called *shugyo*, "self-training." It entails learning a number of simple body movements and sensory stimulations that are repeated in order to induce a trance by bringing about a gradual dimming of both physiological and psychological consciousness, leading to a diminution of ego activities.

In Siberia as well, becoming a shaman requires training, which involves seclusion, reduced calorie intake, and ingestion of hallucinogens (Goodman 1988: 136–143; Balzer 1990:3–45). Children grow up in a shamanic tradition and consider shamanism a plausible career choice. Similarly, in Korea, because group therapy is emphasized, shamans must have the talent to dramatize the presence of the spirits that possess them. The would-be shaman therefore follows a well-recognized "career path" (Yu and Guisso 1988:131–161; Lewis 1986:78–93).

Audrey Butt noted that in South America good-looking young men with a ready understanding, a good sense of humor, and a personality that set them above their peers were most likely to succeed as shamans. Successful shamans are lively, intelligent, sensitive, and responsive to others (Wavell, Butt, and Epton 1967:38–42). It is clear that the shamans in this tradition have very different personalities than those in the Japanese shamanic tradition or the South African and Namibian prophetic tradition.

Shamanic styles are significantly shaped by a people's religious tradition, specific social and cultural setting, and individual and social health problems. In South America shamans are more frequently male than female; in China and Japan it is the reverse. Lewis attributes some of these differences in shamanic style to the fact that in some social settings only women and men of subordinate social status become shamans. He also makes a significant distinction between what he calls peripheral amoral possession cults and central morality cults (Lewis 1971:129–148). Central morality cults are premodern religions that renew and maintain a people's core values. By contrast, peripheral amoral cults refer to those religious practices of a people that are used to assert, and compensate for, existing social inequality.

## Peripheral Amoral and Central Moral Religions

Peripheral amoral religions are usually protest cults that allow the underprivileged to heal themselves and/or make demands on their masters (Lewis 1971). The shamans of these cults are different from shamans in societies where moralistic tribal religions are fully functional, as in certain South American settings. Shamans in Central Asia, South America, and North and East Africa are principally concerned with the moral order of their people, with relationships between individuals, and with the relationship of people to the earth (Seaman and Day 1994; Laderman and Roseman 1996).

During ritual séances these possessed shamans exhort people to shun evils of incest, adultery, sorcery, and homicide and to be harmonious in their social relations. Such shamans are carefully selected and trained, although they, too, follow the typical path to accepting their office. They dream strange dreams that persuade them of the correctness of their choice and seek seclusion in the outdoors to better communicate with the spiritual world.

What Lewis calls peripheral amoral cults tend to develop in societies characterized by world religions such as Christianity or Islam. They spring into life especially in periods of rapid social change and are associated with individuals or classes of socially mobile people whose ambitions are at odds with the prevailing way of life. Together these cults form new religious movements, the leaders of which resemble those who become shamans in tribal settings. Like shamans, these leaders become possessed. Although their possession may begin with an illness, it ends not merely with a cure but, as in the examples above, with divine inspiration of a new view of the world. Leaders with a gifted imagination or an extraordinary capacity for fantasy will elaborate their divine inspiration, as Joseph Smith did in *The Book of Mormon* and the Reverend Moon did in *The Divine Principle*.

Even Fawn M. Brodie's somewhat cynical description of Smith's reaction to his inspiration lets us see the yearning for the global—for an open universe beyond the restriction of the immediate drudgery of life. In her words:

His imagination spilled over like a spring freshet. When he stared into his crystal and saw gold in every odd-shaped hill, he was escaping from the drudgery of farm labour into a glorious opulence. Had he been able to continue his schooling, subjecting his plastic fancy and tremendous dramatic talent to discipline and moulding, his life might never have taken the exotic turn it did. (Brodie 1971:27)

In sum, there are common aspects not only in the case histories of shamans from different parts of the premodern world but also in the case histories of members and founders of new religions in the postmodern world. These are not aspects of what the traditional Western psychological community would characterize as psychopathological. Instead, they are evidence of the discontent that exceptionally bright and sensitive people often experience. These individuals may feel a desire to break out of the small and uninspiring world into the big world of unlimited resources, where they can sense a certain wholeness. Often untrained, these individuals run with their imaginations and dramatic talents.

## Box Myths and Šhuman Religions

In past studies of shamanic or new religions, researchers placed much emphasis on psychological explanations (among many others Hexham and Poewe 1986; Caudill and Lin 1969; Kakar 1982). Although psychological studies have an important function, including that of discovering dissimulation or fraud (Noll 1994), they tend to be too focused on psychopathology. Most new religions, however, have little to do with psychopathology. Instead, they have to do with mythmaking, symbolic expression, creativity, and rhetoric (Young 1991; Poewe 1994).

The operating system of new religions is mythmaking, the fascination of people with what in German is called *Schachtelsage,* or "box myth." A box myth is a myth within a myth. And the particular box-myth-making that attracts contemporary new religionists is that of creating a **personal myth** within a **cosmic myth**. The most famous founders of new religions are those mythmakers who have the creative talent to construct a labyrinthine box myth with the idea of sending their followers through it as if they were embarked on a sacred adventure.

Whether in Japan, Africa, Europe, or America, box-myth-makers always link pre-Enlightenment folk religions with post-Enlightenment trends, giving their religions an interesting quality. None of the founders shows a clear yearning for the **holy** in the sense of **Rudolf Otto**'s meaning of "numinous." These religions do not, in other words, postulate a totally transcendent God who invites absolute abandonment of all things human in selfless discipleship totally dependent on the power that comes solely from, say, a Krishna or Christ. Nor are new religions solely shamanized world religions. Shamanic religions are primarily premodern and thus part of an **animistic** universe. And yet new religions value sanctity and hold some things sacred. But what is it that they hold sacred? The answer is of course the human being.

New religions are what we call **šhuman** religions. They sanctify (š) things human (human). Šhumanists cannot free themselves of nor undo Enlightenment teachings that made the human being and the material world the starting point of all else. True, these religions are pre-Enlightenment in their rescue of the imagination and its mythmaking capacity from the sharp razor of reason. But they are post-Enlightenment in their focus on person and earth, person and nation, person and environment, or person and the material universe. The creative mythmaker is the example par excellence of someone who is confident that he or she has tapped the source of sacred power and, through the creation of a mythological map, can show followers, too, how to find it.

In the remaining sections of this chapter, we briefly look at three mythmakers: Deguchi Onisaburō, Helena Blavatsky, and Shirley MacLaine. Good material is already published about each or by each (Young 1989, 1991; Meade 1980; MacLaine 1983). We therefore give merely a short summary for the purpose of showing readers something about how box myths are made.

## Box-Myth-Making and the Founder of Ōmoto

According to Young (1991:23), the "flamboyant virtuoso" of Japanese folk religion and the brilliant mythmaker of the "Shinto-Christian amalgam" was Deguchi Onisaburō (1871–1948). He was also the cofounder of a new religion called Ōmoto (The Great Foundation). Although Ōmoto is now in decline (Seat 1991), it gave rise to many other "world-renewal" religions, among them Mahikari (True Light) (Young 1989:26). Onisaburō initiated what has since become very popular in Japan, namely, the reclamation and conversion of "numerous divinities and founders of other religions," among them Jesus, into *kami* spirits (Young 1991:23). The question that interests us here is, How did he do it?

Onisaburō was a student of Hirata Shinto. A great synthesizer and charismatic figure, Onisaburō attracted a following and became a modern shaman. Soon he created a personal myth that convinced his followers that he had experienced personally, in another realm, the events he related in his stories. Richard Young does not give us an analysis of the rhetorical figures and symbolic expressions that Onisaburō used "in the formative years of his initiation into religion" to mythologize and modernize texts that tell about a second coming of Christianity to Japan, but he makes clear that Onisaburō was a first-class mythmaker (Young 1991:23–24). He knew logopneumatology ("literally, the study of 'the spirit in [the Japanese] language'"), and he was generally adept at wordplay and allusion (Young 1989:30, 39, 40).

And then Onisaburō did in Japan what we observed frequently in South Africa (Poewe 1993a, 1993b; Luthuli 1962:43–44): He showed that "Christianity was actually not foreign" but rather "had returned to its source" (Young 1991:23). To Japanize Jesus, Onisaburō did a curious thing. The Christ of the Judeo-Christian tradition was, in the view of Onisaburō, "a vacillating and effeminate person who whimpered through his crucifixion" with whom the founder of Ōmoto could not identify (Young 1991:23). Left as such, "Jesus was a 'dead kami' (shinigami), unable even to 'break wind.'" Onisaburō wanted a more Japanese Christ. In 1920 therefore "he declared that the 'Christ' had returned in his own person" (Young 1991:23).

Even in this limited account, we see that the personal myth is not only embedded in a grander or cosmic myth, but the primal experiences that are vital ingredients of a personal myth function like an operating system. They make possible the swift shift between one myth and the other.

## Helena Blavatsky and Mythmaking

Since numerous biographies of Helena Blavatsky exist (Meade 1980; Symonds 1960; Barborka 1966; Noll 1994), we look only at those aspects of her life that make classic material for use in a personal myth. In the process we also note some striking similarities to the lives of founders of new religions mentioned in earlier sections.

According to Marion Meade, whose study is most useful for our purposes, Helena Blavatsky was a nervous, colicky, and high-strung infant. Like other founders and shamans, her earliest memories are of being "perpetually ill" and "ever dying" (Meade 1980:24). Stories have it that Blavatsky was a willful and independent child, in the "habit of automatically defying authority" (Meade 1980:25). Furthermore, she was apparently plagued by a general instability that had something to do with "unconscious psychological conflicts about her parents" (Meade 1980:25). The house serfs believed that she possessed "special magical power," and her family, too, "recognized her abnormalities" (Meade 1980:25, 26).

Most important for her mythmaking talent is the intellectual atmosphere in which she grew up. Although she dismissed it as unimportant, it had much to do with what she became. Blavatsky was blessed with a vivid imagination that found nourishment in the rough military environment in which her father existed. Important for us, however, is that she immersed herself from an early age in occult literature. For some reason, intimate knowledge of the occult tends to be denied in the West. By contrast, would-be founders of religions in Japan have dabbled in it, learned mediumship and divinatory techniques, had visions, and gone into trances. Since all this involves careful instruction and practice, they let their training be known (Hiroko 1979:418–420).

According to Meade (1980), Blavatsky grew up with her grandmother, a zoologist, and her mother, who at an early age wrote novels that depicted the plight of bright women whose brilliance was ignored. Each lived in her own world. Blavatsky's grandmother found fulfillment in marriage and science. Blavatsky's mother wrote literature to relieve her suffering in an unhappy marriage and to fill an intellectual void. Although both these women were self-disciplined, Helena was not.

Largely left to herself and without any formal education beyond a glance at languages and music, Helena Blavatsky invented a spirit world, entering spontaneous trancelike states. She told dramatic tales about herself and about her conversations with her grandmother's stuffed animals, who revealed their former lives to her. Apparently, she felt herself possessed by spirits of the dead; was prone to automatic writing; saw entities no one else saw; heard the voices of pebbles, trees, and decaying timber; and generally had primal experiences that others considered bizarre (Meade 1980:32, 39, 41).

Meade points out that Blavatsky's experiences resembled those of the Irish-born medium Eileen Garrett, who had invisible playmates as a child and was accused of being a liar and crazy. Helena's mother died when Helena was ten years old, and her father left her in the care of her grandmother's house; Garrett's parents committed suicide shortly after her birth, leaving the infant to be raised by an aunt and uncle. At age four, Garrett discovered that she could avert suffering by "retreating into episodes of amnesia" (Meade 1980:42–43). Both Garrett and Blavatsky learned to dream themselves into states of altered consciousness. Throughout her life, Blavatsky invented one invisible protector after another.

Most important for our thesis is that Blavatsky found affirmation of her unconventional ways, primal experiences, and dramatic talents not among her kin but in the enormous library of her grandparents. She was an avid reader, especially of the occult collection that once belonged to her great-grandfather, Prince Paul Dolgorukov (Meade 1980:48). Blavatsky was strongly influenced, for example, by the book *Solomon's Wisdom*, which familiarized her with hypnosis. She was also deeply influenced by the works of medieval alchemists and occult writers generally. But like other founders of new religions (for example, Andrew Jackson Davis), Blavatsky claimed virtual illiteracy (Meade 1980:115, 163). She did this to give the impression that her thoughts, especially those that shaped *Isis Unveiled* and *The Secret Doctrine*, came to her by mysterious means, thus enhancing the authenticity of her books. It is the stuff that fascinated Carl Jung, who attended séances throughout his life (Noll 1994:63). He developed the technique of "**active imagination**," in which he explored notions of **implicit memory**, such as the images individuals see when they have visions, and "transpersonal long-term memory-storage" (Noll 1994:79, 147).

The tendencies and skills she showed in childhood Blavatsky perfected in later years. Like many mythmakers, Blavatsky could not abide dullness or convention. She was fascinated with esoteric and occult knowledge, anything that promised age-old secrets. Blavatsky was not accepted in the Orthodox Christian world of her Russian compatriots, and no doubt she did not want to be. It was much more fascinating for her to find her own divine plan, a more exotic, mystical, and all-encompassing one than that offered by mainline Christianity.

Like those who would follow in her path (Shirley MacLaine, for example), Blavatsky visited as much of the world as her means and dependency on others would allow. She set out on a spiritual adventure that took her to American mediums and spiritualists, American Indians, and gurus in Tibet and India. And if she did not always reach these places in reality, she did so in her imagination.

When Blavatsky could not cope, she would withdraw into trance. When she had needs, she would manipulate people to meet them. Even as a child, she claimed (like a Yanomamo shaman) that "*roussalkas* and invisible beings" were in her power and were "protecting her from harm" (Meade 1980:146). When she was found out in her mischief, she would blame her ill temper and doings on spirits. Since her imagination was more real than reality, she would take credit for the thoughts, actions, and writings of others.

Blavatsky's mission was conceived on a cosmic scale. Her personal myths, wrapped tightly in her cosmic myth, had world implications. In her forties Blavatsky began to understand her intentions, namely, "to restate the entire occult doctrine and salvage the ancient world from the modern stigma of superstition and ignorance" (Meade 1980:156). By the time she completed *Isis Unveiled*, Blavatsky had developed a "venomous hatred of Christianity" and believed "all past wisdom" had its source in India (Meade 1980:169).

## How Myths Are Made: A Brief Example

In the next chapter we point out that myths make statements about the place of the human being in society, the world, and the cosmos. Myths are concerned with relationships among people, other nations, other religions, nature, and the supernatural. Myths have to do with the human being's ability to symbolize. Indeed, in Japan the use of symbolic logic is a fine art, taught, practiced, and cultivated among mediums and founders of new religions (Young 1989:39).

One of our surprising findings, in light of secularization theories, is that our thought patterns and behavior in our postmodern, hi-tech world are deeply symbolic. As Northrop Frye (1982:xviii) says, "Man lives not directly or nakedly in nature like the animals, but within a mythological universe, a body of assumptions and beliefs developed from his existential concerns."

Mythmaking did not cease within biblical times nor with primitive humans, as those who see thought and language in evolutionary terms might expect. Rather, mythmaking is as popular and commonplace an activity as ever. In Japanese world renewal religions, mythmaking is part of a long tradition with roots in Buddhism. Those who join these religions are taught not only various techniques for entering altered states of consciousness but also myths as texts. Although mythmaking is less well organized in Western new religions, it is quite clear that those who are serious about them have considerable mythological knowledge of what is in fact an unbroken tradition of mythmaking (Noll 1994:176).

There are two forms of mythmaking that are particularly popular today. One form has consequences for groups, the other for individuals. Myths with communal consequences are like **revelations**. They tend to share the seven phases of creation, exodus, law, wisdom, prophecy, gospel, and apocalypse. These involve stages of a spiritual pilgrimage and a mythological geography, like exodus, wandering in the wilderness, crossing the Jordan River into the Promised Land, and so on.

Here, however, we are interested particularly in individual mythmaking, commonly found in testimonies by anyone who is on a spiritual quest. A good example of the latter is Shirley MacLaine's (1983) book and film, *Out on a Limb*. The individual mythmakers are artists. They are not only imaginative but blessed with the capability of both universalizing the particular and particularizing the universal. On the one hand, they universalize particular experiences by linking them to fragments of existing myths that are universal. On the other hand, they particularize universal myth fragments by living them out as their own experiences. If an important experience such as unrequited love is in need of meaning, mythmakers give it meaning through its goodness of fit with a mythological fragment, for example, of remembered past lives. Thus Shirley MacLaine explains her intense love for a man she cannot have with a story about a former existence in which they must have known one another. Alternatively, if a mythological fragment, for example, a story about astral travel, seems abstract, mythmakers make it concrete by experiencing it, for example, by having an out-of-body experience.

Second, experiential and historical details are selectively omitted, compressed into dense symbols and powerful images, or turned into a refrain or leitmotif. Thus we might convert the details of the Allied bombing of German cities between 1943 and 1945 into a phrase such as "the year of the big fire" or "the time of the firestorm." That more than one year was involved and that many separate bombings by different forces were carried out becomes incidental. The important thing is to condense time and events into a major symbol, image, or even ideogram. Likewise, the food shortages from 1945 to 1948 may be called "the year of the hunger," just as we have the "year of the locusts," and so on. This compression gives everyday detail universal value yet retains the experiential truth-value or reality.

Third, when individuals intent on creating a personal myth engage in something as commonplace and primal as shamanism, spirit possession, or trance behavior, they can empower these terms—make them more futuristic—by changing the language to suit the times. Shamans or other types of mediums thus claim to be "trance channelers" whose power and wisdom are augmented because they have been displaced by ancient spirits (for instance, a 3,500-year-old spirit called Ramtha). Founders of world renewal religions may have multiple identities: Some claim to be the Buddhist savior figure Maitreya, others Picasso, Christ, and so on. It not only enhances their power and prestige but also sanctions imaginative mythmaking.

Symbolic language is as much subject to fashion as are clothes. And like clothes, language changes to suit the times. The times are no longer merely transcultural and global but hi-tech, interplanetary, and science fictional. Similar transformations apply to an individual, like Ephraim, who comes to represent not only a particular nation or humanity or God but in whom nation, humanity, and God are immanent.

When all is said and done, modern trance channelers are no more powerful than were shamans of old. Behind the drama, the trance, and the media are individuals with life patterns that are similar, in all probability, to Siberian, Japanese, or African shamans and diviners. There is, however, the possibility that what is "real" in a trance channeler was "real" in a shaman. We mean the ability of human beings to enter trance, to let the imagination roam as if it were contacting an ancestral past, and from within this mode, to speak freely a common wisdom.

## Conclusion

The primal experiences described in this chapter seem to be universal, although they are always talked about in terms of particular idioms that are specific to particular communities or religious organizations. That this is so has to do with the intimate link between primal experiences and mythmaking. Primal experiences authenticate the claim that new myths or new mythological revelations have their source in the supernatural.

Just here, however, we find an intriguing and puzzling characteristic of new world renewal religions that Hōyū Ishida (1989) associated particularly with Japan and Buddhism. We, in contrast, see it as a common characteristic of new religions generally. We mean the absence of a sense of the numinous—the holy, in Rudolf Otto's terms. He saw the numinous as a "non-subjective Other which utterly transcends the self and is 'wholly other'" (Ishida 1989:24; Otto 1923). In other words, Otto insisted that God is real and living and can be experienced. To charismatics, for example, the Holy Spirit is a reality that is separate and independent of subjects who experience it. Likewise, God is separate and independent of the natural world that he created. In short, for Otto, "numen was an unambiguously external and independent" reality (Otto 1923:24).

Ishida (1989), following **Ninian Smart**, distinguishes numinous from mystical and, we would add, magical experiences (Smart 1958:79–107; Davis 1980). The latter experiences are the "interior attainment of a certain extraordinary enlightened state of mind" (Ishida 1989:28). One reaches this state of mind through one's own efforts, especially by using manipulative techniques. In such a state of blissful timelessness and spacelessness, there can be no hindrance to the flowing together of any mythological fragments until they form a new, seamless whole.

When spirits are involved, and they often are, given the shamanic influence on new religions, these spirits are but other forms of the human being. They are the ancestors, or what Africans call "the living dead," only now they are associated with the cosmopolitan. They are no longer the ancestors of but one people. Instead, these purveyors of past wisdom are a multicultural lot, a "living dead elite" of a truly global culture. It is for this reason that we coined the word "shuman" religions, meaning religions that venerate and sanctify human beings.

## KEY TERMS

**Active imagination:** A Jungian psychotherapeutic technique of introversion said to allow individuals direct access to the unconscious world of memories and dreams. Creating an analogy with archaeology, Jung argued that the imagination may be used "to make excavations into the phylogeny of the soul" (Noll 1994:178). The idea comes from theosophists, who believed "that the ancestral past could be contacted directly through the imagination" (Noll 1994).

**Animistic:** A term introduced in 1871 by Edward B. Tylor, who argued that from sleep experiences, such as dreams, humans developed the idea of *anima,* or the spiritual principle that animates material objects. Thus rivers, trees, stones, the sun, the moon, and sacred objects such as masks were said to possess spiritual power caused by the indwelling of spirit beings.

**Box myth:** A myth within a myth.

**Cayce, Edgar** (1877–1945): American spiritualist medium and popular writer who was believed to have prophetic gifts.

**Cosmic myth:** A myth based on a story that relates humans to the grand scheme of things.

**Eclectic:** To borrow ideas and practices from any tradition and arbitrarily join them together as though they belong to a unified system.

**Esoteric:** Secret teachings that either belong to secret societies or lie behind the official beliefs that a religious group proclaims to the world.

**Happenings:** Events that can be interpreted as signs or as parts of a whole that caused them. For example, when charismatics are prayed over and fall down, which is referred to as "resting in the spirit," this happening is interpreted as a sign that the Holy Spirit, which caused them to fall, is working in their spirits and lives.

**Holy:** What is set apart and belongs to God because it possesses the character of holiness that is derived from God. See Rudolf Otto, *The Idea of the Holy* (1923).

**Hysteria:** A neurotic mechanism that an individual uses unconsciously in order to avoid the psychological distress associated with emotional conflict. In cultural terms, hysteria is the condition in which a people suffers from a sense of moral injustice so profound that their whole private and symbolic life comes to be centered on an idée fixe, a problem they can imagine being resolved only by an ultimate, dramatic, or sacred solution.

**Implicit memory:** The phenomenon of a kind of spontaneous remembering of information related to repressed past events, possibly in a trancelike state, that is, without conscious or deliberate recollection. The concept is associated with Carl Jung.

***Kami:*** Designating a divine spirit in Japanese Shintoism.

**Lee, Ann** (1736–1784): A "shaking Quaker" who emigrated to America in 1774. She formulated the characteristic beliefs of the Shakers that include celibacy, communism, pacifism, millenarianism, elitism, and spiritual manifestations through barking, dancing, and shaking.

**Lewis, I. M.** (1930–): British social anthropologist and author of *Religion in Context: Cults and Charisma* (1986).

**Oneida Community:** Founded by John Humphrey Noyes (1811–1886) in 1848 on the basis of Christian communism and a belief in human perfectibility. The community disbanded in 1880 when its profitable manufacturing industries became a joint-stock company.

**Otto, Rudolf** (1869–1937): German theologian who pioneered the phenomenology of religion. His *Idea of the Holy* (1923) sets out the thesis that religion is essentially the apprehension of the numinous.

**Personal myth**: A myth that transforms a mundane personal life into a timeless, holistic story that has universal appeal.

**Possession**: The state or experience of being possessed or taken over by a spirit being.

**Primal experiences**: Fundamental spiritual experiences that shatter preconceived notions about the rational order of the universe. These experiences involve dreams, visions, encounters with ghosts or spirits, precognition, and so on.

**Receptive imagination**: The imagination in a state of prayerful surrender and heightened sense perception when insights, intuitions, or visions come to an individual as if from a numinous source that is entirely separate and independent of the individual .

**Revelations**: Crucial insights or acts whereby God discloses himself and/or his will to humankind.

**Shaker community**: A group distinguished by its physical shaking during worship. The community originated with a Quaker revival meeting in 1747.

**Šhuman**: The sacralization of the human; religions that center their beliefs and ritual on the sacred nature of human things.

**Smart, Ninian** (1927–): Scottish philosopher and pioneer of religious studies. His works include *Reasons and Faiths* (1958), *Doctrine and Argument in Indian Philosophy* (1964), and *The World's Religions* (1989), as well as the popular *Long Search* TV series.

*Solomon's Wisdom*: The exact nature of this work is unclear. There is an apocryphal Jewish text with this name plus a number of occult works with the same title. Which of these occult books Blavatsky read is uncertain.

## ❀ 5 ❀

# Myths and Mythological Fragments

*For half a century now, a new consciousness has been entering the human world, a new awareness that can only be called transcendent, spiritual. . . . We all know that life is really about a spiritual unfolding that is personal and enchanting.*

*James Redfield (Redfield 1993:viii)*

$\mathcal{W}$e begin this chapter with a discussion of the meaning of **myth** and present what we consider a useful definition of the term. Then we discuss the lack of a central mythological framework in our society and the function of fragmented myths in the lives of individuals. We show how these fragmented myths form box myths that new religions incorporate into their own operating systems. Finally, we examine the role of **evolution** as a new central mythology that incorporates personal mythological fragments into an integrated perspective.

## Primal Experiences and Myth

What **Abraham Maslow**, in the context of Western modernity, calls peak experiences, others, in the context of non-Western traditions, call primal experiences. Traditional societies mediate the effects of vivid primal experiences through the use of rich mythologies that enable individuals to accept and seemingly understand their psychic condition. But modern human beings suffer from a fragmentation of belief that often leaves those who have primal experiences without any acceptable means of resolving the conflicts associated with them (Maslow 1968).

In medieval Europe people who encountered the primal saw visions of saints and the Virgin Mary. Hindus in India see the gods Krishna and **Rama**, Buddhists meet **Bodhisattvas**, and Muslims share visions of God. By contrast, in industrial society people have raw experiences without readily available imaginative frameworks to give them content and meaning.

Industrial society has no body of shared beliefs, no common mythology. Its members hold onto a collection of disconnected beliefs and are vaguely familiar with fragments of many myths. The advantage that some new religions have in this situation is that they possess powerful integrated mythologies sanctioned by, and sanctioning, primal experiences. The mythologies of new religious movements are created out of numerous disjointed myths found in society generally. By weaving these unrelated myths into coherent wholes, new religions create a sense of continuity with the past. Through the use of traditional myths, they are able to give themselves an apparent historical depth that legitimates their claims to be the carriers of a high culture.

If we are to appreciate how myths are used by leaders and followers of new religions, it is important that we reflect on the function of myth in society. In common speech, to call a story a "myth" is to say that it is untrue. This understanding of the meaning of *myth* dates back to the Greek philosophers of the third century B.C. and was popularized by Enlightenment thinkers in the late eighteenth century. A good example of such a rationalist approach to myths can be found in the works of Plato. In his dialogue *Euthyphro,* Plato depicts his mentor, Socrates, discussing the traditional myths of Greek society with a young man who firmly believes they are true. By a series of clever questions and leading arguments, Socrates soon establishes the contradictory nature of the traditional mythology and so casts doubt on the veracity of the myths themselves. In his book *The Age of Reason,* the eighteenth-century deist Thomas Paine similarly cast doubt on biblical stories, dismissing them as false myths. The skeptical understanding of myths as stories that are essentially untrue permeates rationalist thought. People in our culture find it difficult to think of myths as anything other than fairy tales.

In sharp contrast to common usage, various academics and many popular writers use "myth" to speak about spiritual truths that are hidden within the fabric of ancient stories. This usage allows such writers to promote their own vague defense of spirituality (Eisenberg 1990; Eliade [1954] 1965). In the works of these people and others like them, myths convey some indefinable, transcendental truth or literary value that spiritual people or those who live in nontechnological societies can grasp intuitively but that most modern individuals fail to understand (Ruthven 1976). Although works like these impress people seeking an excuse for religious belief, they are, upon closer analysis, meaningless.

As Hexham has pointed out, because of the problems associated with the term "myth," many social scientists simply abandon it to cranks and attempt to use other, more respectable terms (Greil and Robbins 1994:303–321). This dismissal prevents them from recognizing the way myths color people's thoughts and actions. Not only do myths play a very important role in the interpretation of primal experiences, but they also give meaning to the lives of many people and can even shape entire societies.

## Defining "Myth" Meaningfully

Abandoning the use of the term "myth" to cranks is understandable. But such a retreat causes social scientists to overlook some important aspects of reality that are best understood as myth once the term is meaningfully defined. We can see the value of using myth as an analytic concept when we consider the alternatives.

Instead of talking about myth, we could refer to a *Weltanschauung* (worldview), or we could talk about an **ideology**, **philosophy**, perspective, or paradigm. The problem with all of these and many other similar terms is that they convey the notion of rational argument. Those who live according to their religious beliefs are usually assumed to think and act in a logical manner on the basis of rational arguments. Worldviews are consistent entities, and when their consistency fails or at least is perceived to be failing by either an outsider or an insider, a problem is created for the believer who attempts to show why, despite the apparent contradictions, the worldview is believable.

By contrast, mythological thinking lacks such consistency. Some mythologies may form coherent wholes, but many consist of isolated fragments that coexist in a person's consciousness without the person's feeling any need to express their meaning systematically. Believers often overlook that myths, as myths, lack precise expression because one function of myths is to give coherence to the life of individuals who believe them (Maranda 1972).

What, then, is a myth, and how can we define it without lapsing into the sort of vague nonsense that delights **Mircea Eliade** and others? Probably the most useful definition of "myth" is: *a story with culturally formative power*. This definition emphasizes that a myth is essentially a story—any story—that affects the way people live. Contrary to many writers, we do not believe that a myth is necessarily unhistorical. In itself a story that becomes a myth can be true or false, historical or unhistorical, fact or fiction. What is important is not the story itself but the *function* it serves in the life of an individual, a group, or a whole society.

Myths are stories that serve specific social functions. They enable members of different societies and subgroups within societies to understand themselves and their world. As anthropologist **John Middleton** puts it, "A myth is a statement about society and man's place in it and in the surrounding universe. . . . Myths and cosmological notions are concerned with the relationship of a people with other peoples, with nature and with the supernatural" (Middleton 1967:x).

Thus what makes a story a myth is not its content, as the rationalists thought, but the use to which the story is put. Once accepted, a myth can be used to ennoble the past, explain the present, and hold out hope for the future. It gives individual and social life meaning and direction. This ability to guide action distinguishes myths from **legends, folktales,** and other stories. In short, myths have the power to change lives and shape societies.

## *Myth and Reality*

The importance of a myth lies not with the particular qualities of the story itself but with the use that is made of the story. When a story acts upon the imagination of an individual or collectivity in such a powerful way that it begins to shape their lives, molding their thoughts and directing their actions, then that story has become a myth.

The success of any myth depends upon people's accepting it and acting upon what they consider to be its message. But there is considerable evidence that in fact most people who accept a myth do so because they believe it is true. In other words, their acceptance of the story, before it becomes a myth in their lives, depends upon their assumption that the story is true. Questions of historic, philosophic, or any other form of verifiable truth are therefore important in the creation of mythologies. In fact they precede the creation of myths. What matters is not simply the power of myths to inspire belief and to enable believers to make sense of their experiences but the prior belief that the story is true.

Such a claim contradicts most things written about myth. Nevertheless, years ago, in his essay "Myth in Primitive Psychology," the famous anthropologist **Bronislaw Malinowski** (1884–1942) pointed out that most Western interpreters of myth go wrong precisely because they *do not observe how myths are actually used in social situations* where they are important (Malinowski 1954:96–111).

The validity of individual myths is enhanced when they are incorporated into larger or related myths. In many societies myths are officially sanctioned through public recognition. Thus in medieval Christian Europe many myths, such as those about King Arthur and the Holy Grail, were publicly recognized. In Hindu society myths about Krishna and other deities are given sanction in all areas of life. Christian societies have traditionally given official recognition to Christian mythologies; Islamic societies promote Islamic mythologies; Buddhist societies use Buddhist mythologies; pagan societies draw upon pagan mythologies. In other words, the dominant religion in any given society typically provides its members with a powerful mythology that receives full recognition and social sanction.

Christians tend to be reluctant to admit that myths have important functions in society and that Christianity has provided Western society with official myths for almost 2,000 years. This is because, like rationalists, they usually define "myth" in terms of something that is untrue. They tend to argue that because Hindu stories about Krishna are unhistorical, they are clearly untrue. In contrast, Bible stories are historical narratives and therefore true.

Such reasoning has nothing to do with the status of the Bible stories as myths because, in our usage, the truth of myths is automatically assumed by all believers. The point is that in Europe and North America biblical stories have informed the popular imagination and thus helped mold public opinion to provide society with direction. Thus when we talk about biblical stories creating powerful myths, we are discussing their power to shape the lives of individuals and entire societies.

Speaking of the power of myth, Frye has noted that "certain stories seem to have a peculiar significance: they are stories that tell a society what is important for it to know, whether about its gods, its history, its laws, or its class structure." Commenting on modern society, he says, "In Western Europe the Bible stories had a central mythological significance of this kind until at least the eighteenth century" (Frye 1982:33). By a "central mythological significance," Frye means the power of certain myths to provide a general mythological framework that incorporates all the other myths within a given society. This framework in turn acts as the imaginative and communal operating system of individuals and society by providing them with all the information they need to lead meaningful lives.

From the time of Saint Augustine in the fifth century to the Enlightenment in the eighteenth century, biblical stories provided the framework of European mythology. Other myths found in different parts of Europe were Christianized and incorporated into this framework. Stories such as that of Beowulf and Islandic, Norse, and Germanic sagas were reinterpreted and given Christian meanings. The legend of King Arthur and the quest for the Holy Grail is a striking example (Treharne 1971). The thrust of incorporation may take one of two directions. When Christianity is on the advance, pagan myths are Christianized; when it is in retreat, Bible stories are mythologized, sometimes into foreign myths.

Since the end of the eighteenth century, biblical stories have ceased to provide the central mythology of Western society. Owing to the skepticism of the Enlightenment and nineteenth-century freethinking, most Westerners no longer find in Christianity the basic imaginative and mythological framework by which they understand their place in the world. True, many people still profess to be Christians. But on the whole, Christian belief has been reduced to the realm of private spirituality, and as a result Western mythologies lack a strong Christian content at both their popular and official levels.

Certain subgroups within modern society still retain a strong element of Christian mythology in their understanding of life. It is also true that "Christian values" often inform law and other official elements within different Western societies. But nowhere today do we find biblical mythology providing both the popular and official myths of modern industrial society. As a result, our society appears to lack a strong central mythology capable of integrating mythological fragments into a coherent whole.

Biblical myths appear to have been replaced by a large number of fragmented myths circulating among different subgroups without the benefit of an integrative central mythology. Thus most people hold a mishmash of beliefs that lack cohesion. These beliefs are best described as mythological fragments. We make this observation with some caution, however, because we shall see that a central mythology does in fact exist, although it has not received official sanction outside of the new religions. But before we describe this emerging mythological frame-work, we must first identify the major mythological fragments that are currently popular.

We can identify three major types of personal mythological fragments and three forms of fragmented cosmic myths. These are pseudoscientific myths, myths of fate and prophecy, healing myths, myths of decline, other civilization myths, and myths of transformation.

## *Pseudoscientific Myths*

Myths of **pseudoscience** are stories about what Lyle Watson called *Supernature* (1974). At their core are science-fiction-type stories that reduce people's skepti-cism and their resistance to explain primal experiences in essentially occult terms. When the TV series *Star Trek* first appeared in the 1960s, belief in the occult was at a low ebb. Projecting the story into the far distant future and appealing to an evolutionary framework enabled the writers of *Star Trek* to introduce disembod-ied intelligences and other strange happenings. If these ideas had been placed within a spiritual framework or made to happen in contemporary society, view-ers would have rejected them as ridiculous. But the futuristic orientation and evo-lutionary context made such ideas acceptable because they "might" be possible in the future.

Once people accepted such things as possible within the framework of *Star Trek,* it was an easy and logical step to utilize similar ideas in other stories. It also became easy to make the imaginary shift from extraterrestrial intelligences to spirits and demons. Contemporary occultism owes a good deal of its popularity to **science fiction**. In science-fiction writing proper, the shift from hard **science** to fantasy took place in the mid-1960s. The futuristic scientific interests of older writers such as Isaac Asimov gave way to the cultural and intellectual relativism of younger authors like the anthropologist Ursula LeGuin. LeGuin and other New Wave authors created worlds inhabited by spirit beings motivated by magical spells rather than worlds inhabited by Martians, spaceships, and ray guns.

Another anthropologist who played an important role in popularizing pseudo-science was Carlos Castenada. Unlike LeGuin, who published her works as fiction, he claimed to be writing scientific monographs. Nevertheless, his books about Don Juan invoke a magical world that involves the reader in mystical powers, oc-cult forces, and cosmic battles worthy of LeGuin's fiction. As Jay Courtney Fikes argues in *Carlos Castenada, Academic Opportunism and the Psychedelic Sixties* (1993), Castenada's work is a form of fiction because it lacks the rigor and scien-tific standards found in authentic anthropological treatises. Castenada's great contribution to the development of modern mythology was his claim that "these things happened to me." He changed pseudoscientific stories into personal myths that others could identify with and, by modifying their content, apply to their own lives.

Another man who helped people apply pseudoscientific myths in their own lives was Uri Geller. *The Geller Papers* (Penati 1976) are supposed to contain factual reports about Geller's psychic abilities. Through their publication and numerous public appearances, Geller popularized ideas about psychic forces manipulating physical objects. He is the modern "magician" who claimed to bend spoons and perform other feats through the power of his mind (Puharich 1974). At the time counterclaims by other competent magicians, such as James Randi, who insisted that Geller abused his skills as an entertainer, were conveniently overlooked by the press and gullible believers.

Later, similar ideas were given academic respectability in a more accessible format by Hans Eysenck and Carl Sargent. Their book *Explaining the Unexplained* (1982) is a partisan tract propagating the notions of extrasensory perception (ESP) and psychic phenomena. Although few people claim to have experienced the ability to move objects by mental power, many believe they have had the type of experience Eysenck and Sargent describe. These and similar books enable individuals to appropriate ideas about the psychic powers of human beings into their own personal mythology.

Science-fiction stories, too, provided a bridge between personal and cosmic myths. In 1934 E. E. "Doc" Smith, whose books are still popular, utilized the Atlantis myth and numerous other ideas of theosophy in his fictitious space opera *Triplanetary*. Almost twenty years later, identical ideas appeared as "fact" in George Adamski and Desmond Leslie's best-selling *Flying Saucers Have Landed* (1953).

In their book Adamski and Leslie proclaimed to the world that they actually entered an alien spacecraft where space beings explained to them the secrets of history and the universe. Most later writings about flying saucers and alien visitors to earth draw heavily on the work of Adamski and Leslie, which openly cites theosophical sources (cf. Michell 1967; Steiger 1976). Erich von Daniken's *Chariots of the Gods*? (1968), however, gave these ideas a new twist by omitting the theosophical references. His book in turn influenced the development of Shirley MacLaine's beliefs, who created her own box myth to interpret her life in cosmic terms (MacLaine 1983:339, 341–342).

## Myths of Prophecy and Fate

Prophetic myths involve beliefs about the ability of individuals, with or without the help of certain devices, to foretell the future. The considerable growth in the popularity of this type of personal myth can be seen in the rise in horoscopes featured in U.S. newspapers: In 1940 only 200 daily newspapers carried horoscopes; thirty years later more than 1,750 printed them (Zaretsky and Leone 1974:289).

In addition, there are at least 10,000 full-time and 190,000 part-time astrologers presently working in the United States alone (Melton, Clark, and Kelly 1990:39; Grim 1982:47). One of the most popular of these astrologers is Jeane Dixon, who has successfully manipulated the media to gain a considerable following. The media regularly reports her claims that she can predict events accurately but overlooks her failures, such as her 1979 prediction that U.S. president Jimmy Carter would "suffer a church-related assassination attempt" (MacDougal 1983:35–40). More recently, *Time* magazine (16 May 1988:21–38) examined first lady Nancy Reagan's fascination with astrology. A similar growth in astrological and other occult beliefs is taking place in Germany (Zinzer 1992; *Idea Spektrum,* 5 January 1995).

Equally popular and questionable are the writings of the late Edgar Cayce who, like Helena Blavatsky before him, added a cosmic dimension to his manipulation of personal myths. His predictions were appropriately vague, making it difficult to subject them to proof. His prediction in the 1940s that "sometime between 1958 and 1998" San Francisco would be destroyed by an earthquake did little to enhance his reputation except with the most gullible. Even more difficult to refute and more clearly mythological are the so-called prophecies of the medieval mystic and court astrologer Nostradamus. His cryptic writing style and symbolic language allow people to read almost anything into his works, both wild and plausible predictions.

At a more personal level, teacup readings, tarot cards, the I Ching, and other techniques of divination provide countless individuals with what they take to be experiential confirmation of their belief in prophetic myths. More important, the combined impact of high-profile media prophets like Dixon and the writings of Cayce, Nostradamus, and other "recognized" seers lends credence to the claims of local diviners, whereas personal divination bolsters belief in the better-known figures. Such positive feedback among local, historical, and media prophets mutually reinforces their respective prophecies, making them all seem plausible to anyone who is predisposed to believe in them.

Myths of fate are beliefs in personal and communal luck or fortune. More than the other mythological fragments, these myths point to an increasing belief in a magical and occult universe within Western culture. Belief in luck has always existed in Western society of course, but this general belief was Christianized, and it rarely affected a majority in any given society. Luck was more often associated with gamblers and thus was officially scorned by society. But with the growth of the new mythologies, luck has again found a place in people's outlooks.

In her book *And I Thought I Was Crazy,* Judy Reiser discusses the extent to which belief in luck or in good and bad fortune has become central for many people (Reiser 1979). In this provocative work, Reiser, a social worker, reports interviews with more than 600 people, the majority of whom expressed strong beliefs in common superstitions, good luck charms, and a host of equally irrational ritual actions aimed at fending off evil and misfortune.

Personalized myths of fortune are reinforced by complementary cosmic myths that involve stories about generalized powers. These myths are presented in such movies as *Indiana Jones and the Temple of Doom* and stories about such things as the supposed curse of the long-dead Egyptian king Tutankhamen. The story of

Tutankhamen is typical of how curse myths are generated. When the tomb was excavated in 1922, there was an unexpected delay in the opening of the burial chamber. An overzealous reporter wrote a story saying that this delay was due to the discovery of an "ancient Egyptian inscription" that laid a curse on anyone who entered the tomb. Five months later one of the leaders of the expedition, Lord Carnarvon, died suddenly, and the story of the curse became firmly established in the public mind. In fact no such inscription had been found, and all the other members of the expedition, including those who were the first to enter the main chamber, lived long and successful lives.

Myths of prophecy and fate can also have a social dimension. For example, following the outbreak of World War I a group of white South Africans, known as Afrikaners or Boers, revolted against British rule in support of Germany. Eventually, the British crushed the rebellion and inquired into its roots. To their great surprise, and to the embarrassment of the intelligence officers who investigated the matter, the cause appeared to have been a series of "prophecies" by the farmer Nicolaas van Rensburg, the "prophet" of Lichtenberg.

Van Rensburg is said to have been born with the caul, or afterbirth, over his face. In Boer folklore this indicated the child's psychic powers. He had his first vision at the age of seven. Later, when he served on commando during the Second Anglo-Boer War (1899–1902), he used his psychic abilities to warn Boer commandos of approaching British troops and to guide them to safety. So respected were his abilities that Boer general Jacobus de la Rey is said to have had implicit trust in him.

In July 1913 van Rensburg saw "Europe on fire"; later he had a vision of "two great bulls fighting a struggle of life and death." These bulls were red and gray, and the gray bull was victorious. After the outbreak of World War I, in August 1914, van Rensburg's vision was remembered and interpreted as a prophetic sign that Germany would defeat Britain. As a result, many Afrikaners, including van Rensburg's old commander, de la Rey, rose up against Britain. But this time the vision proved wrong, and both the rebels and Germany were eventually defeated (Nicholls 1987:70–72).

A communal myth of fate that explained personal suffering and national defeat in cosmic terms developed in South Africa following the Second Anglo-Boer War. According to this myth, the Boer republics had been defeated by the British so that they could rise again in the future to fulfill their destiny as the civilizing force in Africa (Hexham 1981). A different type of fate myth developed in Germany following the defeat of 1918 and the unjust Treaty of Versailles. This myth suggested that men who had served in the trenches belonged to a "community of fate," their common destiny drawing them together in a shared future based on past suffering. This myth was first propagated by General von Ludendorff and was later taken up and exploited with great success by Adolf Hitler to gain loyal followers for his cause (Poewe 1996).

## *Healing Myths*

Probably the most influential area for the growth of personal myths is in the realm of health and healing. Healing myths are diverse stories about "spiritual," "holistic," and other alternative forms of healing. They cover a vast range of beliefs, from traditional Christian ideas about prayer to the use of psychic powers and scientology. Many involve claims of miraculous healing, but because of the existence of spontaneous remissions and other natural healing processes, it is impossible to verify such claims. Nevertheless, so great is the appeal of alternative therapies that growing public demand has led to changes in the law that allow alternative practices to flourish (Coker 1995:17). Surveys show that in 1992 26 percent of people in Britain and 60 percent in Germany used some form of **alternative medicine** (Coker 1995:19).

Of course we must differentiate myths of healing from genuine alternative medicines and traditional, nonmagical healing techniques. Herbal remedies, **homeopathy**, massage, and similar methods of healing may not be accepted by all members of the medical profession. They do, however, have a rational basis and do not of necessity involve appeals to occult or mysterious powers, even though they are often cited by magical healers in an attempt to legitimate fantastic claims. Brian Inglis provides a scholarly account of alternative medicines without appealing to or elaborating on their possible mythic significance (Inglis 1964, 1979). His rational approach has helped to make alternative therapies respectable. Consequently, it is now possible to obtain a degree in herbalism from a recognized British university, and a variety of other therapies are widely accepted in British hospitals (Rankin-Box 1995).

What interests us is the role of testimonials about the effectiveness of such methods and the tendency for many practitioners to invoke occult explanations. Most people go to holistic healers because someone has told them about being healed by such and such a method or person. In other words, the popularity of holistic healing is spread through myths. Anyone who doubts this should reflect on the fact that although hundreds of stories circulate about such cures, very few report failure. Yet there is considerable evidence that some forms of holistic healing are harmful (Coker 1995:78–81).

The mythological aspects of alternative healing are a modern version of eighteenth- and nineteenth-century magical health movements, and like ancient healing cults, they have roots in primal experiences. Holistic health is therefore the modern expression of an ancient phenomenon. Its magical quality may not be immediately obvious because many practices tend to be cloaked in evolutionary and pseudoscientific language that gives personal myths a cosmic dimension.

There are obvious links between the modern healing movements and nineteenth-century religious movements that provided personal healing myths with elaborate cosmic explanations. Almost without exception the creeds of major new religions of the past century contained a strong healing element. The magical aspects of Mormonism were expressed in *The Word of Wisdom,* which prohibits the drinking of tea and coffee and advocates various other health laws. They are also present in the Mormon practice of the laying on of hands and in the belief that Mormon priesthood can effect spiritual healings. Christian Science upholds the health beliefs of Mary Baker Eddy's theology, and Christian Science practitioners conduct healing services. Seventh-Day Adventists, theosophists, and even Jehovah's Witnesses, with their prohibition of blood transfusions, all exemplify the tendency to turn religion and spiritual healing into magic (cf. Marty and Vaux 1982).

Because of their seemingly greater affinity to science, the most important "healing" phenomena are the mythological elaborations of the new psychotherapies. This magico-moral cult activity has given expression to myriad new therapies that have turned the West, as Martin L. Gross has suggested, into a "psychological society" (Gross 1978). Psychological healing myths have generated a systematic and identifiable social structure consisting of new messiahs, new therapies, and citizen-patients.

In the Third World, all these body-based shamanic techniques are used to treat physical ailments and psychological problems that have become somatic. In the West, the emphasis is on encouraging the body to eliminate, ejaculate, vibrate, palpitate, and so on in order to increase awareness and to carry the human spirit closer to its goal of ultimate spiritual liberation. To reach the beyond of our ultramodern imagination, we are told to return to ancient techniques of gyrating the body because these actions create a bond or link to some vast cosmic scheme.

## Myths of Decline and Transformation

Myths of decline are elements of popular mythology that provide a cosmic dimension to personal myths by expressing pessimism concerning modern society. They are generalized stories about the decline of civilization and the end of the world. Essentially they hold that society as we know it is doomed. They claim that ecological disaster and/or atomic war are imminent. Should we escape these, then a *1984,* Big Brother–style dictatorship awaits humankind. Doom or world catastrophe is an essential aspect not only of mythological structure but also of the structure of private visionary or conversion dreams.

The pessimism of decline beliefs is supported by a range of stories and ideas from religious writers speculating about the return of Christ, scientists worrying about ecology, and observers forecasting imminent economic collapse (Lindsey 1970; Meadows et al. 1972; Ruff 1980; Davidson and Rees-Mogg 1994). Threats of financial instability and reports and rumors of wars and new diseases all feed the hunger for vicarious drama that creates a culture of hysteria. In the 1970s the Watergate scandal, the oil crisis, and inflation created a sense of impending doom. In the 1980s optimism began to return, only to be dashed in the 1990s by slow economic growth, new epidemics (like the Ebola virus), terrorism, and increasing chaos throughout the world.

The mentality of doom provides those who participate in new religions with a new sense of mission. Members of the Solar Temple and even some members of the Mormon Church stockpile at least two years' supply of food in their basements. So-called survivalists and militia groups retreat to remote locations to prepare for the coming end of modern civilization. Their journals and specialist shops selling dehydrated foods and modern weapons grow as rapidly as the mythology (Abanes 1996:73–109; Barkun 1994:75–119).

As human imagination reaches forward into doom, so it stretches backward into a glorious past and outward to embrace other planets. The second element of the emerging mythology consists of beliefs in other civilizations, usually civilizations greater than our own. The mythic significance of these ideas is that they form a theoretical bridge between the pessimism of decline beliefs and the optimism of transformative beliefs. Here again, as Michael Barkun points out, there are "striking parallels" between "New Age literature" and that of the militias (Barkun 1994:248). Barkun also shows that contrary to popular belief, groups such as Christian Identity are strongly opposed to Christian fundamentalism. In other words, the militias *are not* an outgrowth of traditional Christianity. Rather, they are an amalgam of new religious movements, blending in many occult themes (Barkun 1994:103–105, 243–253).

Myths of transformation bring together a profound mistrust of modern science with a deep respect for science as myth and a belief in the immanent cosmic transformation of humans. Proponents of such myths often speak about a golden age, which they project either into the far distant past or onto an extraterrestrial civilization. The latter involves a vision of humankind's future. The former involves a nostalgic vision of the past that allows people to indulge vicariously in thoughts about prehistoric humans who lived in harmony with nature and possessed vast powers because they cooperated with natural forces to build great and enduring civilizations.

Myth merchants argue that hints of the powers of lost civilizations are found among Filipino psychic healers, the San in southern Africa, and other native communities worldwide that retain some knowledge of nature's spirits and forces. Why humans as a whole lost these wonderful powers and why those who possess them today live in abject poverty are never adequately explained. However, the fall of primal civilizations is typically accounted for in terms of pride and the misuse of magic.

Proponents of such myths maintain that the failure of orthodox archaeologists to affirm this romanticization of civilizations simply proves how sterile modern science is and how much it needs the "creative" investigations of spiritual people. And so spiritualists conjure up visions of Atlantis, **Mu**, **Lemura**, and other lost civilizations, embellishing them with complex comparisons and apparent erudition.

L. Sprague de Camp's book *Lost Continents* (1970) relates these myths to nineteenth-century religious groups. *The Book of Mormon* is based on the existence of a lost civilization built by North American Indians, and theosophy appeals to stories about Atlantis. Other groups, too, invoke the idea of lost or extraterrestrial civilizations to objectify their claims. Many **neopagan** groups demonstrate a preoccupation with pyramids and sacred measurements. It would seem, in short, that myths of other civilizations perform an apologetic function by weaving observable "evidence," such as the **Mayan** ruins, into a web of beliefs that entangles doubts in its very complexity. And once believers accept the existence or possibility of the existence of these civilizations, they further believe in UFOs.

Thus both UFO sightings and other primal experiences receive "scientific" or "historical" confirmation from the general mythology. Without the mythology, many primal experiences would lack context and would probably assume little significance in the life of an individual. But through the intervention of myth, primal experiences are seemingly confirmed by procedures that are deceptively like those of orthodox science. The result is a powerful belief system that is self-confirming. But the myths do not serve only to authenticate primal experiences; in a more important sense, they encourage people to have primal experiences in the first place while at the same time amplifying their importance.

Another form of transformative myth involves a vision of death followed by rebirth. Proponents of these myths hold that the night of doom will be followed by the dawn of a new era at the level of both individuals and society because it will embrace the entire cosmos. The myth of a "New Age," which is often called "the Age of Aquarius," goes back to Swedenborg (Beaman [1881] 1971:7). From his followers it was passed on through New Thought and theosophy to become part of the received wisdom of the occult revival in the early twentieth century (Webb 1971:188–217; Wessinger 1988:6–8, 336–344). Consequently, the idea of the dawning of the Age of Aquarius became popular in occult circles early in the 1930s (Brandt 1936:12–26; Howe 1972), flourished in the 1960s, and was revived in the 1980s after the publication of MacLaine's *Out on a Limb* (1983).

The sense of expectancy engendered by a strong belief in the New Age is sustained and augmented by talk about the return of Christ. In such a context, this orthodox Christian notion does not refer to the literal return of Jesus and a Last Judgment but to a code expressing the hope of transformation. Some place their hope in a new religious leader who symbolizes the mission of Jesus and creates an ideal world. Annie Besant associated such an understanding of Christ's return with her protégé, Krishnamurti (Wessinger 1988:74–78). The Unification Church equates the Reverend Sun Myung Moon with Christ through a commonality of purpose.

Still others talk of Christ's return in terms of a Christ spirit that will permeate the world. Certain fundamentalist biblical groups hold that Jesus will return bodily and fulfill a number of specific prophecies. And various other groups combine elements of all versions of Christ's return in a confident but vague belief that someday things will miraculously get better.

In addition to beliefs about Christ, there are beliefs about the coming of space lords and other aliens who will liberate humankind and save us from the threat of planetary destruction. Once again, we should note that science fiction has played a key role in propagating and popularizing such views. Novels such as Arthur C. Clarke's *Childhood's End* (1963) and his more recent works suggest this theme in powerful ways. Although science fiction started the trend, new religions quickly developed and promoted beliefs in a variety of salvations brought about by space beings (Barkun 1994:248).

Other savior figures also feature in the myths of transformation. For many counterculture people in the late 1960s, the mythic figure of Gandalf, the white wizard in J. R. R. Tolkien's *Lord of the Rings* (1966), became a symbol of the New Age. Others have developed beliefs about King Arthur and similar legendary heroes. We find "Buddhas" and "Krishnas" and such personalized saviors as the "Bhagwans." All are liberators sanctioned by one or another of these major coalescing myths.

Whoever the savior is to be and whatever the terms in which he or she is described, the mythic structure of beliefs surrounding the central figure is essentially the same: The savior is coming to change the world, to make it good and free from the terrors of modern life. Humankind will no longer be alone in a hostile universe but will once more live in a personalized context in which human values will ultimately triumph. The assurance of the final victory of good over evil comes from traditional legends, religious stories, and newly invented myths. But their authenticity within the mythology generally, and in new religions particularly, is always assured by the intervention of shamanistic leaders who create what we have called box myths. These people are agents or shamans who initiate change.

One such agent of consciousness is **David Spangler** of the Findhorn Community, cofounded by Peter Caddy. He is described by many writers as one of the foremost spiritual leaders today. In his book *Emergence: The Rebirth of the Sacred* (1984), Spangler gives an account of the new mythology as seen by an insider. His works and many similar ones impose a coherence on the fragmented myths of modern society that brings these fragments together in a pattern similar to the one we have outlined. Another highly successful mythmaker and transformer of consciousness was L. Ron Hubbard, the founder of scientology. His early science fiction paved the way for a complex mythology that encouraged the use of technological rituals that both explain and evoke primal experiences.

Both Spangler and Hubbard added the final ingredient that provides their myths with the potential they need to become integrative mythologies. This element is the expectation of evolutionary transformation. It is to this theme of the overall integration of the myths into a central framework that we now turn.

## Toward a New Central Mythology

So far we have identified various myth fragments that people use to form box myths. During the nineteenth century and again in the counterculture of the late 1960s, these unrelated myth fragments were brought together to form a more cohesive mythology. The union of mythic fragments into a more general, self-reinforcing mythology involved integrating them with an overarching myth of evolution. In a sense, the myth of evolution became a new operating system that opened new windows on people and society.

Evolution as myth must be distinguished from evolution as science. The difference lies in the type of question each tries to answer. Scientific evolution explains "how." Evolutionary myths explain "why." The mythology of evolution provides religious answers to ultimate human questions about meaning and purpose, whereas evolutionary science is simply meant to help us understand natural processes. Swift shifts from the "how" to the "why" become possible today because many people *believe in* rather than *understand* modern science. Our culture is characterized more by a *faith in science* than by an appreciation, or understanding, of the **scientific method** and rational thought. What this means in essence is that we have allowed magic to replace science as knowledge and procedure.

In the literature of new religions, faith in science has been transformed into a faith in a "new science" that is associated with an "emerging evolutionary consciousness." The shift in language reflects both a popular belief in science and a distrust of science as it is actually practiced by scientists. People distrust modern science because it has brought us the atomic bomb and ecological crises. But the faith in science remains. Instead of questioning the use of modern science or learning how science works, many people take the easy route of believing in the new science.

The transition from belief in science to faith in a new science is most clearly made in Theodore Roszak's classic *Making of a Counter-Culture* (1969). Roszak attacks modern science because of its "objective consciousness" and control by experts. He then advocates the democratization of science by encouraging a return to a holistic vision based upon intuitive feelings, magic, and the way of the shaman. Spangler merges popular mysticism and faith in science with New Age beliefs in a similar fashion by using the language of evolution to make shamanic conversations with nature spirits and disembodied intelligences appear reasonable (Spangler 1984). William Irwin Thompson takes much the same approach, drawing on Freud's concept of the repressiveness of civilization:

> Now that the failure of the Green Revolution has dramatized the failure of the industrialization of agriculture, the underground traditions of animism can surface without any sense of embarrassment. . . . The iron winter of the industrial era is beginning its end. . . . Animism and electronics is the landscape of the New Age. . . . The people of Findhorn understand the place of technology in nature, and if they forget, the elves will soon let them know. (Thompson 1975:ix–x)

## The Nineteenth-Century Roots of Evolutionary Mythology

In many ways the situation we face today in terms of our collection of disconnected myths is similar to that the inhabitants of New England faced in the early part of the nineteenth century. Like us, these New Englanders experienced rapid social change, including revolutions in transportation and communication. Their society was transient and uprooted. Traditional beliefs were on the wane, and new ones vied for acceptance.

In the late 1820s, Thomas Dick wrote about the possibility of life on other planets in a book entitled *Philosophy of a Future State* (1828). Swedenborgians speculated about spiritual "worlds." Ethan Smith pondered the origin of the American Indians in his book *A View of the Hebrews* (1825). People were fascinated with the Indian mounds that dotted the landscape. Stories about the pyramids of Egypt and lost civilizations were common.

Against this confused and confusing background, Joseph Smith Jr. claimed to have discovered a book that explained the true facts about many of the puzzles that intrigued his contemporaries. In *The Book of Mormon* (1830), Smith laid the basis of a powerful mythology that wove together many diverse myths into an integrated whole. In his later "revelations," Smith elaborated these myths so that the developed mythology of Mormonism not only explained the origin of American Indians but also spoke about the significance of their archaeological sites and speculated about life on other planets.

Brodie contends that Smith "was groping for a new metaphysics that would somehow take into account the new world of science. In his primitive and egocentric fashion he was trying to resolve the most troublesome philosophic problem of the nineteenth century" (Brodie 1963:172). Thomas O'Dea has argued that although *The Book of Mormon* leaves much to be desired as literature, in its own terms and the context in which it was written it was a challenging document "concerned fundamentally with the problem of good and evil" (O'Dea 1964:26).

O'Dea cautions us against simply rejecting *The Book of Mormon* as an unbelievable and therefore unintelligible story. Rather, he maintains, it has an important intellectual element that gives its mythology an appeal far beyond the mere telling of tales. This element consists in the folksy but rational way in which Smith presents different viewpoints and argues for and against them. An important but often overlooked element of Mormon mythology that gives it a continuing appeal is its use of evolutionary ideas.

## The Evolutionary Mythology of New Religions

Smith wrote some thirty years before Darwin, but even at this time evolutionary ideas were being hotly debated and widely disseminated. The influence of these ideas is especially evident in Smith's later work, *The Book of Abraham* (1842), which, with *The Book of Mormon*, Mormons regard as divinely inspired scripture.

Even more clear in its use of evolution as a mythological device is the book *Key to the Science of Theology* (1855), written by the Mormon apostle Parley P. Pratt. Pratt speculates about humankind's visiting other worlds in the future and places Mormon views of human life within the framework of spiritual evolution (Pratt

[1855] 1973:153–159). According to Mormon theology, humans are spiritual beings whose existence predates their physical birth. Mormons believe that our spirit bodies originated in eternity and that we progressed to earth to "gain a body" and undergo a probationary period that determines our future state. This spiritual evolution is covered by the "law of eternal progression." As their early leader **Lorenzo Snow** said, "As man is, God was; as God is man may become." This well-known saying appears in many Mormon publications (Hansen 1981:103). The idea of evolution gives Mormon theology its essential unity by providing Mormon beliefs with an all-embracing operating system.

Similar views about eternal progression and spiritual evolution are found in other nineteenth-century new religions. Although her focus differed, Mary Baker Eddy, the founder of Christian Science, also used evolution to unify her creed. In the first edition of her fundamental work *Science and Health* (1875), she stated quite clearly that "Mr. Darwin is right with regard to mortal man or matter, but he should have made a distinction between these and the immortal, whose basis is Spirit" (cited by Peel 1958:91).

Evolution was even more thoroughly adapted to religious needs by Blavatsky, the founder of theosophy. In her book *The Secret Doctrine* (1888), she speaks of moral development and individual lives in terms of cosmic evolution. Theosophy suggests that the inner, spiritual growth of humankind constitutes the heart and dynamics of the whole evolutionary process. Commenting on this, Bruce F. Campbell, a recent historian of theosophy, says "a core of Theosophical teachings emerged. They are a synthesis of the idea of evolution with religious concepts chiefly from Hinduism and Buddhism" (Campbell 1980:61).

Thus nineteenth-century religious movements were developed and systematized by way of an evolutionary mythology. The evolutionary framework has also been popular in the twentieth century, as, for example, in the writings of the British biologist Julian Huxley and Roman Catholic scholar Pierre Teilhard de Chardin (King 1980). More important, it is a central theme in the literature of the new religious movements, as **Timothy Leary** recognized in his seminal work *The Politics of Ecstasy* (1970:182–193).

Leary repeatedly linked the use of psychedelic drugs to the evolution of consciousness and the development of new religions. He argued that the popular use of drugs heralded the next great evolutionary step for humans. In his more recent work *Changing My Mind, Among Others* (1982), Leary develops the idea of evolution as a cultural myth by giving the reader a vision of a religious consciousness that will lead to the creation of a new humanity.

Various other general works that reflect contemporary spirituality are structured by the mythological framework of evolution that binds together fragmented myths and provides the basis for a new religious consciousness. Marilyn Ferguson speaks of evolution as "the new paradigm" and expresses faith that humankind is entering a new evolutionary phase during which we will control our evolutionary destinies. It is no surprise that Ferguson cites *Childhood's End* as an apt "literary metaphor" for what she claims "many serious scientists" actually believe is happening today (Ferguson 1980:157–162).

More recently, James Redfield's phenomenal success, *The Celestine Prophecy* (1993), merges prophetic myths of fate and fortune with evolution as a central mythology for guiding people's lives. Of course Redfield wrote his book as a novel. But for many readers it is clearly far more. No wonder the *New York Review of Books* has regularly listed it in both its fiction and nonfiction sections. Many people read the book as a novel, and that ends their interest. Others, however, allow it to speak to them and organize their lives according to its teachings because they believe that behind the veil of a novel lies a real discovery of personal and cosmic significance. Thus the novel functions as a modern myth, integrating individual experiences into a greater whole or operating system.

When she developed theosophy, Helena Blavatsky quickly discovered that although myths speak to people and help integrate their experiences into a meaningful web, they ultimately leave the believer without intellectual satisfaction. This is because myths alone ultimately lack substance. Consequently, Blavatsky learned to integrate her mythology with doctrinal teachings from the great world religions.

Numerous other founders of new religions have followed or repeated Blavatsky's example. Therefore to understand the process by which new religions come into being, we must know the broad outlines of the historic religious traditions. It is to this task that we turn in Chapter 6.

## KEY TERMS

**Alternative medicine:** Traditional medicines and modern therapies that exist outside the modern medical establishment. The term includes such things as herbalism, homeopathy, and various spiritual techniques of healing.

**Atlantis:** An imaginary land in the Atlantic Ocean that the Greek philosopher Plato first used as a metaphor. Several hundred years later, people began to take Plato's myth literally and started to look for a real Atlantis.

**Bodhisattvas:** Beings who aspire to enlightenment or Buddhahood. In the Mahāyāna Buddhist tradition, the idea refers to a savior figure who forgoes enlightenment to bring salvation to all sentient beings.

**Eliade, Mircea** (1907–1988): Romanian scholar and professor of religious studies at the University of Chicago, best known for books such as *The Myth of the Eternal Return* (1954).

**Evolution:** A scientific theory of evolution first proposed by Charles Bonnet (1720–1793), who discovered that an embryo already contains all the parts of the mature organism. The theory was developed by Charles Lyell (1797–1874), who in 1832 speculated on the evolution of land animals. It gained popularity with the publication of Charles Darwin's *Origin of Species* (1859).

**Folktale:** Popular stories told to entertain. They often have religious and moral or immoral connotations.

**Holistic:** Literally, "of the whole." A term J. C. Smuts invented in his book *Holism and Evolution* [1926] (1987).

**Homeopathy**: A nineteenth-century alternative to allopathy (medical treatment using drugs), which is based on the principle that like cures like. Homeopaths use very small doses of specially prepared essences to treat illness. In North America homeopathy is generally considered quackery. In Britain it is part of the national health scheme because of the support of the royal family. In Germany it is generally accepted alongside allopathic medicine.

**Ideology**: Beliefs that shape a person's outlook, whether or not the individual is conscious of the influence. Marxists define ideology as abstract, false thought; illusion; false consciousness; unreality; something that leads people away from reality.

**Leary, Timothy** (1920–1996): American psychologist who became the guru of the 1960s drug culture. He is famous for his motto "Turn on, tune in, and drop out."

**Legends**: Traditional stories from the far distant past dealing with cultural heroes and significant events in the life of a people.

**Lemura**: A "lost" culture invented by Helena Blavatsky as one of the sources of ancient civilizations like that of the Egyptians.

**Malinowski, Bronislaw** (1884–1942): One of the founders of social anthropology who wrote *Argonauts of the Western Pacific* (1922).

**Maslow, Abraham** (1908–1970): Well-known American psychologist who did extensive work on trance states and similar phenomena; the author of *Religions, Values, and Peak-experiences* (1964).

**Mayan**: The ancient civilization of Mexico. Many occult writers link the growth of Mayan civilization through a common source, such as Atlantis, to that of ancient Egypt. In fact Mayan civilization developed centuries after the decline of ancient Egypt and never attained the technological skills of the Egyptians.

**Middleton, John** (1921–): British social anthropologist who has written extensively on religion. He is the author of *Lugbara Religion* (1960).

**Mu**: A land similar to Atlantis that the Englishman James Churchwarden argued once existed in the middle of the Pacific Ocean.

**Myth**: A story with culturally formative power that can shape the lives of individuals and even entire societies.

**Neopagan**: Traditionally a pagan was a non-Christian. Today the term is used by various new religions, including Wicca, Celtic, and Germanic religions, and modern shamans.

**Philosophy**: From the Greek, meaning "love of wisdom," the study and knowledge of things and their causes. The term is commonly used as a general name for any system of ideas or even way of life.

**Pseudoscience**: Various practices, many of them involving magic, that claim to be scientific but in fact reject standard scientific tests and procedures.

**Rama**: One of the most popular Hindu gods who figures in the classic Indian epic *The Rāmāyana*.

**Science**: The pursuit and classification of knowledge through systematic methods that permit repeatability. Science is not scientific knowledge, technology, or discoveries but rather the method used in acquiring that knowledge and in making discoveries.

**Science fiction**: Futuristic stories that explore the possible application of science to human affairs and often involve space travel to other worlds or galaxies.

**Scientific method**: That process of systematic inquiry that proceeds in a logical manner and involves the testing of theories against the available evidence.

**Snow, Lorenzo** (1814–1901): Mormon apostle and religious leader who articulated the "law of eternal progression."

**Spangler, David** (1945–): A spiritual writer who became the leader of the Findhorn community.

**Weltanschauung:** A German philosophical term that refers to an overarching perspective of the world, its people, and its problems.

*The Word of Wisdom*: Dietary rules and advice for living proclaimed by Joseph Smith and followed by Mormons.

# 6

## Yogic and Abramic Religions

*A doctrinal system can be ultimately and essentially false, and yet contain an immense amount of knowledge and intuition.*

*Aurel Kolnai (1938:57)*

*Findhorn was built on a direct apprehension of Tradition rather than on reliance on one of the many traditions that seek to express the Presence. . . . The function of all traditions is to bring us safely and wholly into the presence of that Tradition, or, if you prefer, into the knowing of that God-Presence which embraces ourselves and the universe and is dynamic reality.*

*David Spangler (1976:242)*

*I*n this chapter we review some key doctrines found in the two major world traditions: the Yogic and Abramic traditions. It is these traditions that inspire creative individuals to construct new religions. The **Yogic tradition** originated in India. It involves belief in karma, rebirth, samsāra, māyā, dharma, moksha, astrology, the practice of yoga, and devotion to a guru. The Abramic tradition traces its roots to the patriarch **Abraham. Abramic religions** preach a doctrine of creation, fall, and redemption. Because fundamentalist Christianity has given birth to numerous new religions, we also examine some Christian teachings about faith, the return of Christ, and eschatology. Finally, we explore charismatic gifts, the search for community, and prophetic leadership.

New religions incorporate doctrines from world religions to interpret and give intellectual content to primal experiences and new mythologies. At first glance it might appear that there are hundreds if not thousands of religious traditions in the world. But upon closer examination, we see that all religions fall into the categories of two major traditions. We call these traditions Yogic and Abramic. The best-known religions of the Yogic tradition are Jainism, Hinduism, and Buddhism. Those of the Abramic are Judaism, Christianity, and Islam. We use the term "Yogic" because the practice of yoga represents the strand of this complex tradition that most influences new religions in the West. The term "Abramic" has been used to describe Judaism, Christianity, and Islam because these religions trace their origins to Abraham. The discussion of Yogic and Abramic beliefs that follows is aimed at producing a typology for understanding new religions in Western societies. It is not meant to be a description of "pure" or historic versions of world religions. We are simply presenting some aspects of religious belief that are commonly found in new religions.

## Yogic Religions

The Yogic tradition originated in India. Themes of quest and **pilgrimage** are key features of its pointedly **transcendental** worldview. Yogic religions assume this world to be a veil of sorrow that must be endured and escaped. Swami A. C. Bhaktivedanta Prabhupāda (usually called Prabhupāda), the founder of the Hare Krishna movement, sums up the negativity of the Yogic tradition when he says of the world that "this place is not meant for happiness. . . . It is a place of miseries and . . . is temporary" (Prabhupāda 1982:10). Similarly, **Edward Conze** writes:

> The Buddhist point of view will appeal only to those people who are completely disillusioned with the world as it is, and with themselves, who are extremely sensitive to pain, suffering, and any kind of turmoil, who have an extreme desire for happiness, and a considerable capacity for renunciation. . . . The Buddhist seeks for a total happiness beyond this world. (Conze 1951:22)

As we have noted, these perspectives are common among those who join new religions.

To most Westerners, the Yogic view of the human condition seems extremely pessimistic, but practitioners of Yogic religions would disagree. Eliade, for example, has stated that Yogic **soteriological** doctrines "may appear 'pessimistic' to Westerners, for whom personality remains, in the last analysis, the foundation of all morality and mysticism. But, for India, what matters most is not so much the salvation of the *personality* as obtaining *absolute freedom*" (Eliade 1969:35). Yogic religions portray a very different view of salvation than do Abramic religions. The latter place primary value on human personality and emphasize the salvation of the individual, whereas Yogic religions speak of salvation *away from* individuality. As Ninian Smart has written, Yogic thinking holds that

> Men and other living beings are continually being reborn. With death, the individual is reborn in a different form. This everlasting recurrence of births and deaths can only be stopped by transcending it by attaining a liberation in a transcendental sphere where the self is freed from mental and bodily encumbrances. Typically, this

is achieved by the practice of austerity and yoga: self-denial and self-discipline are means of destroying that which leads to rebirth—Karma. (Smart 1969:70)

## Karma

What exactly is **karma**, and what role do it and other key doctrines play in the new religious consciousness of the West? At its crudest, karma is viewed as a physical substance that literally sticks to people's souls, binding them to the material world. Karma is the cosmic law of cause and effect that ensures that whatever a person does, good or bad, has ultimate consequences. If we do good, we produce good karma. If we do evil, we produce bad karma. Good karma frees us from the illusions of the material world and makes liberation possible. Bad karma binds us to life and creates illusions of happiness.

The source of Yogic belief in karma is the ancient Brhadaranyaka **Upanishad**, which says that "according as one acts, according as one conducts himself, so does he become. The doer of good becomes good. The doer of evil becomes evil. One becomes virtuous by virtuous action, bad by bad action" (Day 1982:73). In the foreword to his translation of the Bhagavad Gita, Prabhupāda explains the action of karma as follows: "Suppose I am a businessman and have worked very hard with intelligence and have amassed a great bank balance. Then I am an enjoyer. But then say I have lost all my money in business; then I am a sufferer. Similarly, in every field of life we enjoy the results of our works, or we suffer the results. This is called karma" (Prabhupāda 1968:xix).

In the West Blavatsky was the first to extend the idea of karma from the realm of personal fortune to that of global events. In *The Key to Theosophy* she wrote:

> We must not lose sight of the fact that every atom is subject to the general law governing the whole body to which it belongs, and here we come upon the wider track of Karmic law. Do you not perceive that the aggregate of individual karma becomes that of the nation to which individuals belong, and further, that the sum total of National Karma is that of the World? (Blavatsky 1972b:202)

In the counterculture of the 1960s, this theosophical understanding of the effects of karma was used to explain the Vietnam War and later the environmental crisis. Countless articles reflecting this outlook were published in such journals as *New Age* and *Co-Evolution Quarterly*. All interpret elements of the new mythology in terms of karma to produce a strong nature mysticism.

## Rebirth

Within the Yogic tradition, ideas of **rebirth** are logically related to belief in karma. Traditionally, rebirth is explained in two ways. Hindus believe that when human beings die, their souls pass—**"transmigrate"**—into another body. Buddhists, in contrast, deny the existence of the soul. They believe that the continuation of sense impressions at the point of death deludes those who suffer near-death experiences into thinking that they have an essence or soul. Buddhists postulate reincarnation rather than transmigration. Those who popularize new religions in the West, however, typically fail to convey these distinctions. They tend to define reincarnation as rebirth in human form and transmigration as rebirth in nonhuman form.

Western belief in reincarnation typically has nothing to do with karma. It is usually called upon as a means of explaining claims that some people remember past lives. Past-life experiences have been widely popularized of late in books such as Shirley MacLaine's *Out on a Limb* (MacLaine 1983).

Within Yogic religions, karma and rebirth provide a powerful basis for social morality and offer an explanation for inequalities in society. In the West, however, the moral element of these beliefs is usually deemphasized in favor of a strong romanticism: Its popularity lies in the fact that it meets psychological rather than moral needs. It is this sort of emphasis that accounts for claims in popular literature that karma can bring lovers together or enable us to meet people we knew in previous lives.

Many members of new religions say that they remember past lives and adventures. Their "memories" give them a false sense of personal worth and enable them to escape difficult personal relationships with the excuse that they have not yet found their "soul mate." Simply put, the idea of rebirth is often used to avoid moral obligations.

For most Westerners and members of new religions, belief in reincarnation is an exciting idea that seems to offer past adventures and future hope. Few relate the idea of rebirth to the need for salvation or the possibility of being reborn in hell. Once a person makes the move from a generalized belief in reincarnation to joining a new religion of Yogic origin, she or he quickly becomes aware of the need for salvation and the moral implications of reincarnation and karma.

## *Samsāra, Māyā, Dharma, and Moksha*

**Samsāra,** or the "wheel of existence," is the name given a vast network of births and deaths through endless lifetimes involving incarnations in many worlds, heavens, and hells. Those who believe in samsāra assume that everything and every being is bound together in the infinite repetition of birth and death through karma.

People do not ordinarily experience the bonds of karma or become aware of the wheel of existence. Instead they experience their individual lives as a fleeting moment of consciousness to which they ascribe ultimate significance. But this awareness of one's individuality and belief in the significance of one's present life is an illusion brought about by the effects of karma. Karma blinds us to the reality of samsāra and thus to the possibility of escaping our karmic bonds and attaining liberation. Karma creates the illusion of individuality and of a permanent creation, when in reality everything is in a state of constant flux. The illusory nature of our experience of reality is brought about by **māyā**, which magically conjures up an unreal world. Once we see through the illusion, however, we realize that we need to be liberated from samsāra and the bonds of karma.

In Hinduism **dharma** is a religious way of life that embraces all one does and all of society. Dharma implies the idea of a fixed standard of divine conduct that is a sacred law by which human beings must live. In the West, though, dharma has come to be understood primarily in terms of its Buddhist meaning as teaching about what is right or the truth about reality. When members of new religions speak of the dharma, they are most often referring to the way to liberation according to their own particular beliefs.

Liberation, or freedom from the bonds of karma and release from samsāra, is known as **moksha**. Moksha takes many forms in the Hindu tradition. Those who believe in it contend that it can be experienced as absorption into the whole or God, as entry into life with a particular god such as Krishna, or simply as annihilation. In Buddhism liberation is called **nirvāna**. It is said that we cannot really say what nirvāna is because it is not conditioned by our universe of cause and effect and is consequently beyond our comprehension. We can do no more than affirm our belief in it. All we can really know is that nirvāna is freedom from the wheel of samsāra and the bonds of karma. It is the cessation of our present mode of existence. Buddhist teaching also maintains that although we cannot explain what nirvāna is, we can know what enables people to attain it.

New religions have linked ideas about nirvāna and liberation generally with the concept of an evolving human consciousness. Marilyn Ferguson expresses this idea in a secular way in *The Aquarian Conspiracy* (1980). David Spangler sacralizes it in *Emergence* (1984). Lawrence Blair offers a self-consciously religious understanding of liberation as a higher evolutionary state in *Rhythms of Vision* (1975). T. Lobsang Rampa, a former British plumber who has claimed to be a Tibetan lama, aptly describes the importance of these ideas when he writes that "to live one has to progress.... Nirvana is the stage in humans where all faults are eliminated ... the state where there is no evil" (Rampa 1967:197). To religious purists, the mythologizing of Yogic beliefs in these ways may appear shocking, but they represent a common theme in the new religions.

## Astrology

Many Western scholars have chosen to ignore the magical aspects of Yogic religions. Scholars such as C. A. F. Rhys-Davids in the nineteenth century and Christmas Humphries in our own have attempted to present religions like Buddhism as the height of rationality (Rhys-Davids 1894; Humphries 1964). Other scholars, such as Conze and Eliade, have rightly drawn attention to the magical aspects of Yogic religions and particularly to the importance of belief in **astrology** (Conze 1979; Prebish 1979).

As Eliade points out, belief in astrology arises naturally from a belief in karma and rebirth. In the West people may accept astrology largely because it works rather than because of its relationship to other beliefs. Once accepted as a reality, however, astrology naturally reinforces belief in such things as karma, and it dramatizes Yogic beliefs generally.

Belief in astrology was widespread in the Greco-Roman world. It declined with the rise of Christianity and was ridiculed by early Christian writers. Astrological ideas were revived during the sixteenth-century Renaissance, but they were severely criticized by both the Protestant Reformers and leaders of the **Catholic Counter-Reformation**. By the time of the Enlightenment in the eighteenth century, European astrology had virtually died out. In the nineteenth century it was generally regarded as a failed science, although it was revived toward the end of the century by movements such as theosophy. Today astrology is increasingly popular. Some 15 percent of Americans, for example, seriously believe in astrology, and a much larger number of people dabble in it (Gallup and Castelli 1989:75–77). Outside of Europe, in India, China, and the Islamic world, astrology seems to have retained its popularity with relatively little criticism.

It is important to recognize that there are two distinct forms of astrology: natal and mundane. Natal astrology concerns individuals and their personal lives. Mundane astrology deals with cultural development and world history. The best-known belief associated with mundane astrology is that of the dawning of the Age of Aquarius, which is part of the operating system of the new mythology.

Astrology has been thoroughly discredited by scientific testing (McGervey 1977; Bastedo 1978). Richard Cavendish documents some of these failures in his book *The Black Arts,* correctly observing that "astrology is essentially a magical art" linked to irrational beliefs and a desire to gain control over seemingly uncontrollable events (Cavendish 1967:219). Contemporary Western interest in astrology demonstrates a deep desire for certainty in the context of a fear of the future. In the Yogic tradition, astrology fits well with shamanistic practices and beliefs about human beings with superhuman powers. Within the new religions, astrology and shamanism unite to confirm the authenticity of the group's leader. Members of new religions, from Scientology to the Unification Church and the **Children of God,** commonly appeal to astrological signs in an attempt to prove that their leader has a divine mission.

## The Meaning of Yoga

We have noted various Yogic beliefs and mentioned the practice of **yoga** as unifying Yogic religions. But what is yoga? Meditators and members of new religions claim that yoga is a way of life, an experience, a healthy exercise, and simply a form of **meditation**. In fact all of these descriptions are correct. Eliade states that "etymologically *yoga* derives from the root *yuj*, 'to bind together,' 'hold fast,' 'yoke.' . . . The word *yoga* serves, in general, to describe any *ascetic technique* and any *method of meditation*" (Eliade 1969:4). The popular author Richard Hittleman admits that prior to the mid-1960s he used the idea that yoga was healthy to hook Americans and get them interested in Hindu religious ideas (Hittleman 1969:9–14).

Meditation, or yoga, can be described as an inward journey on which the meditator leaves behind the rational mind and enters a new realm of consciousness. Many methods of yoga are popular today. Most involve mental concentration, breathing exercises, or devotional activities such as the dances and chants of the **Osho movement**. The results of meditation vary from person to person and are modified by the particular beliefs the meditator claims to hold. Generally, however, practitioners say meditation results in "enlightenment" and freedom from the confines of the everyday world. In Yogic terminology, it leads to a release from the bonds of karma.

New religions offer various explanations of what one should expect in meditation. Transcendental meditation (TM) teaches that meditators reach a deep peace as a result of tapping the inner resources of the human mind. Eastern religious cults and sects that have taken root in the West, such as the **Western Buddhist Order** and Hare Krishna, hold traditional beliefs in nirvāna and the glories of Krishna consciousness. Other meditators speak about a sense of absorption or a loss of consciousness and bliss. Those who meditate universally maintain that words cannot fully express the sort of liberation they feel. When meditators do attempt to describe what they undergo, they repeatedly depict states of consciousness we associate with primal experiences and the use of drugs.

Central to modern Yogic beliefs is the acceptance of a holistic vision of the universe that incorporates an evolutionary perspective, which gives it an apparent scientific validity. Behind this vision is an assumption that the whole of reality is ultimately *one* and that our material world is really illusory because the true reality is on a different, nonmaterial plane.

The version of the Yogic tradition found in the West is more unified and clearcut in its monism than is Eastern Yogic philosophy. Many of the schools of philosophy in India, Japan, and other Eastern nations do propound the essential oneness of everything—**nondualism**, as it is known in the Indian philosophic tradition. But elements of materialism and other views are also strong in the Indian tradition. The preeminence of the Upanishads, the philosophy of Śankara, and Buddhism in the Western perception of Eastern religions has led Westerners to assume that nondualism constitutes the essence of Yogic thinking.

Steven M. Tipton sums up the worldview of the Westernized Yogic tradition as follows: "Conceptions of the divine, where they exist, tend to be nontheistic or at least they describe a nonprophetic sort of god who issues no commandments. . . . There is the fundamental assumption of an acosmic monism, that 'all is one,' pure energy or existence without any enduring structure or *logos*." This difference between the new religions and the culture at large is also reflected, notes Tipton, in the counterculture's "rejection of the conventional Christian outlook" (Tipton 1981:14).

Salvation in the Western Yogic tradition is a matter of overcoming our awareness of **dualism** and **individualism** in order to experience oneness. Thus it conceives of the human plight as essentially an **ontological** problem, a matter of our fundamental way of being and our belief in individualism. We are delivered when we lose our identity as individuals and our consciousness of personhood. As Eliade puts it, "The wretchedness of human life is not owing to divine punishment or to an original sin, but to *ignorance* . . . metaphysical ignorance" (Eliade 1969:14). Life is wretched because we experience it as separation, and we will continue to do so until we understand and experience the oneness of all things, until we merge with the Absolute.

Practitioners of yoga maintain that the discipline is the essential means by which one can regain one's true ontological status and lose individual personhood. But yoga is difficult. One needs the instruction of a **guru**.

## The Guru

Yogic practices produce trances or similar psychological states that could easily harm the uninitiated without the protection of one who is more experienced. The guru is a person who has already been initiated into the spiritual world and is therefore able to help the uninitiated. Eliade hints at the historical relationship between the yogic tradition and shamanism but never really examines the role of each character in detail (Eliade 1969:318–326). Peter Brent gives a more vivid account of gurus in his book *Godmen of India* (Brent 1973). He shows that gurus demand an inflexible relationship in which their disciples surrender totally to their authority. Gurus teach and facilitate. They have gone before and experienced the terrors of psychological disorientation that meditation can bring. In the language of Yogic religion, the guru encounters spiritual beings, battles demons, and embraces gods. Each guru shares a tradition with other gurus, and none speaks for him- or herself. Each guru has his or her own guru, living or dead, so that a succession of teachers share esoteric knowledge and communicate ancient techniques of psychic manipulation.

Gurus are not prophets who declare the will of God and appeal to propositions found in a Scripture. Rather, they are said to be greater than God because they lead to God. Gurus have shared the essence of the Absolute and experienced the oneness of being, which endows them with divine powers and the ability to master people and things in this world.

In India the true guru is held to be a god-human with superhuman powers and is recognized as a sacred being. But in the West there is a clear distinction between the explicit and implicit claims to divinity of contemporary gurus. L. Ron Hubbard did not explicitly claim divine status, but it is clear from the way committed scientologists speak that they regard him as more than human. Similarly,

Werner Erhard, the founder of EST (for Erhard seminar training), claimed simply to have discovered a way to make life work better through a technique of humanistic psychology. Outsiders report, however, that in Erhard's presence his followers clearly treated him as though he were a divine being.

At the other end of the spectrum are the followers of Prabhupāda, who claim that their deceased guru has ascended to the spiritual world, where he has become a god. Members of the Divine Light Mission went even further. They declared that their leader, the thirteen-year-old guru Maharaj Ji, was a living god.

The idea of a human being claiming to be, or to be on the way to becoming, God is common in both Yogic and new religions. But this popular idea is anathema to the Abramic tradition, even though many new religions that use Abramic terminology incorporate into their theologies the idea that humans are gods. With these thoughts in mind, we now need to understand how the Abramic tradition differs from the Yogic.

## The Abramic Tradition

Abramic religions trace their ancestry to the person of Abraham, whose story is recorded in the **Hebrew Scriptures**. The major religions of this tradition are Judaism, Christianity, and Islam, which have a common understanding of God. In these religions there is only one God, who is the Creator of all things. Although some forms of these religions may speak about "deification" in a specialized sense, at their heart all three deny the essentially Yogic idea, found in many new religions, that humans are gods.

The Abramic religions also share such related concepts as creation, fall, redemption, and revelation. The meanings of these doctrines differ somewhat from one religion to the next. Because we wish to understand new religions in Western society, we will concentrate on the Christian interpretation of the Abramic tradition because today's new Abramic religions draw their ideas principally from Christianity, particularly conservative Protestant Christianity (cf. Campbell 1968; Griffith-Thomas 1930; Henry 1976).

There are new religious movements among Jews and Muslims, Roman Catholics and Eastern Orthodox Christians, but they are for the most part revitalization movements that essentially remain faithful to the tradition from which they arose. The Protestant equivalent of these new types of orthodox religions is Christian fundamentalism rather than groups like the Unificationists, the Way, or the Children of God. We will not focus on fundamentalism or any contemporary religions that affirm a traditional form of religious orthodoxy.

## The Doctrine of Creation

The **doctrine of creation** sets Abramic religions apart from Yogic religions. Following the Hebrew Bible, Abramic religions teach that God brought the entire universe into existence by an act of will. He did not reform already-existing matter or use a part of himself to make material things. Rather, "what is seen was not made out of what was visible" (Hebrews 11:3). As the **Nicene Creed** states, God is "the Creator of heaven and earth, and of all things visible and invisible."

But the Abramic tradition conceives of creation as far more than just an original creative act that started the universe. The scriptures of the Abramic religions—the Judeo-Christian Bible and the Islamic **Qur'ān**—construe creation as involving God's *continuing* providence as well. They assert that God made the worlds and continues to uphold them by his will, which is expressed in terms of law. God rules the universe by his law, which governs every aspect of life. If God were to cease to will the continuation of all things, they would cease to exist.

All Abramic religions contend that God is not dependent upon the universe. The universe is dependent upon God. He is the sovereign ruler of the universe; everything is subordinate to him. God is absolute, and all else is relative. We owe our existence to God; as created beings, we are finite, whereas God is infinite. There is therefore an absolute distinction between the creature and the Creator.

Another important aspect of the Abramic doctrine of creation is that when God created the universe, he pronounced it to be good. Abramic religions agree that God's original creation was without blemish. They also agree that the present state of human alienation from God and the presence of evil and suffering in the world were not part of God's original intention. These things resulted from an act of human will that had cosmic implications: **the fall**. Finally, according to biblical and Islamic concepts of creation, all human beings belong to one race. Abramic religions firmly reject the idea of **polygenesis**, or multiple human races evolving at different times and in different places, and with it **biological racism**.

## The Fall

The Abramic religions differ in their understanding of the fall and God's subsequent acts of **redemption**. The basis for Christian interpretations of the fall is found in Chapters 2 and 3 of the book of **Genesis**, which relate the story of the Garden of Eden. Adam was told that he could eat of any tree except the "tree of the knowledge of good and evil" because "in the day that thou eatest thereof thou shalt surely die." Then the serpent entered the story and convinced Adam and Eve that eating the forbidden fruit would not lead to death but would make them into gods "knowing good and evil." They ate, discovered their mistake, and lost communication with God. Death entered the world.

Setting aside the issue of the historicity of this story, we might ask what it teaches us about the human condition. In other words, what is the significance of the story as a myth? Adam and Eve were given freedom within the limits of human finitude and were placed in an ideal environment. They were warned about the danger of death but were otherwise left alone to explore the world. The serpent then urged them to ignore God's warning. Since animals do not normally talk, the story might be suggesting that human beings were misled by their senses into doubting God.

The central theme in the story is distrust. Adam and Eve desire the "knowledge of good and evil" that would make them "like God." This suggests not only that they were discontent with their dependent status as finite creatures but also that they desired independence from God through knowledge gained by the ritual act of eating rather than through growth and thought. If this interpretation is correct, the story symbolizes the ever present human desire for magical shortcuts to knowledge and power at the expense of trust and understanding.

At the heart of the story of the fall is the human desire for sudden and total freedom and power, unrestricted by the limits of the human condition. As we have seen, this is precisely what the Yogic religions claim to offer their followers. The Bible presents the fall as an act of unrestricted self-indulgence based on the impossible desire to be like God. Instead of leading to freedom, it results in bondage.

Following the fall, material things rather than personal relationships come to dominate human existence. The desire for power disrupts human relationships. Distrust of God leads to distrust of human neighbors, and anxiety about life leads to a continued search for the means to control other people. After the fall, humanity is marked by a magical understanding of the world and a desire to manipulate knowledge in a manner indistinguishable from sorcery. If this were the end of the story, our plight as humans would be sad indeed. But the Bible goes on to say that after the fall God took active steps to restore the relationship between humankind and himself. These steps are known as redemption.

## Redemption

Together with the fall, the **incarnation** and **resurrection** of Jesus are the central doctrines of the Christian faith. For the purposes of this discussion, we can say that they form a major Christian theological unit defining God and human. If the actions of Adam and Eve broke the trust between human and God, God restored it with the birth and death of Jesus. In the process, human beings learned who they are: finite creatures who nevertheless have a freedom of choice. And humans learned who God is: a being both infinite and divine.

As we noted earlier, mistrust entered the relationship between humanity and God with the fall. God became suspect. To redeem us from suspicion and regression, God redeemed humankind with an act of infinite love. He gave humans Jesus, leaving them free to choose their attitude and relationship to him. By dwelling on the recollection of having crucified him, humans might have been left wallowing in guilt. But by resurrecting him, God not only redeemed humans but also showed them that he is infinite. God redeemed humankind by redeeming himself at the same time, defining humans as distinct and different from himself, subject to his divinity yet free in their humanity.

The Christian notion of redemption, as we interpret it in this admittedly limited way, fits well with Western attitudes toward science and knowledge. It grants believers knowledge and choice within the confines of God's universe but dictates that since humans are not granted ultimate or Godlike knowledge, human pursuit of knowledge can never be complete. It does not allow humans to rest in the comfort of having attained union with the One, as the believers of many Eastern religions do, but it thereby prevents Christians from stagnation. Its emphasis is not on *being* (except in the sense of being at peace) but rather on *becoming*, in that the pursuit of knowledge and exploration is never-ending for humanity, that humans will always be able to experience growth, development, and above all hope.

Nor does the Christian sense of becoming necessarily have anything to do with evolution, especially not with the myth of evolution. Humans' becoming may be regressive or progressive, good or bad. This central Christian theme assures believers that they were given the wherewithal to build and destroy and the opportunity to choose whether to build or destroy. It leaves believers with the hope of finding ever new frontiers to conquer without the delusion that all "conquest" will be ipso facto "higher" and "better." The paths humans travel are a matter of their choosing. These Christian doctrines leave believers with a feeling of exhilaration, for they indicate that they have the opportunity to direct all that God has given them. And they can do so without having to hallucinate spirit helpers. Choice is conscious, not fortuitous, not subject to the occult, not even subject to a belief in the evil powers of humanity. It allows Christians to act in the world from the healthy perspective of trust.

## The Importance of Faith

Christians believe that the way humans reenter a living relationship with God is through **faith**, an act of trust based upon knowledge of God and his deeds. It is not a blind leap into the unknown but a confident step into enlightenment about the nature and love of God. Faith is the opposite of doubt and magical power. Faith is to redemption what magic and doubt are to the fall. It frees believers of anxiety because it entails their accepting their identity as creatures made in God's image.

Theistic faith is an expression of trust. It leads to a new way of life based on a living relationship with God. The inspiration for the distinctively Christian understanding of faith is found in the story of Abraham, who left the security of Ur of the Chaldees to become a wanderer and nomad in response to God's call (Genesis 12–24 and Hebrews 11:8–19). The longest exposition in the Bible of the meaning of faith is found in the book of **Romans**. It starts with Paul's observation that people have renounced truth and served "the creature more than the Creator." The essence of Paul's argument is that human beings, having lost the ability to trust God, made gods out of created things. In so doing, they lost the ability to trust each other, with disastrous results. But faith restores not only believers' relationship with God but also their relationship with their neighbors.

It is difficult to have faith. Many people choose to be satisfied with the sort of apparent reconciliation to God and neighbors that can be achieved by observing rigid codes, ritual actions, and prescribed ways of living. They look to laws rather than faith for instruction concerning how all people must live. These laws appear to restore human relationships and create communion with God, but in fact they produce a new kind of servitude. Paul calls this servitude "**legalism**" and discusses it at length in **Galatians**.

Legalism leads to magical practices and the observance of "feasts, sacred days, and Sabbaths," which are justified by appeals to what Paul calls "philosophy and vain deceit after the tradition of men" (Colossians 2:8, 16). The "law" also includes such things as observing genealogies, continuing ancient rituals such as circumcision, and keeping dietary rules. Paul and other New Testament writers condemn all of these ritual observances, denouncing them as bondage (see Acts 10, 15:1–29; Galatians 2–4; 1 Timothy 1:4).

In Galatians 3:1 Paul describes people who have submitted to legalism as "bewitched." Usually we regard this phrase as a figure of speech. But when we read it in conjunction with Galatians 5:20, in which "witchcraft," by which Paul means the sorcery of the Roman world, is classified with idolatry and other sins as "the works of the flesh," a different interpretation suggests itself. In Paul's view, legalism is akin to bewitchment and is therefore nothing other than the power of sorcery. In the Christian tradition, faith is presumed to free people to enter meaningful, nonexploitative relationships, whereas legalism is presumed to create dependence, addiction, and exploitation. The essence of legalism is the replacement of trust in God with manipulation through rituals. Legalism is therefore the continual reenactment of the fall (Lloyd-Jones 1984).

As Tipton points out, one reason the counterculture and new religions have grown is that many young people have turned to them after having rejected the legalism of Christian churches. And yet by joining new religions they enter even more repressive and legalistic situations. In effect, they are simply exchanging one form of legalism for another.

## Creation, Fall, Redemption, and New Religions

The new religious movements that grow out of the Abramic tradition typically deny the necessity of a faith relationship in favor of new forms of legalism. Biblical views of creation, which view the material world as good, are replaced by quasi-Yogic conceptions of the world as evil. Groups such as the **Local Church** have developed spirituality to the point that salvation of the soul becomes the sole objective in life. The traditional Christian emphasis on "glorifying God" and enjoying his creation is lost, and practices are introduced that encourage mystical visions that deny bodily experiences.

Many new religions find sexuality problematic. The Unification Church, for example, explains the fall in terms of wrongful sex. The church seeks to redeem sex, however, by staging elaborate shamanistic marriage rituals. Other groups shun sex altogether or, conversely, maintain that it is the means to ultimate liberation. Both of these emphases subvert the biblical vision of human beings as the image bearers of God. They lead couples who should be concentrating their efforts on establishing a loving relationship to focus instead on the desire to escape this world.

## Types of Eschatology

Ideas about the "return of Christ" give many contemporary religions their distinctive emphasis. These ideas arise out of the interpretation of the **eschatological** passages of the Bible, such as those in the books of **Daniel** and **Revelation** as well as key passages in the Gospels, such as Chapter 24 of **Matthew**. Attempting to understand the "true" meaning of prophetic passages in the Bible, new religious movements ignore established methods of exegesis and often use novel interpretive tools. For example, Charles Taze Russell, the founder of the Jehovah's Witnesses, claimed that the Great Pyramid of Egypt involved "sacred measurements" that he believed unlocked the meaning of the Bible.

The key to this type of esoteric interpretation is the magical manipulation of numbers. In essence it involves ways of thinking that display an obsession with coincidence and the creation of sacred patterns. Such ways of viewing the world are typical of people under severe stress or those who are suffering from hysteria.

To understand the ways in which new religions develop their ideas about the return of Christ, we need to look more closely at traditional Christian eschatological teachings. There are three basic theological understandings of biblical eschatology: **postmillennialism**, **premillennialism**, and **amillennialism**. For our purposes, it will only be necessary to look at the first two.

The postmillennialist position and its variations are the most orthodox, held by the majority of Christians throughout history. Postmillennialism holds that the gospel must be preached to every nation, after which there will be 1,000 years of peace before Christ returns to judge humans and nations. The Puritans held a particularly optimistic version of this view, maintaining that the millennium would be a period of continuous progress and human advancement.

The premillennialist position has had few supporters throughout church history, achieving popularity only as recently as the nineteenth century. Today it represents the dominant mode of interpretation in North America. One of the best-known presentations of this position is Hal Lindsey's book *The Late Great Planet Earth* (1970). Essentially, premillennialists believe that society will disintegrate into chaos before the Second Coming of Christ. Instead of 1,000 years of peace, there will be universal unrest and widespread persecution of Christians. In recent years this view has been directly linked with the expectation of atomic war because the New Testament speaks of the world being destroyed by fire (2 Peter 3:10).

**Dispensationalism** is a variation of premillennialism that was popularized by the *Scofield Reference Bible* (1909) and is taught at such places as the influential

**Dallas Theological Seminary**. Dispensationalism adopts the basic premillennial scheme but divides history into seven time periods, or dispensations, during which God is said to have dealt with humanity on the basis of different expectations and offered different ways of obtaining salvation.

An important issue on which postmillennialists and premillennialists disagree is the biblical teaching about Israel. Premillennialists contend that biblical references to Israel are references to the Jewish people. They maintain that the return of the Jewish people to Palestine and the establishment of the state of Israel in 1948 was a fulfillment of biblical prophecy. Consequently, they are strongly pro-Israel. More important, they expect a battle between Israel and the Arab nations and/or Russia to signal the end of the world.

Postmillennialists reject this type of interpretation, maintaining that the Jews who returned to Palestine cannot be identified with the biblical nation of Israel, which was destroyed in the sixth century B.C. The Jews who subsequently returned to Palestine are not really the people of Israel, they argue, but descendants of the tribe of Judah. Postmillennialists also argue that the references to the nation of Israel in New Testament prophecies are in fact references to the church of Christ. The reference to Israel in Hebrew scripture cited in 1 Peter 2:9, for instance, is meant to be applied to Christians, and when Paul ponders the fate of Israel in Romans 9–11, he is referring to the church, the new Israel into which God has "grafted" Gentiles (Romans 11:13–24).

## The Effects of Eschatology

To many people, arguments about eschatology may seem unimportant. But many new religious movements cannot be fully understood apart from their eschatological beliefs. The notorious Children of God began as a premillennialist, fundamentalist sect. They believed that the end of the world was imminent and that their leader, **David Berg**, had visions confirming it. Acting on their belief, they adopted an itinerant lifestyle and lived as a people waiting for the end. Many of their excesses can be understood in the light of the sense of urgency their premillennialism created (cf. Travis 1974).

By contrast, the Unification Church espouses a traditional postmillennial eschatology. Its members are optimistic about the future and work exceptionally hard to usher in the era of peace. Their political, business, and other activities are intended to be steps toward creating a heavenly kingdom on earth in keeping with their postmillennialist eschatology.

## Eschatology and Charismatic Gifts

The eschatology of the Abramic tradition has also given rise to significant prophetic and charismatic movements. Christians who call themselves "charismatics" believe that glossolalia, healing the sick, prophecy, and other "gifts of the spirit" are signs of "the last days." Verses from Acts 2, John 14–16, and many other passages of Scripture are used to justify such expectations.

In the 1960s, books such as David Wilkerson's *The Cross and the Switchblade* (1963) and John Sherrill's *They Speak with Other Tongues* (1964) popularized the notion that God's spirit is at work today in preparation for the end. The implications of this belief are that established, noncharismatic churches are spiritually dead and that to be a true Christian one must rely directly upon the leading of God's spirit.

Charismatics contend that spiritual "leading" is manifested in miraculous acts, visions, prophecies, and other supernatural phenomena. Such teachings have the effect of undermining the established authorities and rational procedures of traditional churches. Spontaneous charismatic leadership, devoid of specific qualifications, is made respectable by appeals to the Bible and becomes the source of authority and direction in small groups, prayer cells, and independent churches. Some of these fellowships like the Children of God have developed further into new religions.

## The Search for Community

Eschatological and charismatic beliefs have led to the formation of many community-oriented Christian groups. A concern with community is another of the hallmarks of the Abramic tradition. In Judaism and Islam, community is clearly identified with ethnic, national, or religious groups, as Christianity was until the Reformation. During the Reformation the emphasis on the importance of faith led many Christians to return to a concept of community found in the New Testament, which stresses the idea of the fellowship of true believers sharing a common faith in an essentially hostile and unbelieving world.

The Puritans of the sixteenth century and the Pietists of the seventeenth century are examples of Christian groups that sought to establish new communities of faith. Other outstanding examples of the quest for community include the monastic movements in Roman Catholic, Anglican, Lutheran, and Orthodox traditions and also such groups as the **Mennonites**, **Hutterites**, and **Doukhobors**. Today the idea of community has reappeared with new vigor in charismatic circles.

Christian interest in community takes many forms. In the traditional Protestant denominations, it has surfaced in revitalization movements that seek to recreate a sense of fellowship among church members. These movements tend to be rational, well controlled, and essentially moderate in beliefs and practices. Within some traditional churches, such as the Roman Catholic and Anglican, charismatic gifts are tolerated and at times even encouraged. They are placed within a framework of tradition and history, however, that tends to encourage respect for rational authority and common sense, thus preventing enthusiasm and cultic practices. The leaders of these mainstream movements tend to be well educated and have considerable theological and biblical knowledge.

By contrast, charismatic groups that emphasize community outside of established denominations tend to arise spontaneously as the result of the conversion experiences of their members. These groups acquire self-appointed leaders who are often poorly educated and theologically unsophisticated. It is out of such groups that many new religions, such as the Children of God, the Local Church, and the Way, have arisen. Both the Children of God and the Local Church place great emphasis on the spiritual nature of leadership. The Way differed from these groups in that its founder was a professor of theology whose search for meaningful community led him to break denominational ties and establish his own group.

## Prophetic Leadership

The question of authentic leadership and religious authority is clearly important in judging new religions. Religions of the Yogic tradition revere gurus who gain complete authority over their disciples. Abramic religions have no gurus. Instead, they have the institution of the prophet. A prophet differs from a guru in that the prophet simply declares the Word of God.

Prophets are not held to be gods or to share in the essence of God or even to lead the way to God. They simply serve to remind people of God's Word. Prophets take existing revelation and apply it to particular situations, in the process reminding people of their failures and calling them to restore their relationship with God. Prophets traditionally did not develop new doctrines or techniques for attaining salvation but applied existing knowledge and allowed their words to be tested against the Scriptures.

The testing of prophecy is an important theme throughout the Bible. Prophets are called to conform to God's revelation, and the conclusions they draw from particular passages must be fulfilled if their words are to be regarded as authentic. Unlike the guru's teaching, which is tested only by experience, the prophet's teaching is tested by Scripture and history as well as experience.

In many new religions, however, the office of prophet has developed away from biblical norms. Prophets in new religions, like the Mormon Joseph Smith, develop new doctrines and fundamentally change existing traditions through the incorporation of beliefs and practices from other traditions and folk religions. Other new religions, such as Scientology, appear to merge the office of prophet and guru to create a new leader who both proclaims the truth and becomes the object of devotion.

Standing between the god figure of Yogic religions and the Abramic prophet are individuals, such as the Reverend Moon and Isaiah Shembe, with spiritual power and holy missions. Members of the Unification Church and ama-Nazarites do not believe that their savior is a god, but they do believe that he is more than a mere prophet. For Unificationists, Moon is the Lord of the Second Advent. He has become a Christ figure by assuming the office of the Messiah and fulfilling

God's will on earth. To the ama-Nazarites, Shembe is the Servant of Sorrows who reveals God to his people.

## Conclusion

Virtually all new religions are largely shaped by the world's two great religious traditions, the Yogic and Abramic. These traditions are very different from one another in their evaluation of human life and destiny. The major difference between new religions and the Abramic tradition lies in the fact that all new religions implicitly or explicitly reject Abramic teachings about God and human responsibility, denying individual choice and replacing trust in God with magical notions that breed authoritarian organizations and personal dependence. The major difference between most new religions and the Yogic tradition is the rejection of the implications of karma and samsāra. Instead of seeking enlightenment to escape the bonds of karma, new religions tend to interpret karma in a mythic evolutionary framework that sees rebirth as an inevitable step toward personal perfection.

### KEY TERMS

**Abraham**: The biblical patriarch and founder of the Jewish people whose story is told in the Book of Genesis.

**Abramic religions**: Religions that claim Abraham as their common ancestor. These are Christianity, Islam, and Judaism.

**Amillennialism**: The theological position that argues the Bible teaches Christ will return at the end of history, but humans have no way of knowing how or when, and it is better not to speculate.

**Astrology**: The occult belief "as above, so below," which relates the movement and position of stars to the destiny of individuals and entire peoples. Natal astrology deals with people, mundane with nations.

**Berg, David** (1919–1994?): The founder of the Children of God and visionary guru to his followers. He assumed the name "Moses," or "Mo," under which he wrote a series of sexually explicit *Mo Letters* detailing his revelations.

**Biological racism**: The nineteenth-century development of racism that relates cultural differences to fundamental biological differences among peoples, first advocated by the French author Joseph Arthur Comte de Gobineau (1816–1882).

**Catholic Counter-Reformation**: A sixteenth-century Roman Catholic revitalization movement spearheaded by the Jesuits to reclaim Europe from Protestantism.

**Children of God**: One of the most notorious new religions of the 1960s founded by David Berg. At one point his followers practiced "flirty fishing," or ritual prostitution.

**Conze, Edward** (1904–1983): English-born German communist who in 1933 fled Nazi Germany to take refuge in England, where he converted to Buddhism. His book *Buddhism: Its Essence and Development* (1951) is the best single introduction to Buddhism, whereas his autobiography *The Memoirs of a Modern Gnostic* (1979) is entertaining reading.

**Dallas Theological Seminary**: The leading evangelical/fundamentalist seminary in the United States to teach dispensationalism.

**Daniel:** One of the prophetic books of the Old Testament that contains various visions of the future.

**Dharma:** That which is established law; the wheel of existence; ultimate truth. A term used by Buddhists, Hindus, and Jains to describe the human situation and the way or means of salvation.

**Dispensationalism:** A fundamentalist form of premillennialism that divides God's dealings with humankind into distinct time periods, or dispensations. It is associated with creationism and the *Scofield Reference Bible.*

**Doctrine of creation:** The Abramic belief that God created the universe and that all humans are descended from common ancestors.

**Doukhobors:** A Russian religious sect founded in the eighteenth century known as the "spirit wrestlers."

**Dualism:** Any system that explains the facts of the world, or particular facts, by belief in two different ultimate and irreducible principles. Two major forms of dualism are seeing the universe as a cosmic battleground between the principles of good and evil, and the strict division of human nature into spirit and matter.

**Eschatological:** Concerning the last things, the final end of humans and the world.

**Faith:** Understood in two ways in traditional Christian thought: first, as belief or mental assent to the truth; second, as the orientation of the total person, best described as trust, confidence, or loyalty.

**The fall:** The traditional Christian explanation for the present state of the world. According to Genesis 3, the first humans rebelled against God, creating moral chaos and bringing evil into the world.

**Galatians:** Next to Romans, the most important of Paul's letters, containing more of his teachings on faith.

**Genesis:** The first book of the Bible.

**Guru:** A spiritual teacher in Yogic religions.

**Hebrew Scriptures:** Those books of the Bible that Christians call the Old Testament.

**Hutterites:** An Anabaptist sect that emerged in Moravia in 1529 and was reorganized by Jakob Hutter in 1553. Anabaptists insisted on the baptism of adult believers only, as they considered baptism a profession of faith. Today there are around 10,000 Hutterites, who are distinguished by their communal living, traditional dress, and hostility to modern culture.

**Incarnation:** The taking of human form by God in the person of Jesus Christ; in more general terms, any manifestation of God or gods in human form.

**Individualism:** A philosophic system that values the individual over the community.

**Karma:** One of the central doctrines of Yogic religion that is probably best described as a belief in a universal cause and effect that embraces all things.

**Legalism:** Any religious system driven by laws at the expense of grace and human understanding.

**Local Church:** The name of an evangelical Christian group of Chinese origin that has numerous distinctive features that cause some other Christians to regard it as a cult.

**Matthew:** The first of the four New Testament Gospels that portray the life of Jesus.

**Māyā:** The concept of cosmic "illusion" that plays an important role in Hinduism.

**Meditation:** The practice of self-reflection, concentration on a sacred object, yoga, or prayer for spiritual enlightenment.

**Mennonites**: A Christian community descended from the Anabaptist movement of the sixteenth century. The movement owes its name to the Dutch religious leader Menno Simons (1492–1559).

**Moksha**: The achievement of enlightenment and release from the bonds of karma; spiritual liberation.

**Nicene Creed**: The traditional Christian creed, or statement of belief, formulated by the Council of Nicaea (A.D. 325). It defined the person of Christ as equally God and human.

**Nirvāna**: The ideal of salvation in Buddhism, attained through meditation. Its meaning is "blowing out" or "cooling"; Western writers sometimes describe it as annihilation, although Buddhists often deny this meaning.

**Nondualism**: A more correct understanding of Yogic philosophy than suggested by the term "monism." It implies the rejection of dualism but not necessarily a universal oneness.

**Ontological**: Related to ontology, the science of the essential properties, nature, and relations of being as such; a branch of metaphysics.

**Osho movement**: The new name adopted after his death by the followers of Rajneesh.

**Pilgrimage**: A journey undertaken for sacred purposes to reach a spiritual goal.

**Polygenesis**: The scientific theory that the human race evolved in several places to produce not one race but many different races.

**Postmillennialism**: The theological position that argues that there will be 1,000 years of peace on earth, which will establish the Kingdom of God, before the return of Christ. It identifies biblical promises to Israel with the Church.

**Premillennialism**: The theological position that argues that life on earth will increasingly worsen until there is an almost complete collapse of civilization, at which point Christ will return. It identifies biblical passages about Israel with the modern nation of Israel.

**Qur'ān**: The holy book of Islam that contains the revelation of God's will for humankind.

**Rebirth**: In Yogic religions, reincarnation, transmigration, or some other form of metempsychosis. Christians use it to speak about the experience of conversion, being born again, or regeneration.

**Redemption**: The salvation of humankind by God. In Christian theology this comes about through faith in the saving work of Christ.

**Resurrection**: The restoration of a body, sometimes transformed, to human beings after the death of their physical bodies. The great example of resurrection in Christian theology is that of Jesus three days after his execution by the Romans.

**Revelation**: The last book of the New Testament, containing many passages that are difficult to interpret. It is often taken as a blueprint for foretelling the future.

**Romans**: Probably the most important of the apostle Paul's writing. His teachings on faith, found in Chapter 3, formed the basis of Martin Luther's theology and the driving force behind the Reformation.

**Samsāra**: The wheel of rebirth in Yogic religions. Believers seek liberation from the bonds of both karma and samsāra.

***Scofield Reference Bible***: A very popular fundamentalist version of the Bible first published in 1909 that includes copious notes that "explain" biblical passages and proclaims a dispensational view of eschatology.

**Soteriological**: Having to do with theology that deals with salvation and the liberation of humans.

**Transcendental:** That which is prior to, independent of, and exalted over the universe of space and time.

**Transmigrate:** The act of metempsychosis, the soul's leaving the body at death to be reborn in another body as a baby. Transmigration is closely associated and often confused with reincarnation.

**Upanishad:** A collection of texts that since the eighth century B.C. have been known as the last of the Vedas, or sacred books, of the Hindu tradition. The content and doctrine of the Upanishads vary considerably, from treaties that promote atheism to devotional theism.

**Western Buddhist Order:** A highly successful European Buddhist missionary movement based in England.

**Yoga:** A Sanskrit term meaning "to yoke," which is used to describe a process of spiritual discipline or harnessing of physical and mental powers to attain self-control and ultimate enlightenment.

**Yogic tradition:** Religions originating in India that have yoga as their central practice.

# 7

## The Membership Process

*After a year watching people join ... I have yet to see anyone lured in by any-
thing other than their own hunger to believe. As far as I could see everyone
joined out of choice. . . . If they stayed it was because they wanted to. . . . Life
is an endless round of meetings, prayers and ceremonies to keep the flame
alive. It is all or nothing.*

William Shaw (1995:185–186)

*T*his quote from William Shaw's *Spying in Guru Land* summarizes the way new
religions bring together a total way of life that meets spiritual needs. In this chapter we discuss the process by which new religions make daily life sacred, and we
provide four case histories to illustrate our argument. We conclude with a theory
of conversion to new religions in terms of personal reorganization and a global
vision.

### Experience, Myth, and Ideology

So far we have argued that the new mythology predisposes individuals to accept
the validity of their own primal experiences. At the same time, primal experiences
give the mythology a life of its own and often cause people to seek such experiences for themselves. But to gain and sustain membership, new religions need to
add an intellectual element. This doctrinal dimension provides members with a
cognitive resource that allows them to integrate their experiences and mythologies into a living community. The doctrines of new religions are created by adapt-
ing teachings from historic religious traditions. These teachings are integrated
into an interpretive framework that explains the relationship between myth and
experience in specific ways.

When we wrote our earlier book *Understanding Cults and New Religions*, we
were committed to a psychological theory of conversion based on **schismogene-**

sis. Now we recognize that membership in new religions is more complex. Rather than one mode of conversion, becoming a member involves a wide spectrum of "conversions." At one end of this continuum are dramatic, Pauline-type conversions. At the other are people who join a group as a result of friendship networks and casual contact. In Fred Welbourn's words, these people have simply found a "place to feel at home" (Welbourn 1961:201–213).

We also recognize that new religions fall into various organizational patterns. Once again we are dealing with a spectrum from what Stark and Bainbridge call "**audience cults**," which involve little or no commitment, to "**cult movements**" with high expectations in terms of the commitment of their members (Stark and Bainbridge 1985:27–30). These different types of new religions also affect the type of conversion people report.

Nevertheless, for most people, but especially the first generation of members, the shift from secular rationalism to the acceptance of a supernatural worldview involves a form of conversion. This transition to the acceptance of religious realities involves both myth and experience. Yet on their own, primal experiences and a rich mythology rarely maintain commitment over time. Nor do they lead people to join specific religious groups.

To demonstrate that the new mythology cannot by itself provide direction to a group, even when it is reinforced by repeated primal experiences, we might look at the example of the religious community that formed near the town of Glastonbury, England, in the mid-1960s and early 1970s. English and American hippies came together in this setting because of its rich mythological background, incorporating medieval legends about **King Arthur** and Jesus. Many individuals reported encounters with these and other legendary figures, yet no organized movement developed out of this gathering.

The early Findhorn Community headed by Peter Caddy was similarly rich in primal experiences and myth but lacked definite ideology. Only after the arrival of David Spangler did the community develop a distinct ideology based on a combination of futurism and various Eastern philosophies. Later still, in the early 1980s, the Findhorn group obtained property in Glastonbury and proceeded to propagate a unified ideology. Even if they support vivid primal experiences and rich eclectic mythologies, groups like the early Glastonbury and Findhorn communities will not coalesce into new religious movements. To do so, they must draw upon some established theological or ideological framework that structures both the experiences and the myths. We should turn next, then, to the sources of these overarching frameworks.

## Joining a New Religion: The Šhuman Process

Having learned how myths and doctrines help create new religions by providing the means to interpret experiences, we now need to examine the personal and social characteristics of people who join new religions. We can best do so by taking a closer look at the sort of individual who becomes involved in the šhuman process, the sacralizing of the human to invest everyday life with religious meaning.

In order to give an indication of both the variation and similarities in the life histories of members, we present four case histories using the fictional "**New Dispensation movement**" as a representative new religion. We selected these cases from a large number of interviews undertaken during extended research trips in North America during 1984 and 1985 because they epitomize conversion stories. Later, in 1987 and 1989, we gathered very similar data from interviews with members of new religions in South Africa. We have continued to observe essentially the same patterns in other interviews in Europe and North America in the 1990s.

The reader should note the significant role that primal experiences and fragments of mythology play in the lives of all four individuals either before the individual joins the new religion (as is most often the case) or after. Nor are our findings unique (Beckford 1985; Barker 1984). We present them because most authors who document the occurrence of similar primal experiences fail to recognize that interviewees interpret them as evidence of the reality of the new mythology. It is this power of primal experiences to transform extraordinary mythology into ordinary reality that helps propel potential converts into a group of their choice.

## Raymond: Spiritual Seeker

Raymond was born into poverty in 1953 in central Canada. He had a family, including two brothers, but he cannot remember them. By the time he was two years old, he was in a foster home. His memory starts there, in that Pentecostal foster home, with the regular beatings he received from the family's adolescent son.

Once he was beaten into unconsciousness, an event he remembers to this day as the occasion on which he developed a deep and abiding resentment. It was then, when he was about five years old, that he concocted a scheme to kill the son of his foster parents by placing razor blades in his bed. He was saved from this act of revenge when his mother kidnapped him. What he did not escape, however, was poverty, for he remembers that his mother took him to a dump to find blankets for him. The stay with his mother was brief—a few months, maybe a year. All he remembers is that she was very religious and taught him to pray. He began to believe in something.

He was soon taken to a new foster home and found it to be worse than the first. He fought frequently, at the same time fearing the evil within him that made him fight. And when his foster parents chained him to a doghouse and fed him dog food for days at a time, he began to feel it was right. Chained, he felt at peace, as if the chain restrained his otherwise unchecked self-hate. He remembers running away somehow and living among Cree Indians for a few months. He remembers being among animals and feeling befriended by them. He remembers talking to them and feeling less lonely among them. And he remembers learning about

**Manitou**, the Cree Indian conception of the divine. His association with Cree Indians heightened his suggestibility.

When he was seven, he was back with his real family. His appendix was removed. During the operation, he remembers quite clearly a feeling that he was outside of his body. By age eight he was in another foster home. One event from this period stays in his memory: He ate a full jar of honey, became sick, and was in a coma for a week. During that coma he entered a loving world that would be his alone for many years to come. He calls it the spirit world. It was filled with "friends" who would visit him in recurrent dreams and in his subsequent retreats to it.

At age nine he was back with his family. Hate, isolation, and tension formed the essence of family life. They also gave rise to his first stomach ulcer. So difficult was his reality that he learned to visit the spirit world regularly. He was in fact preoccupied with it. He would sit on his bed, visualize the spirit world, fashion it to his liking, and enter it. Once inside, he would be reunited with his friends. His spiritual preoccupations became obvious. When he was ten, his brother discovered him talking to his invisible friends. The brother alerted his parents who must have listened in, for they took Raymond first to a psychiatrist and then to an exorcist; they resented the expense of these visits. Raymond became an altar boy in the Catholic Church, but he found no solace.

Shortly before his eleventh birthday, he decided to end his life. It was his intention to commit suicide on the day of his birth. The day arrived. He was on his way to throw himself in front of a bus at a chosen street corner when he was struck by a question: "What if I am the returned Christ?" He had heard a fair amount about the Second Coming of Christ just previously, and he was captivated by the idea. He forgot suicide. Christ was suffering, and he was Christ. He came to believe he had been Christ for two years, a period, he remembers, that had been filled with questions to God. He asked, and God answered through his inner voice. "And the answers," he added, "resembled the teachings of the New Dispensation movement."

He had never told his mother that he believed himself to be Christ. But once, when he was thirteen and she was beating him for something, she said, "And you are not the returned Christ." That was it. He began to question who Christ really was. He read the Bible and asked priests, but their answers seemed hollow, and he felt that they were accusing him of dabbling in satanism. Disillusioned, he gave up attending the Catholic Church. Seeing himself as somehow chosen, and filled with a sense of moral injustice in the world, he joined the Socialist Student League. To his mind, Christ was a socialist. And socialists shared. This fit in with his deep resentment against the wealthy.

He started taking LSD and then marijuana and then hashish. He also studied the martial arts. During this phase he shifted between retreats into his spirit world and increasingly open displays of violence. Christ and God were dead. He was a socialist and felt embittered toward the rich. At age sixteen he mobilized over 600 students from three schools. His brief moment of glory was soon over, though, because he dealt in drugs, was in frequent trouble with the police, and was quickly abandoned by his socialist friends.

His violence increased, and he looked for a philosophy that would accommodate it. He found it in **Kung Fu** and the martial arts, at which he was now adept. By the time he was twenty, his spiritual development had halted, but his violence was increasing. He resented the Catholic Church, scorned priestly celibacy, lived with one woman after another, dealt with drugs, and participated in the underworld. As he grew older, the condition of imbalance shifted from retreat into his spiritual world to violent confrontation with the social world. The pattern continued until he found himself without friends.

It was his Kung Fu teacher more than anyone else who made him aware of his mean, antisocial behavior. Raymond had felt uncomfortable about his inability to maintain friendships, but he justified his cruelty by blaming a cruel world. His teacher, however, insisted that the fault lay as much in his personality. Believing that Raymond's untoward behavior had something to do with fear of death, his Kung Fu teacher had Raymond beaten up. In the midst of his beating, Raymond had another out-of-body experience. The effect of the experience made him lose his fear of death and persuaded him to begin a serious spiritual search. Like many others, Raymond entered his spiritual career by joining and leaving numerous groups, among them Pentecostals, Baptists, Scientologists, Krishnas, and Buddhists. He took some of his guidance from such occult practices as palm and tarot card reading.

Finally, to overcome his hatred of rich people, he began socializing with various local politicians. At age twenty-five he began having spiritual experiences that dealt more with a sense of mission. Disembodied voices and apparitions would tell him, "Come and save us." At a strenuous session of Kung Fu training in the wintry mountains of Canada, he had a vision of cosmic importance. The world changed suddenly and became surrounded with light. He knew that something was about to happen. These experiences continued. Sipping a cup of coffee, Raymond told us that a stranger had walked up to him and asked, "Would you give your life for the world?"

Everything he described subsequently consisted of coincidences into which he read great meaning. He felt strongly that he must leave the farm where he was a laborer; a day later it was hit by a hurricane. Then he heard a distinct voice tell him to "go sit on that bench and a blonde will come and speak to you." She came, and she was wearing a watch that counted hours in colors, which he had also foreseen. The young woman talked to him of God. Coincidences continued until he joined a controversial new religion: the New Dispensation movement. Since then, he has had to work hard to reduce his aggression. Raymond said that each morning God would speak to him in a very specific way, telling him that he had "to develop a parental heart for others by accepting the right of three different people today to have a different viewpoint" from his own. God was working on his personality, Raymond told us, showing him what it means to become a brother in the New Dispensation family.

During a bout of sickness, Raymond had further revelations about the fall of humankind, having an "unconditional heart," and being objective toward God. At the time, he said, he entered the spirit world, and "the spirits gave testimony to the Promise." He also had a vision of a golden city, a new Jerusalem, in which the Promise given by the leader of the New Dispensation was about to be realized. He went to a Promise ceremony and was betrothed to a wife. To this day, Raymond is still struggling with aggression, bitterness, and suspicion and with his excessive spiritual openness.

## Poppie: Looking for Relationships

Poppie's story is shorter and less complex than Raymond's. She was born in 1955 into a working-class home in England. Her family's Anglican affiliation would indicate that they were aspiring toward a higher-class status. Her parents scraped and saved money and sent Poppie to a private school. Her experience at this school left Poppie with considerable feelings of bitterness and constituted enough of an imbalance to become an idée fixe. Having successfully completed an international secretarial course that made her competent in several languages, Poppie left England for Spain. At first, she told us, she associated with "leftists" because she "shared some of their bitterness." Their irresponsibility in practical matters and personal relationships, however, persuaded her to leave them.

She wanted to gain "mind power." To that end, she associated with a group called the **Infinite Way**. She reported that her working-class background left her with little appreciation for meditation, however: "One has to do more in life than just sit around and meditate." Above all, she resented the pretensions of perfection among the other members and described them as lacking in morality and knowledge about relationships. Considerably disturbed by the bitterness that she seemed unable to conquer, she studied journalism with the aim of entering a new career. She also practiced yoga to "purify her life" and clean up her personality. With these decisions she turned around a drifting (though dramatic) life and made it purposeful.

Modestly successful at her new job, she set off for the western United States in order to write articles about the American spiritual smorgasbord. She had quite clearly geared her work to help her straighten out personal imbalances. In San Francisco she met members of the New Dispensation movement and was from the first excited about their relational dynamics. She attended one of the movement's retreats, studied its **"principle of providence"** at another church camp for three weeks, spent eight weeks on a work crew, and ended by witnessing in another city for nearly two years. Appropriately enough, she worked in the city's Spanish district, distributing food and teaching. When her visa expired, she returned to Britain, where she worked for an oil company while remaining a member of the New Dispensation movement. The following year she came to Canada.

## Tim: The Rational Quest

Tim was born in 1955 to parents who were both scientists in an agricultural community. All four children of this family were very bright. Tim told us that he skipped a grade and took university math by correspondence while still in high school. He was verbally facile and extroverted and had a sense of humor that he used primarily to defend himself, to shock others, and generally to gain attention. He was clumsy in expressing his emotions, which made him appear to be somewhat insensitive.

Tim appeared to have experienced the world and his relationships in it as castrating. He remembers a formative incident in his life that occurred in the fourth grade: Four boys ganged up on him and attempted to castrate him. The emotional void in his life is perhaps best indicated by his claim that when he told his parents of the fearful incident, they suggested that he probably did something to deserve it.

The intellectual atmosphere in his home left Tim with a feeling of inner hollowness that was only worsened by the hostility he experienced from his peers. The other children in the rural environment appeared to be more robust and less intellectual than he. The pervasive alienation of his school years persisted. During his second year in college, he developed chronic back problems. His first bout with this ailment left him bedridden for six weeks. He was, however, beginning to realize some benefits from his verbal skills. He reports that he was able to dissuade four individuals from committing suicide. This gift convinced him that there was a mission for him somewhere.

People like Tim characteristically describe their relationships to others and the world in repetitive, impulsive, and stereotyped ways, and they often exhibit a peculiar fascination with the occult. Tim's repetitive reference to the number four is a significant point in this regard. He grew up in a family of four children. Four boys ganged up on him in the fourth grade. And four times he saved someone from suicide. At the age of twenty-four, he had major conflicts with a New Dispensation movement leader who was also twenty-four years old. Before he joined the movement the fourth and final time, he prayed for twelve minutes each night for forty nights to discover whether his decision was right.

As is common among those with such a personality, Tim spoke of his relations and experiences in a stylized manner. He characteristically described stereotypical child-parent and victim-aggressor relationships, often involving rescues. He also produced fantasy-like explanations of situations that entailed caricatured roles for himself and others. His relationship to his parents turned him into a victim, a theme replayed throughout his short life. There was the aggressor-victim theme with his peers in high school. Inside the New Dispensation movement, he felt victimized by what he called "middle-management leaders," which he cited as the reason he left the movement the second time. He met a new leader named Taylor when he attended the movement's Great Lakes Center, and he said that a talk with Taylor saved him. He rejoined the movement as "Taylor's chauffeur" and for a short period completely idolized the leader, referring to him as a saving master from whom flowed a healing love. In the end, however, the relationship soured. Tim sank into depression and was plagued by a recurrence of his chronic backache. He left the New Dispensation movement again, returned to college, and got a degree in industrial engineering.

Unable to reach a decision about whether to return to the New Dispensation movement, he set up various tests that might help "strike him" with what to do. The forty days of prayer failed to provide him with any clear guidance, so he formulated a second test, then a third and a fourth. During the third test, he opened the Bible randomly and was struck by the passage he happened upon: "Again I will be your God and you will be my people." He considered this a great revelation, and he felt that the message was confirmed the next week when he had a series of great dreams about God, Christ, and the founder of the New Dispensation movement.

This period seems to have resulted in some healing for Tim. He reported that "for the first time God had become real and personal, and I could relate to him intimately." He experienced the love of God, and the great emotional void in his life was at last filled. He also lost his fixation with cult figures and Lucifer-like middle-management types. Earlier in his career with the New Dispensation movement, Tim had a vision "about developing Third World industry for the sake of the Third World itself." Now he found the courage to relate that vision to others and act upon it. Several of his personal problems neared resolution: He opened a printing business to develop his business skills for the benefit of the Third World. He became engaged to a Jamaican. Then he had a tumor removed from his knee, which seemed to clear up his back problem as well.

Tim still remembers having major dreams two or three times a year, and he usually uses them as an aid to solving dilemmas. He also has visions of strange animals coming toward him. When they are sinister, he strengthens his prayer.

## Brian: Emotional Confusion

In psychological terms, Brian suffers from an antisocial personality disorder that is, in varying degrees of severity, quite common among males who join new religions. He was born out of wedlock in 1961. His natural father left during the pregnancy, and Brian never knew him. Sometime later, his mother married a man who then adopted Brian. They had four other children together. Brian's adoptive father beat him and his mother frequently. Their home was the source of constant emotional chaos. Brian remembers experiencing peace only when his grandparents took him to Sunday school.

Brian did not learn that he had been adopted until he was twelve, when his adoptive father left the family. He says that learning that the man who had beaten him all those years was not even his real father infuriated him, making him a "seedbed of hatred." He vowed to kill the man and plotted for three years to do so. Brian had always taken after his adoptive father, and after the man left he became even more wild. He put another child "into the hospital." He started taking heroin but then switched to speed (methamphetamine) "because it was less expensive."

Brian's mother complained that both he and his two stepbrothers "were out of control." Since his mother was unable to control the boys, Brian's adoptive father was given custody of them when Brian was fourteen. He stayed with the man for two years, which he describes as "absolute hell." He reports that there were "constant physical fights between father and me." Brian went to jail three times, primarily for theft and forgery. He lost hope that he would ever reform and "prayed and cried to God to reveal himself." The degree of his unhappiness with his violence is evident in that he instructed a friend outside to buy a gun he could use to do away with himself if he had not reformed within two and a half years, the length of his last jail sentence.

After three months in jail, Brian met a member of the New Dispensation movement who was also imprisoned. Brian says that he learned something about a spiritual life from this man. He did not, however, undergo a transformation (nor has he yet). Instead, he continued "to drink, smoke, and swear." The jail psychiatrist did, however, help him come to terms with his hatred for his father. After Brian left jail, he had a reunion with him, and he says that both he and his father "opened up and cried." His former hatred for his father was not so much dissipated as redirected. When he learned that his psychiatrist had told his father about Brian's wish to kill him, he felt betrayed and experienced an urge "to kill the psychiatrist."

Brian went to stay at a New Dispensation movement center, but he did not have an easy time there. He resented the discipline and tried to avoid witnessing. It was suggested that he move out and return to school. Within six months, he realized that he had fallen back into his old destructive pattern. He asked to move back to the center. Since his return he has done primarily manual labor on the farm or at the center. At the time of the interview, Brian was still struggling.

There has been no dramatic transformation of his personality, although he has become more self-aware. He recognizes that he is "unstable" and that he "stretches the truth," and he is aware of his "volatile temper." He claims to be "repulsed by the idea of violence," however, and says that he "could never hurt anyone again." According to some of the movement's members who live with Brian, "He doesn't really love God, but he sure hates Satan." Brian reports feeling particularly close to two members of the New Dispensation movement and says that their closeness and warmth steady him. So does fantasy. He told us that he loves science-fiction movies and books by Tolkien, LeGuin, and Donaldson, among others.

His violence, once directed toward specific people, seems to have undergone a transformation. It is now his aspiration to play a central role in "the triumph over communism." Words and acts that once made him violent now make him laugh. Brian's growth is slow and arduous. Far from being spiritual, except as a voyeur, he is only learning to diversify his narrowly focused and violent emotions. He has added "warmth," "openness," "willingness to be vulnerable," "fantasy," and "laughter" to a catalogue of emotions once restricted principally to hatred.

## Our Theory of Conversion to New Religions

People who shop for new religions typically do so because they are experiencing some kind of disorganization in their relationships to themselves, other people, and the world. In this state they recognize their need to reorient their lives and make a new beginning. We have identified two major categories of such reorganization—relational and psychological.

People who see a need to reorganize their relationships are sometimes said to experience relational double binds. The case of Poppie above provides an example of such a person: a child from a poor, working-class background who was sent to a private school where she felt uncomfortable and developed a deep and abiding bitterness. As she became aware that her attitude was costing her friends, she began to search for a solution. When rational and secular solutions didn't work, she began to look for religious solutions. She tried different cults and new religious groups until she found one that accommodated her attitudes, behaviors, and views.

People who feel the need to reorganize their chaotic emotions are sometimes said to experience psychological double binds. Different types of psychological reorganization arise from three major and rather separate kinds of discord or conflict. Spiritual reorganization arises from a conflict between an inner spiritual world and the external world of reason or unreason and usually leads people to retreat increasingly into a private world of visions, voices, or hallucinations (as in the case of Raymond). Rational reorganization is the result of a conflict between reason and emotion (or lost emotion) and usually leads people to engage increasingly in rationalizations that give evidence of their having lost touch with their emotional and physical reality (as in the case of Tim). Emotional reorganization grows out of a conflict between emotion and reality and usually leads people to vent their emotions with increasing frenzy or violence (as in the case of Brian).

An awareness of the need for spiritual reorganization tends to occur in people who are physically and/or mentally mistreated early in their lives, often prior to age six. Many such individuals are denied parental love and have been raised in foster homes, some shuttled from one home to another. This condition is especially prevalent in ghettos in both North America and the Third World, but it is also found among poor whites.

However mild or severe the rejection they suffer, these people quickly learn to live in an elaborate private world of spirits, voices, visions, vivid dreams, hallucinations, and out-of-body experiences. With increasing age they may become more bitter and more violent or, alternatively, more withdrawn. Uncomfortable with their personality and lacking self-esteem, they embark on a spiritual search.

Such primal experiences as visions, coincidences, and revelatory dreams lead individuals to attempt consciously or unconsciously to change their personalities. Primal experiences are usually associated with primal religions and traditional societies. Research indicates their prevalence among white North Americans, Europeans, and people usually classed as schizophrenic, substantiating Boisen's point that certain types of mental disorders and certain types of religious experience constitute similar attempts at reorganization. For those undergoing spiritual reorganization, temporary mental disorders and religious experiences may indicate a healing process.

Rational reorganization is similar to the condition that R. D. Laing calls schizoid, and on the whole it entails a less dramatic conflict than spiritual reorganization (Laing 1965). People in this situation often come from upper-middle-class or professional homes, and they tend not to feel at home in their own physical body. Typically highly intelligent, they tend to be emotionally clumsy or immature, covering their inadequacy with brash humor, verbal cleverness, or skillful rationalization. These strategies usually serve only to exaggerate their sense of a disrupted relation with their self and the world of more robust individuals around them. Uneasy with their emotions and physical being but aware of somehow having to come to terms with them, such people tend to drift toward new religions that emphasize self-realization through meditation and emotional muting.

Some are made aware of their need for personal reorganization not through psychedelic drugs, meditation, or a religious subculture but by the criticism of other people. Often such individuals feel that others are characterizing them as physically weak, effeminate, inadequate, or sickly. Sometimes family circumstances necessitate their being raised among a different class of peers—often less intellectual and more physical—and the differences give rise to disparaging comparisons that they cannot deal with easily.

Emotional reorganization occurs when people are so overwhelmed by life that they fall apart and sink into emotional chaos. This condition is found frequently in ghettos of the Third World. It occurs less frequently in the West because caretaker professions and institutions tend to prevent extreme emotional confusion.

Individuals who find themselves in states of emotional turbulence are rarely able to voice, and still less to analyze, their problems. This makes them susceptible to panic, a condition common among black women in southern Africa. They are drawn to new religions that integrate aspects of Christianity with African traditional beliefs and practices to "heal" their condition. In these movements ritual massaging, pummeling, shaking, washing, dancing, and the incantation of sacred songs are common. It is as if "sense" were knocked into them, panic shaken out of them, and joy danced and sung until it surrounds them. Once their panic recedes, these women are encouraged to maintain their balance by following further rituals during the course of their daily activities. Holy water is thought to be particularly efficacious.

To sum up, many people who are uncomfortable with their circumstances enter a long search for a religious community in which they can feel at home. In the West feelings that our world is too impersonal, too rational, and too insincere often give rise to a longing for relational, spiritual, and rational reorganization. In the Third World, in contrast, material and cultural deprivations and social upheavals often give rise to the need for emotional reorganization through independent faith healing or magical religions.

## The Globality of Personal Reorganization

In our culture a large number of scholars in the disciplines of religion, philosophy, and the social and physical sciences continue to perceive men and women primarily as rational beings. As **Kenelm Burridge** suggests, the dominant anthropological framework still views the human being as a thinker who (1) experiences conflict primarily as mental conflict; (2) becomes aware of this conflict through a process of rationalization, intellectualization, and symbolic representation; and (3) transcends the conflict through a process of rerationalization, antithetical argument, and moral critique (Burridge 1979:7).

According to Burridge, the individual is a self that consists of a *person* and an *individual*. By "person" he means the conformist aspect of one's personality that is given to reproduce in word and deed the norms and relations of a given tradition. By "individual" Burridge means that aspect of the self that manifests "relations opposed to those indicated by the person." A self is an individual to the extent that it is a "normal critic who envisages another kind of moral order, the creative spark poised and ready to change tradition." But Burridge contends that this creative spark originates in one's rational faculties (Burridge 1979:5–7).

Peter Berger argues that religion is an "immense projection of human meanings into the empty vastness of the universe—a projection, to be sure, which comes back as an alien reality to haunt its producers" (Berger 1969:106). He, too, considers only the rational aspects of human beings, contending that sociologists of religion must suspend judgment concerning "the question as to whether these projections may not *also* be something else"—which is to say that they must adopt an atheistic methodology. But such an approach projects the rationality of the observer (the only faculty scientists are supposed to use in their work) onto those being observed. Many social scientists adopt Berger's approach. In doing so, however, they ignore in themselves and in their analyses important aspects of the human being, aspects that William Barrett has referred to as the "Furies": forces *underneath* intellect and reason (Barrett 1958:276–279). It is precisely this aspect of human nature, these subrational forces, that individuals who search for and join new religions are trying to deal with.

We would do well, then, to explore the perspective of individual *experiences* and quest for personal reorganization. Our studies of the life histories of shamans, diviners, "prophets," and members of new religions have led us to the conclusion that the structures of their personal lives are remarkably similar, regardless of where these "seekers" or religious practitioners lived—in Africa, Japan, China, Siberia, America, or anywhere else—and regardless of the era in which they lived. This structural similarity holds up despite differences in idiom, imagery, and cultural contexts. What is more, these life histories frequently contradict traditional sociological analyses of both the new religions and their adherents.

We suspect that the constancy in personal lives of these individuals, despite the variety of cultures in which they lived and the variety of social scientists who observed them, has something to do with the structure of the human psyche. Beneath the diversity of different cultures, we observe, like Sudhir Kakar, psychological universals (Kakar 1981:10).

It should be noted that there is considerable hostility among members of many new religions to those who want to analyze the psychological state of initiates and more established members. The hostility naturally arises from the tendency of analysts to attribute the primal experiences of the members exclusively to the biochemistry and psychological makeup of the individuals who have the experiences, whereas members of new religions prefer to attribute them to the existence of a separate spirit world. The former contend that primal experiences are evidence of deviance, whereas the latter contend that they constitute privileged communication.

Ordinary members of new religions have primal experiences quite frequently and in some communities are encouraged to record and circulate them. Leaders of the Unification Church now deemphasize the importance of primal experiences—but they do so not because they have been intimidated by outsiders but because they fear that such experiences might keep members from accomplishing their primary tasks. In a talk entitled "Piety and Spirituality," Unification Church leader Patricia Zulkowsky made this explicit, stating that "such activities are often discouraged since they may distract a person from his mission." In line with an increased emphasis among Unification Church leadership on social action, she concluded by saying, "The restoration of the people in the physical world is most important—as the physical world is restored, the persons in the spirit world will also be restored" (Zulkowsky 1980). Such a conclusion bears strong resemblance to material determinism.

During the discussion accompanying Zulkowsky's talk, however, the sociologist Thomas McGowan pointed out that of seventy-four Unificationists he had interviewed, 73 percent reported having had spiritual experiences. Many of them described visionary dreams. In our random interviews of fifteen Unification Church members in Toronto, all but one mentioned spiritual experiences, some of which were quite negative. Two individuals said that they had left the

Unification Church for a year or two because they were "spiritually burned out" or had "a breakdown." One sought psychological help outside the Unification Church and later rejoined when he felt "stronger." Yet when McGowan made his observation, Zulkowsky politely dismissed it. "When I said that we deemphasized these things," she said, "I meant that our behavior is more important than spiritual experiences."

Many ordinary members do not seem to agree with these leaders. Indeed, Unification Church leaders are becoming adept in the game of intellectual dissimulation. They refer to hallucinations, visionary dreams, and hearing voices as Unification mysticism. That burned-out youths leave the group to recover would seem to suggest that their psychological problems go unnoticed within the church. What is lacking of course is a willingness of Unification Church leaders to reflect seriously upon, and of sympathetic observers to view critically, the obvious discrepancies between reports from ordinary members and those from leaders.

And yet when a member of the Toronto Unification Church group reported recently that he had a vision, others in the group were prompted to speak of "the need to move away from intellectualism and to recommit oneself to the *practical* everyday expression of love." One can almost sense the longing for a charismatic revival in this as yet very new charismatic religious movement. It would not be surprising if the day came when some young recruits of the Unification Church split away over the issue of intellectualization versus spirituality. Fortunately for the movement, the young members are kept so busy working that they have little time to reflect seriously about what ails them. In the meantime, and in the name of tolerance, most observers politely refrain from studying the psychological condition of youthful sect members.

## Variations in New Religious Movements

Different religious groups have different affirmations, renunciations, rituals, core symbols, and dogmas that promote and maintain personal reorganization. And just as we stand in judgment of members of new religions, so they stand in judgment of us. At the very least they present a powerful reminder of those human characteristics and behaviors that our scientific theories fail to explain and our mundane, rational world tends to exclude. Nor can we afford to characterize all new religious movements as simply anti-intellectual, antimodern, or antiscience. What they renounce or affirm are frequently quite subtle shifts in attitude or behavior.

For example, the Osho movement, which was originally founded by Rajneesh, does not renounce wealth but affirms it (Thompson and Heelas 1986). Adherents of the movement differ from mainstream society in the means they advocate for acquiring wealth and the attitude they have toward using it, but on the whole they stand with mainstream society in contrast to more traditional religious groups. Consider, for instance, **Saint Francis of Assisi,** who idealized poverty, using nakedness as the master symbol of emancipation from structural and economic bondage. The Rajneeshies hold the color pink, a symbol of spontaneity, freedom, love, and joy, to be the master symbol of emancipation from the seriousness of the world.

Some new religions attempt to unite inner experience with scientific activity. The Unification Church, the transcendental meditation movement, and those who continue in the way of Rajneesh all attempt to reunite the subjective with the objective in various ways, achieving various results. They all embrace the fruits of science—technology, medicine, and psychotherapy—but they have different attitudes toward science itself as methodology and a means of explanation. The Rajneesh movement rejects it, the Unification Church seeks a synthesis, and the TM movement hides its rather traditional religiosity behind it.

Some new religions argue that truth is attained by nonpropositional revelation—that is, by something other than a set of rational propositions. They contend that truth has little to do with ideas but a lot to do with meditation or silence. As the Bhagwan Shree Rajneesh puts it, "Spirituality simply means that you have gone beyond the mind. Ideas as such are transcended" (Rajneesh 1983:31). The Reverend Moon favors a more rational approach to truth in his *Divine Principle* (1973). Similarly, different new religions meet different psychological needs. Some attempt to reorganize a universe that has come crashing down. Others try to fertilize and enliven a universe that has become sterile and routine. Some pride themselves in their ability to reduce stress and rebalance a world they previously experienced as "schizoid." Others create psychic experiences as a way of healing, breaking down the demands of social conformity and bringing new enthusiasm to what was once an unreal situation.

## The Conversion State of the Individual

Many Americans who join new religions, such as the various meditation groups, come from upper-middle-class homes in which intellectual and/or professional achievements are highly valued. The vast majority of such people have had some college education. Their backgrounds are not typically marked by the sort of drastic turmoil found in the ghettos of the cities of the West and throughout the Third World generally.

It is not surprising that the substantial hardships of the Third World produce the sorts of confusion and breakdown that lead its victims to search for spiritual healing (Poewe 1985). It is surprising to discover analogous if not entirely similar conditions in wealthier populations. And yet many upper-middle-class youths report that they feel their rational selves have been split from their bodies, emotions, and the rest of their world. They say that they feel restricted to the rational part of the self, which they refer to as a "cover-up," a "lid," or a "theatrical number." They complain that this unreal self conceals either a void or an underlying reality that they view as their true self, which they claim has somehow been lost under the prattle of rationalizations at which people have become so adept. The rationalizations no longer have anything to do with the true self; what there is left of the self is an "act" held together by rational processes that threaten to break down, plunging them into chaos. They say that they have become "hollow forms" devoid of "content."

Many such individuals report that before they entered a new religion their rational thought had become estranged from their physical being, that they no longer experienced thoughts expressed in movements, habits, acts, and feelings. In short, they were troubled because they felt they had lost *experience* or, more precisely, lost the experience of "thinking and cognition as **psychosomatic**." A central feature of most new religions is some sort of ritual practice that meets this need to reunify reason with body, mood, and feeling. Many individuals find that such practices allow them to experience life fully in each simple act, in each moment of silence, in being (Tipton 1981).

The active estrangement of reason from body to the point that people experience themselves as "false selves" adapted to "false realities" is echoed in the way many members of new religions describe their attitude toward scholarship and the professions prior to joining their particular group. New converts become aware of having sacrificed their notion of the scholar as seeker to that of one who merely "kept up" and "did well." Indeed, they are voicing a valid criticism of much modern education. Many academics have forgotten that knowledge is exciting precisely because it identifies and encompasses "real" problems in an experiential world.

Like Laing in *The Divided Self* (1965), many converts to new religions say that they invert divisions in order to balance them. They say that speech is silence, for instance, and speak of understanding being acted out. Work becomes practice, ritual, or play. Doctrine becomes a practical interpretive framework secondary to the experience of meditation. The individual in relation to "practice" is elevated above the nuclear family. The person becomes the foundation of social life. Interpersonal intimacy is muted to become "transpersonal" intimacy. The future becomes the here and now. The self, once torn by desire and suffering, becomes an unattached and all-accepting consciousness.

### Preconversion Conditions and the Search for Integration

The way of being-in-the-world of those who join new religions is clearly divided. In the discussion that follows, we call it the divided self. As we have seen, the concept of reorganization is important. We have found that the reorganization of those who join new religions is different from the reorganization of those who do not. Some people experience and/or internalize the world's tensions and convert; others experience the same tensions but don't convert.

For example, those who join new religions that primarily use Yogic doctrines often note that before they joined their tendency to rationalize had produced within them a sense of "terrifying emptiness." But now, they say, the practice of meditation has turned this emptiness into "blissful nothing." In the past they repressed or resisted the terror of feeling empty by filling it with words. In the new religion, they no longer repress the feeling with rationalizations. Their emptiness has become not just normal but the very essence of spirituality. Instead of resisting it, they are encouraged to surrender to it until they experience it as bliss. The silence that was once hastily covered with words is now bared or even entered into voluntarily through meditation. The major symptom is transformed into the major experience, and their condition is reintegrated into the cosmic order. They feel whole.

Although we can't test it here, it is our hypothesis that those who convert to new religions do so because they can reorganize only with the help of something external. By joining a new religion, they regain a sense of balance and well-being at the same time that they come to live in a community of others just like them. They and the new religion constitute their reorganization. New religions tend to dissolve them into a sense of saving spirituality. Rather than thwart the drive for self-realization in those who experience a disorganized way of being-in-the-world, new religions bring about a calm self-acceptance.

But some people never reach the point of feeling the need to convert. Although these individuals feel the world's tensions and go through crises just like those who convert, we suspect that they are able to maintain or reestablish a dynamic balance by themselves with relative ease. It would appear that they experience an intraindividual reorganization. They find that they are able to integrate and even grow with unusual experiences as easily as they can integrate and grow with familiar ones.

People who experience their existence as in crisis may turn to nonreligious ways to deal with their condition. Some receive psychiatric help. Others drift until they reach a state of deterioration that requires hospitalization. Generally, however, people enter a period of searching and find bits and pieces of a new mythology among friends, in literature, drugs, or dharma. They discover, in other words, hints of the possibility of personal wholeness in integral religions.

The psychedelic experience of the 1960s introduced a large number of people to a state of consciousness that demanded a spiritual explanation. They found their new awareness to be a mixed blessing, offering not only ecstasy but dread. As Tipton stated, "Drugs dissolve the relatively rational, reified sense of self maintained by the conscious mind: Drugs take the lid off who you think you are" (Tipton 1981:123). Such "uncovering" makes one aware of a formerly concealed underlying reality, the exact form of which may well be problematic. As one youth said, "Dope opens you up, for sure, but it also spaces you out."

The psychedelic experience has a significant impact on people. Having surrendered the rational self, they are left with the problem of how to grasp and reintegrate the nonrational self. Seekers typically search for a way to alter their selfhood. The search often involves an exploration of Eastern philosophy and religions, specifically such ideas as reincarnation, dharma, karma, and yoga. Some seekers visit different cult centers and new religious communities. They participate in feasts, camping weekends, and workshops where they experience new feelings of warmth under the care of devotees. Most eventually find a spiritual home of their own with the group that best meets their needs.

## Personal Reorganization Redefined

At this point we need to further clarify our conceptualization of the membership process. "Personal reorganization," as we are using the term, refers to the complex process of (1) the perception of a split in one's relation with the world, others, and oneself; (2) a cumulative, runaway inclination to function within and focus on a single way of being-in-the-world, usually the opposite of the way that is most common among those in one's immediate environment; and (3) an awareness that something is out of balance within oneself. Individuals experiencing personal reorganization characteristically perceive this imbalance as "evil" and consider themselves to be in need of "purification." Having come to this conclusion, they usually start looking for ways to "right" themselves.

A key point, we want to stress, is that because individuals are aware that they no longer follow or adhere to the social conventions, they become aware of their need for personal reorganization. It is crucial to the process that these individuals *experience* their reorganization as a saving event.

We identify several kinds of intraindividual reorganization and indicate how each reduces the individual's ability to function socially and the relevant solutions that different new religions provide. Some upper-middle-class individuals experience no more than a mild form of rational personal reorganization. Less fortunate individuals suffer from several forms of personal reorganization simultaneously. In general, the poor and ghettoized tend to undergo more complex emotional reorganization.

The šhuman process is fascinating because it forces theologians and social scientists to deal with those subterranean aspects of the individual that they usually prefer to ignore—the phenomena of fragmented beliefs and shattered worldviews. These are characteristically accompanied by anxiety, dread, emotional instability, tension, ennui, and various personal crises.

Personal crises frequently motivate people to search for a meaning system to explain their condition and afford peace; many seek fulfillment within a new social reality. Beyond a meaning system, many also look for a framework of practice in which to express the new meaning. Belief and practice—in short, a new lifestyle—enable an individual to engage his or her whole self, so that each movement, each feeling, each thought is reintegrated into a sense of "spiritualized acceptance."

Analytically speaking, the process of establishing a new religion comprises four major phases. First, a new religion starts when a leader and some close associates externalize and objectify a worldview. They publicize their beliefs, collect followers, and build an organization. Second, individuals experiencing personal crises or generally significant tensions in their environment start to search for a worldview and social setting that will dissolve these tensions and save them and the world from its evils. Third, the searching individuals find the new religion and are socialized into it. Fourth, society generally or those close to these new members (parents, friends, community) react favorably or unfavorably to their commitment and to the new religion. Thus the šhuman process includes the combined innovations of the **religious entrepreneur**, spiritual therapist, lifestyle designer, and of course the seeker. With these points in mind, we need to examine the change of outlook that personal reorganization produces in the convert. That is our topic in Chapter 8.

## KEY TERMS

**Audience cults**: A term coined by Rodney Stark to refer to religious movements that exist as seminars, lecture series, or similar events where a speaker, trance channeler, or guru addresses an audience, which may pay for the privilege of hearing the master. After the event, those in attendance return home without joining a movement.

**Burridge, Kenelm** (1922–): British-born Canadian anthropologist and author of numerous books on religion.

**Cult movements**: Stark's term for new religions that form definite organizations with an identifiable membership.

**Francis of Assisi, Saint** (1181?–1226): Founder of the Franciscan order. After a vision in 1209, he began preaching brotherly love, apostolic poverty, and repentance His family and the local Roman Catholic bishop thought he had gone mad and tried to deprogram him.

**Infinite Way**: A small theosophical/New Thought new religion.

**King Arthur**: The legendary king of ancient Britain who is said to have been spirited away by mystical maidens before his death. He is believed to be buried in the Glastonbury area, from where he will emerge to restore order when Britain faces its darkest hour.

**Kung Fu**: Chinese martial art developed by Buddhist monks.

**Manitou**: Traditional name for God among some Plains Indians.

**New Dispensation movement**: The name we give to a large new religion to mask its identity.

**Principle of providence**: The belief that all things and every person lives according to the predetermined, which can be known through meditation and spiritual practices.

**Psychosomatic**: Referring to the interaction between physical and mental states resulting in health or illness.

**Religious entrepreneur**: Creator of a new religion.

**Schismogenesis**: A term coined by anthropologist Gregory Bateson to denote the social and psychological state that leads to conversion or other drastic personality changes.

# 8

## New Religions: New Visions

*After my conversion, my sense of divine things gradually increased, and became more and more lively, and had more of that inward sweetness. The appearance of everything was altered; there seemed to be, as it were, a calm, sweet cast, or appearance of divine glory, in almost everything.*

Jonathan Edwards (1962:60)

*When this knowledge, this insight, had arisen within me, my heart was set free from intoxication of lusts, set free from the intoxication of becoming, set free from the intoxication of ignorance. . . . And I came to know rebirth is at an end.*

From the ancient Buddhist text
the Maha-saccaka (Underwood 1925:69)

So far we have emphasized the ways in which new religions meet basic human needs through creatively uniting primal experiences, myths, and doctrines to encourage and sustain religious conversion. Now we must examine some problems and potential problems associated with new religions. We begin by looking again at the effect of conversion. Our discussion is followed by an examination of the nature of religious language, which brings us back to the issue of modernity. Here we argue new religions represent a revolt against science as knowledge in favor of faith in science. New religionists use modern technology while rejecting the rationality that created the modern world. Recognizing that most North American readers come from Christian backgrounds, even if they personally reject Christianity, we then examine some Christian criticisms of new religions. Finally, we conclude with the observation that although it is possible to admire the creativity of new religions, caution is needed in assessing their potential social impact.

## The Effect of Conversion

Saint Paul describes the conversion experience of Christians by saying, "If anyone is in Christ, he is a new creation; the old has gone, the new has come" (2 Corinthians 5:17). John Wesley sums this up in his hymn "And Can It Be," in which he expresses the emotions of the convert as follows: "My chains fell off, my heart was free; I rose, went forth, and followed thee."

These descriptions and many more portray Christian conversion as an experience of being "born again." Converts undergo a change that results in their seeing the world in a new light. A typical reaction of Christian converts is to claim that their conversion made sense of the Bible and their life because both took on new meaning. Many Christians speak of how the Bible seemed meaningless until they were converted. Conversion, they say, removed blinders from their eyes and enabled them to see the truth. Converts to new religions make almost exactly the same claims. Mormons explain how *The Book of Mormon* made the Bible come alive; Unificationists say the same thing about the power of *The Divine Principle*. In each case the emphasis is on the way conversion causes people to reinterpret their lives in light of the teachings of a religious tradition.

Like the mother of Saint Augustine, some parents of Christian converts are themselves Christians. They long for their child's conversion. More often, however, the parents of a new convert to Christianity are not Christians, and many react to the conversion of their child with confusion or horror. To them it seems that their child has gone mad. Often they do what they can to discourage their offspring's newfound faith. For unconverted parents, spouses, and friends of a new convert, the worst experience is their sense that they can no longer understand the person. Suddenly the convert's world has changed. It is shaped by a new outlook, dominated by new goals.

Outsiders find it very difficult to understand and appreciate evangelical Christianity. Many psychiatrists contend that Christians are deviants who need help. The common psychiatric explanation of conversion is that converts are passive, dependent people who seek an easy out or a crutch. Christian attitudes (especially sexual attitudes) are commonly held to be "unhealthy," and many embittered people are quick to blame Christianity for all their problems. Non-Christians often react to Christianity in essentially the same way that outsiders, both Christian and non-Christian, react to new religions.

## Understanding New Religions

Reflection on the biblical depiction of conversion ought to help us understand the conversion process of members of new religions (Ferm n.d.; Brandon 1960). Examples of well-known converts to Christianity throughout the history of the Church should also help. New religious movements are no more incomprehensible than foreign cultures or, indeed, Christian conversion, with which most North

Americans are at least familiar. With a little effort, we can appreciate the world-view of new religions.

To the outsider, the world of the believer is an alien culture. The easiest and safest reaction to an unfamiliar worldview of this sort is simply to say that it makes no sense, that it is irrational. Attempting to understand those unlike us entails looking closely at our own beliefs and way of life, and many people find that a threatening prospect. Modern philosophy and anthropology can help us grasp the threats and benefits we encounter when we immerse ourselves in an alien belief system or culture.

It is easy to dismiss members of new religions on the grounds that they joined because they ceased to think, but this assumption is unwarranted. In his classic anthropological study *Witchcraft, Oracles, and Magic Among the Azande* (1937), E. E. Evans-Pritchard showed that popular European reactions to African witchcraft ignore the psychology and logic of this belief system. Europeans fail to recognize that witchcraft is a *rational* way of dealing with the *irrational* forces of envy and hatred. As explanation, witchcraft is incompatible with European thought; as symptom of social disease, it is real.

Witchcraft beliefs, although scientifically false, follow a recognizable logic. Once we understand the logic of witchcraft, we can predict the reactions of people who believe in it. And an acceptance of the reality of witchcraft as both symptom and belief system is essential for anyone who wishes to understand the traditional Azande.

In a similar way, anyone who wants to communicate effectively with members of new religions must enter their thought-world, which can be done only by recognizing the logic of their beliefs. This is not to say that entering other thought-worlds involves abandoning one's own or accepting the beliefs of the religion in question as beyond criticism. But it does call upon the investigator to show genuine respect for the other person's beliefs and a willingness to risk understanding them. It demands, in short, that both the Christian and the member of the new religion become aware of what exactly it is that they believe. Not infrequently, such an encounter will lead to a better understanding of both themselves and each other.

## The Language of Faith

The philosophical insights of the Austrian philosopher **Ludwig Wittgenstein** can help us understand the language and beliefs of new religions. In his *Philosophical Investigations*, he discusses what he calls "language games," using that phrase "to bring into prominence the fact that the speaking of language is part of an activity, or of a form of life" (Wittgenstein 1963:11). In essence, he argues that various "language games" or "forms of life" exist within society, each having its own intelligibility and internal coherence.

According to Wittgenstein, religion constitutes one such language game. Those who understand it hold the key to the community of believers. The British philosopher Peter Winch further developed Wittgenstein's notion of understanding, suggesting that "the notion of intelligibility is systematically ambiguous. . . . Its sense varies systematically according to the particular context in which it is being used" (Winch 1958:18). Yet another philosopher, D. Z. Phillips, emphasizes the importance of participation as well as contextualization. In his book *The Concept of Prayer,* for example, he states that the "believer must be a participant [because] . . . to know how to use the language is to know God" (Phillips 1966:50).

The importance of context and participation for religious language was also recognized by **Paul Tillich**, who wrote that "faith needs its language, as does every act of personality." He argued, in other words, that the language of faith is "created in the community of believers" (Tillich 1957:24). Many American evangelical Christians reacted strongly against Tillich's assertions. And fundamentalist writers accused him of being an atheist. Others more charitably said that whatever his beliefs, his written works are definitely un-Christian. But no matter what we think of Tillich's theology, we must acknowledge his profound insight into the workings of religious language. Both Tillich and Wittgenstein point out that religious communities create and use their own languages and that believers find meaning within these languages. To the outsider, the language of the religious community is likely to sound meaningless and confused, but to the believer it represents a systematically coherent way of understanding. How to convey this understanding to outsiders is a key problem.

Because religious or spiritual experiences are highly individual and potentially idiosyncratic, language plays another important role. It socializes and makes public what would otherwise remain highly subjective and noncommunicable. Language is used in similar ways in nonreligious groups. Paul Hellas, for example, points out that the language of residents of Marin County, California, transforms extreme individualism into a social phenomenon (Barker 1982:69–85). The "psychobabble" that these individuals use to describe their experiences makes them feel that they are part of "a group mind" (Barker 1982:79).

## Rationality and Basic Assumptions

The intimate tie between language and the community of believers suggests that we may not be quite as rational as we generally suppose ourselves to be. Until recently, most people in the Western world assumed that sensible and intelligent people operated in terms of reason. The assumption was that there is only one objective truth and that we can determine that truth by employing inductive, deductive, or abductive reasoning. Not just modern science but also much of Christian thought follows these principles of reasoning. We tend to reject other ways of building symbolic universes as irrational.

But the rational model of the world is not as straightforward as most of its advocates would have us believe. Both Wittgenstein and Tillich offer alternative ways of understanding rationality. Although talk about "alternative rationalities" may alarm some people, it becomes clear that reasonable individuals deduce the workings of their universe from a variety of different assumptions. People build on these assumptions because they presume them to be self-evident, and presuming them to be self-evident they rarely question them. Yet we find that what is self-evident to one person may well not be self-evident to another. And of course the viability of any given symbolic universe depends on its assumptions. So long as the Azande, for example, believe in the active intervention of the dead in the lives of the living, their sacred beliefs, which center on the worship of ancestors or other unseen forces, remain altogether understandable (Dooyeweerd 1953).

## The Discarded Image

Since new religions typically arise in reaction to the prevailing worldview, it will be worthwhile to look at the nature of the scientific worldview and to assess its— and our—place in the larger global cultural context.

As C. S. Lewis points out in his book *The Discarded Image* (1964) and Arthur O. Lovejoy in his *Great Chain of Being* (1960), medieval European thought was vastly different from our modern Western worldview. Essentially, people in the premodern West assumed that the earth was the center of a universe created and governed by God through the agency of angelic beings. In this creation everything had its allotted place, from the lowliest single-cell organism to the loftiest archangel. All things, including human society, were presumed to be ordered by God on a hierarchical scale that reflected a cosmic structure and divine purpose. The earth was held to be a fallen realm of death and decay at the center of the universe. Above the earth were the heavenly, changeless realms of perfection and angelic beings. Below the earth was hell for sinners and fallen angels. On earth God maintained order through the authority of his Church and duly appointed political rulers, who owed their place to the will of God.

This premodern worldview, or "myth," has of course been largely discarded and replaced by new myths. Owing to the easy cross-cultural contact of people today, the new myths, discussed above, make up colorful mosaics. They incorporate symbols that are taken from any and all of the world's principal spiritual traditions.

In the sixteenth century, the Western European, Christian God-centered vision of life was shattered by a series of events and new ideas that gave birth to the modern world. **Nicolaus Copernicus** (1473–1543) challenged the notion that the earth was the center of the universe. Even more significant was the discovery of **Galileo Galilei** (1564–1642) that the heavens, the moon, and planets were material realms subject to change and decay just like the earth. The cosmological basis of the old order was dealt a deathblow from which it never recovered (Boas 1962; Hall 1963).

Martin Luther (1483–1546) and John Calvin (1509–1564) cast doubt on the claims of the Roman Catholic Church and thus undermined the intellectual authority of the old order. By insisting that all people read the Bible for themselves and act according to their conscience as directed by Scripture, the Reformers initiated serious questioning of the social order. This questioning began with religious institutions but soon embraced secular structures as well. Once the Roman Catholic Church lost its religious authority, secular institutions that it legitimated were open to criticism. Calvin's followers, the Puritans, began by criticizing church government and ended by doubting the judgment of kings.

The rapid development of religious criticism into philosophic and political criticism is discussed in numerous works on the sixteenth and seventeenth centuries (for example, Walzer 1965; Hill 1965; Kuhn 1962). These works show how a view of the world as ordered and hierarchical as that which had existed since Roman times was replaced by a new worldview based on radically different assumptions. Democratic thinking replaced hierarchical authority, and the vision of nature ordered by spiritual beings gave way to a universe governed by God's law. A renewed Christian ethic, based on a perception of God as transcendent and exemplary, enabled the unleashing of human creative powers. The anxieties about the envy and jealousies of one's neighbors generated by belief in witchcraft were conquered by the moral message of Christianity.

## Science and Reason

**Isaac Newton** (1642–1727) believed that God ordered nature through divine law. His system of natural philosophy gave a strong impetus to the development of ideas about the laws of nature. Newton's scientific work led to the emergence of what became known as the Newtonian worldview, which pictures the universe as a closed system, rather like a mechanical toy or watch, regulated by natural laws. Such a worldview suggests that it is the task of science to discover natural laws by **empirical** investigation.

Newton was deeply religious and studied Scripture along with the natural world. He did not find contradictions between the truths he discovered by scientific investigation on the one hand and study of the Bible on the other. His successors, however, increasingly rejected the Bible as a means to attain knowledge; they valued the truths uncovered by empirical investigation more than the truths received from **special revelation**. In time reason came to replace revelation as the accepted source of true knowledge, and natural philosophy grew into modern science.

By the middle of the nineteenth century, technological advances and medical discoveries seemed to confirm the value of science and reason. Religion was progressively relegated to the realm of personal devotion and ethical beliefs within the larger framework of an essentially rational, ordered, and nonsupernatural universe. As they developed, modern school systems increasingly sanctioned the assumptions of the Western scientific worldview while discrediting other views (Richardson 1961; Hall 1963). Although the leaders of certain intellectual movements revolted against the domination of scientific rationalism, state educational systems ensured its survival. Since the mid-1960s, however, scientific rationalism has come under increasing attack. And some of these attacks, as we shall see, have been led by inventors of new religions and their adherents.

Today the basic assumptions of Western society are threatened by change. **Quantum theory** and other scientific advances have led many scientists to abandon notions of a closed and mechanistic universe. Instead of talking about natural laws, scientists are content to operate in terms of generalizations in the form of statistical probabilities (Hoffmann 1960).

The general public, however, is less comfortable with the uncertainties of these generalizations. People are not satisfied with the world as depicted by empiricism. They rebel against viewing the world as a mechanism composed of a multitude of parts that seem to grow more numerous and less comprehensible as research progresses. They rebel against a view that reduces even social reality to biochemical processes. One senses a craving for a new holism. The response of some social scientists is to produce a new *scientific* holism that not only leaves the social and cultural context intact but shows its influence on human well-being, even physical health. Likewise, some religious entrepreneurs have endeavored to produce a new *religious* holism that promotes a new spiritual or religious ideology to "put right" the imbalance and disharmony that result in so many forms of social disease (Capra 1982; Reisser, Teri, and Weldon 1983; Bednarowski 1989; Steyn 1994).

The danger of holism is that it can easily be transformed into **totalitarianism**. German national socialism in the 1930s and 1940s remains the most potent recent example of a holism gone awry. National socialists intended to cure German "soul sickness" by promoting a new worldview that united the spheres of science and spirituality into a single politico-religious system of thought and practice (Rhodes 1980; Nanko 1993).

The widespread discontent with modern science in current Western society and the sorts of measures being taken to correct it raise two questions that are especially important in the context of this book. First, is a totalitarianism that is in its initial impetus political in nature different from one that is in its initial impetus religious? And second, is the content of historic religious traditions more conducive to furthering human freedom than is that of new religions? We look at possible answers to these questions in the final chapter.

## Overview of the Changes to Modernity

As the roles of science, religion, and, with them, the Western worldview changed, so the perception of the nature of the human being changed. According to **Peter F. Drucker** (1939, 1942), Western peoples have perceived themselves differently in each historical period. In the thirteenth century, the paradigm was the spiritual human. By the sixteenth century, this image had changed to the intellectual human. In the eighteenth century, the image of the economic human became popular. This image persists even today, although it is somewhat tarnished. We have also recently developed a considerable variety of images to define ourselves. Existential philosophy introduced the image of the irrational human, Marxism that of the social human, national socialism that of the heroic human, the new mythology that of the experiential human, and the new science that of the holistic human.

The profusion of images has much to do with the mobility and fluidity of modern life. People have shown themselves willing to give up the security associated with adopting a single identity for life in order to gain the flexibility and choice afforded by a less rigidly defined identity—even at the cost of some uncertainty and anxiety. Robert Jay Lifton argues that the prevailing modern image is that of the Protean human, Proteus being the Greek god who can change his identity at will (Lifton 1968:13–27).

Of course not everyone is content with exchanging security for flexibility. Scholars argue that some people join new religions because they are distressed by and dissatisfied with the prospect of the Protean human. It seems clear that at least some young people have been drawn to the conservative Unification Church, for instance, precisely because it stands for commitment. They know implicitly, if not explicitly, that making choices, remaining true to those choices, and living with the consequences of those choices have much to do with becoming a person and developing character. A different sort of reaction against the prevailing values of our society is evident in some of those who have joined the Osho movement. They concur with the larger culture in valuing flexibility in attitudes and experiences, but they avoid our culture's emphasis on extreme individualism by living in a community with others who share their views. In this kind of utopian movement, the individual can enjoy the benefits of self-actualization without paying the cost of social isolation.

We have noted just a few of the attitudes that distinguish contemporary Western culture from its counterparts in earlier eras. There are many such attitudes and values that set today's new religions apart from the religious movements that arose several centuries ago. In those earlier movements, there was on the whole a much more pronounced emphasis on the spiritual value of such things as suffering, sorrow, duty, effort, perseverance, decision, commitment, and in general asceticism. Current movements, in contrast, tend to place greater emphasis on peak experiences, euphoria, surrender, adaptability, fluidity, tentativeness, and in general self-actualization. It is not that the ascetic attitudes no longer exist; it is that they have on the whole become unfashionable and suspect. People today do not generally assume that the sort of self-sacrifice involved in, say, voluntarily living a life of poverty or even seeking martyrdom will bring spiritual exultation.

Examples of the new attitudes are clearly evident in the writings of Abraham Maslow, an individual who has deeply influenced the current religious ethos and contributed to the California "psychobabble" phenomenon. Maslow talks about a new brand of psychology, the psychology of the fully evolved and authentic self. It should parallel if not replace, he says, the "psychopathology of the average." In his book *Toward a Psychology of Being* (1968), Maslow dismisses European existentialists for "harping" on "dread, anguish, and despair," for being "high IQ whimperers on a cosmic scale." These "whimperers" should have known, argues Maslow, that the discovery of identity is exhilarating and strengthening and comes from experiences of joy and ecstasy.

But Maslow, an American in California, simply overlooks much of history and the living conditions in the Third World. He ignores the fact that much of European history *was* grim and anxiety-ridden. It shaped Europeans as surely as the extreme conditions and cultural despair in the Third World shapes much of the world's population now. He also overlooks the fact that people—Saint Francis of Assisi, for example—have voluntarily assumed poverty and managed to transform it into freedom, even frivolity (Turner 1969).

When we study the singular emphasis on joy, peak experiences, and exultation of some new religions, such as the Osho, we cannot but agree with **G. K. Chesterton**, who wondered whether religion, when simplified "all to a single idea," does not "so lose the breadth and balance of Catholicism" (Chesterton 1957:35). Nevertheless, ours is a different world. It is inevitable that new forms of self-perception and new attitudes should accompany the spirit of our times. Some new religions, perhaps more freely than many of us individually, acknowledge the shift from the predominance of a mechanical model of the universe to the model of an open universe, from the predominance of major traditions to the ascendance of new religions, from a focus on God to a focus on a more generalized spirituality, from Western cultural triumphalism to cross-cultural accommodation, from the economic human to the holistic human, from catholicism to internationalism. In this sense, however, the new religious movements of today, like those of times past, share at least one major function: They stand as a corrective to astonish and awaken the world to spiritual realities.

## From Modernity to Postmodernism

In the nineteenth century, such thinkers as **Thomas Henry Huxley** (1825–1895) and Karl Marx (1818–1883) believed that science could replace religion as the universal source of meaning for humans. Others, like **Auguste Comte** (1798–1857), sought to create new religions of science to satisfy the human need for transcendence, meaning, and purpose. As the twentieth century dawned, Comte's wisdom became clear as the limitations of secular science could no longer be avoided. Although science excelled in answering questions about the how of things, it had no answers concerning their why. Instead of providing new meaning, it accelerated the loss of faith. Ultimate questions remained unasked and unanswered. In the long run, people find such a situation unbearable, especially when primal experiences, joys, and tragedies shake their complacency. In such a context, religion finds a ready response—and new religions, which speak the idiom of modernity, thrive.

In the past when a people's confidence in modernity and a purely secular existence was shaken, it was expected that they would return to traditional Christianity. Such an expectation is no longer valid, for it underestimates the appeal of modernity. People are not much inclined to turn to the Church because from childhood they have been taught that Christianity is old-fashioned, that it has been disproved. Predictably, such people are more likely to turn to new religions or new forms of old religions, which are attractive in their very newness.

Some new religions reject scientific aspects of modernity without rejecting its technology. They deny scientific findings on the grounds that such findings contradict the "true religion" that they claim to represent. Converts to these new religions rarely realize that they are not really embracing a historical tradition. The gurus of these new religions claim continuity with the tradition, but in fact they are like the gurus of other new religions that have no real ties to any historical past. They have rejected history and reason, and in doing so they have rejected all forms of genuine tradition as well. They are, in short, postmodern.

If new religious movements consisted simply of a creative interaction among mythology, primal experiences, and aspects of the great religious traditions, they would be interesting but not particularly new. Throughout history, religious movements have arisen through a recombination of existing ideas and experiences. Today's new religions are new in the sense that their development is different from historic religions. Specifically, their novelty consists in the ways they incorporate modern technology and cross-cultural knowledge. High technology has not only been mythologized but has fundamentally changed our attitudes toward the past, present, and future.

Defining modernity is difficult. In common parlance it is usually associated with what is up-to-date, with trendy fashions, with an attitude of commitment to the future in its full connotative sense of looking outward in time and space rather than backward to the past. Roger Scruton has suggested that "modernity" signifies "the transformed consciousness of the word and the self that comes from living *now* rather than *then*" (Scruton 1983:302–303). A preference for things of the future rather than things of the past is essential to the concept of modernity. Modernists place more value on the advancement of industry, science, and technology than on their history generally and on religious authority specifically.

Some have interpreted the counterculture phenomenon of the 1960s as a romantic revolt against science and modernity, but in fact it was not. At most, it was a revolt against the grip that Western history—the past—has had on our society's methods of production and institutions. Today new global religions continue to express concern about technological progress, capitalism, and specific issues (e.g., genetic engineering), but it seems the vast majority quietly take advantage of high technology. Technology makes use of old traditions along with the new. The important thing to remember is that these old traditions have been dislocated in time and space. What has really been done away with is a sense of history; it has been replaced by a form of eclecticism.

## Veneration of the Past

This inclination to accept modernity and science and their religious implications is relatively new. In fact most religious people, including prominent theologians, have done little in the way of assessing the intellectual and social significance of modernity. The majority of religious scholars still view history as a process of unbroken development from the time of Jesus to the present. Such an attitude fundamentally distorts their understanding of our time and prevents their fully appreciating the significance of new religious movements.

As we have noted, the idea of enlightenment and the sense of a radical break with the past are key to the notion of modernity. This sense of rupture is evident in the contrast between today's popular attitudes toward the here and now and those of former generations. Until the last two decades of the eighteenth century, most people in our culture viewed the past with a sense of loss. European schools taught the works of classical Greek and Roman authors, and only the most optimistic educators dared to hope that their generation might attain the heights of achievement of classical civilization. Scarcely any thought was given to the possibility of surpassing the ancients. Every educated person took it as a matter of course that the glory of European civilization—and all other great civilizations, for that matter—lay in the past.

In the premodern world, ancient things and ideas were revered. Veneration of the past was a social reality because technological change was painfully slow: A history of technological change shows relatively little innovation in the period from Roman times to the eighteenth century. Educated people were aware that Roman civilization was more advanced than anything their own culture might achieve. Indeed, many Roman architectural feats were not repeated for hundreds of years because the art of manufacturing such things as concrete had been lost with the collapse of the Western empire. Like Solomon, premodern sages could assert confidently that there was nothing new under the sun. It was assumed that a fortunate person might see everything anyone could possibly hope to see in the course of a lifetime.

Of course technological change was not entirely absent—the invention of the modern printing press in the middle of the fifteenth century, for instance, altered many aspects of society. But such changes were the exception, not the rule. In many areas of life, technological skills actually deteriorated from the heights attained in Roman times.

It was not until the latter part of the eighteenth century that real technological progress began to occur. With the discovery of various metalworking techniques, it became possible to manufacture steam engines and put them to use. It is the speed of this translation of discovery and invention into use that is remarkable. For example, within one year of its invention, the steam engine was used to power boats; within three years it was used to spin cotton; within forty years it was used to power railroad locomotives.

More than anything else, the expansion of the railways in the nineteenth century changed the social composition of countries and the outlook of their peoples. Travel was no longer a privilege of the few, nor was it dangerous or uncomfortable. A whole new way of seeing the world had been created. For the first time since the Roman legions withdrew from Britain in A.D. 410, it was possible not only to travel from London to Rome safely but to travel faster than had ever before been possible. The realization grew that in one respect, anyway, the once-vaunted Romans had been surpassed by a succeeding generation.

The effects of many such apparently simple changes were far-reaching if little appreciated at the time. A new outlook on life emerged. Instead of looking to the past for guidance and direction, people began to look to the future. It is not surprising that the works of Jules Verne (1828–1905) and other futuristic writers became popular. And for the first time scientists became folk heroes. The entire basis of daily life changed as agricultural societies were transformed into urban industrial societies.

## Christianity and the Implications
## of Technological Change

The change of attitude toward the past and the future was paralleled by a profound but little recognized change of attitude toward religion in general and Christianity in particular. Prior to the nineteenth century, Christians identified with the wisdom of the ages and claimed the heritage of Roman civilization. Christians were able to argue that the Romans were the most advanced people on earth and that at the height of their achievements they had chosen Christianity. If Christianity was good enough for the advanced and sophisticated Romans, it should surely be adequate for less advanced and more barbaric peoples.

Miracles, prophecy, and a host of other beliefs that modern people find problematic were not an issue for our ancestors. Indeed, Christian apologists freely appealed to miracles and prophecy as evidence of the truth of Christianity. In the period from the fall of Rome to the nineteenth century, very few people questioned the essential claims of the church. Such skeptics as did make their presence felt were generally considered misfits who were objecting to the whole trend of European civilization. If the Romans could accept the validity of miracles, then how could less educated people with a lower level of scientific and technological skill possibly doubt them?

All of this changed in the 1800s. The intellectual doubts of a few individuals in the eighteenth century became a torrent of skepticism as ordinary people experienced the impact of technological change in their daily lives. The Greeks and the

Romans suddenly appeared ignorant and prescientific. We became more aware of their superstitions and irrationality. The conversion of Roman civilization to Christianity was no longer considered remarkable; it simply confirmed the credulity of ignorant people. Religion was, in other words, old-fashioned; Christians found themselves on the defensive against progress and the findings of science. Miracles and prophecies that had once been convincing became embarrassments. It was as if science had declared biblical reality a primitive illusion.

Few people fully appreciate the rapidity with which Christianity lost its dominant position as the preserver of civilization and knowledge in the West. Indeed, one might say the Church is still in a state of culture shock following its loss of respect and authority. Nevertheless, there is no disputing that the Church is no longer at the center of Western culture. It has been replaced by the sciences, creating a spiritual vacuum now being filled by new religions.

## Mormonism: A New Religion Based on a New Mythology

During the nineteenth century there emerged a number of religious movements that responded in creative ways to modernity. Most of these movements were short-lived. Others, such as Christian Science, are still with us. Mormonism, or the Church of Jesus Christ of Latter-Day Saints, was one of the first religious movements to display clearly the influence of modernity. Founded in 1830, this new religion is an intriguing blend of old and new. *The Book of Mormon* tells the story of two groups of Jews who left Jerusalem and eventually settled in the Americas. Their descendants then experienced periods of revival and apostasy until finally Jesus preached the gospel to them following his resurrection. Finally, however, the apostates massacred the true believers and degenerated into a state of barbarism.

As a romantic novel, *The Book of Mormon* is basically Christian. With the exception of its teaching about the fall, its theology is simple and fundamentally orthodox. It does, however, embellish the biblical account when it details certain points that are seemingly unclear in the Bible (e.g., the proper mode of baptism). Nevertheless, its overall orthodoxy is used to great advantage by Mormon missionaries in presentations to unsuspecting people who come from Christian backgrounds. It is of course more difficult to convince the potential convert of the "historical" truth of the book in light of its rather unusual and far-fetched story about the migration of Jewish peoples to the Americas. On the whole, however, Mormons encounter fewer objections concerning doctrinal deviations than do disciples of other new religions.

The effects of modernity on Mormonism are best seen in the later "revelations" of Joseph Smith and the "Scriptures" he claimed to have discovered. A prime example is *The Book of Abraham,* which is found in the Mormon *Pearl of Great Price.* These works, as we have seen, develop the theme of eternal progression—the doctrine that human souls exist prior to their earthly lives. This doctrine, which is the cornerstone of modern Mormon theology, is clearly a mythologization of the idea of progress and evolutionary philosophy.

The genius of Smith was his ability to appeal to the common person, to people with little to no education. He took progressive and fashionable ideas, embedded them in specific contexts of "new revelations," and told these in the form of stories resembling those of the biblical writers. As Brodie shows in her brilliant biography of Smith, he was a popularizer of new ideas (Brodie 1963). More important, he was able to turn the confusion produced by intellectual and social change into new certainty, and he did so by being sensitive to the idiom of his audience. Although its theology draws on ideas from the Abramic tradition, Mormonism gave modernity its first great religious expression.

## The Myth of Modernity: A Summation

The myth of modernity consists of an acceptance of high technology and continued responsible technological progress. Its gurus reject the notion that everything can be explained solely in terms of reason and intellect. Its gurus and their followers alike have tired of professional explanations of private, social, or political conditions. Modern mythologizers rarely idealize our historical past, although sometimes they project an imagined "golden tradition" into the future. Yet most members of new religions romanticize the remnants of the traditional—especially the non-Western traditional world. Modern romanticism and pastoralism together constitute the modern mythological idiom, a way of thinking centered not on our historical past but rather on other cultures.

Many people today are particularly susceptible to the new mythological idiom because it is, at its best, at once up-to-date, cross-cultural, experiential, and deeply spiritual in nature. In this sense, much as sects once did, new religions constitute an expression of revolt against the unquestioned central authority not only of orthodox Christianity but also of a life explained and ordered by specialists and dominated by the intellect.

Among the disadvantages of this loyalty to the new mythological idiom is that just as the religious emphasis is currently no longer on suffering but on health, positive energy, euphoria, and peak experiences, so the mythological emphasis is no longer on a painstaking adherence to scientific method but on its fruits—namely, high technology and the comfortable lifestyles it can afford. This attitude is dangerous, for no tree can bear fruit without nourishment from its roots. No society is able to enjoy the fruits of the work of past generations for long if it does not make contributions of its own.

## Some Differences Between Christianity and New Religions

One suspects that many individuals in America's mainline churches and in Western society generally no longer appreciate the real significance of the Christian doctrine of justification by faith. But the religious void that is thus created is being filled not by a renewal of religious traditions, as Stark and Bainbridge (1985:116–120, 506–530) contend, but by the creation of new religions.

One major distinction between Christianity and new religions has to do with the difference between theistic *faith* and nontheistic *magic*. The distinction is not, it should be noted, between God on the one hand and faith in magic on the other. Faith in magic is a psychological impossibility. At most *belief* in magic may pacify suspicion, jealousy, and insecurity. But it cannot produce faith, because by definition faith excludes belief in magic. People who lose their faith often replace it almost unconsciously with belief in magic and intense allegiance to modern-day magicians, individuals with exemplary charisma and extraordinary personalities.

The belief in an acosmic monism, the oneness of all things, that pervades many new religions is far removed from the Christian understanding that there is a significant distinction between God and his creation. The two perspectives have profoundly different implications. Acosmic monism implies imminent magic. The Christian distinction between God and his creation implies the need for transcendent faith.

In keeping with their acosmic monism, most new religions advocate a mystical version of universal love and respect for all things. From this perspective, spontaneous and total self-expressiveness appears safe and even desirable. If all things are one, self-expressiveness is the proper cement with which to unite the community. In contrast, Christianity clearly distinguishes good from evil and maintains that there is a potential for either in all acts, beliefs, and attitudes. All self-expression is a matter of choice, and every choice entails a moral responsibility. It is naive to suppose that every choice we make, every way we choose to express ourselves, will necessarily be good.

The centrality of choice in Christianity has to do with what Arthur F. Holmes calls the *ad extra* of Christianity: All created things are *ad extra*—created by God "to the outside" of himself (Holmes 1983:64). Holmes suggests that God gave the world its own reality, granted it delegated power, and now cares for it with special acts of providence and miracles to achieve what otherwise would not occur. The fact that such providence is divinely added discourages Christians from belief in magic. There is nothing intrinsic in the creation that will guide our destinies; *we* are responsible, and we must exercise our responsibility and choice.

Christianity stresses that God has delegated power in creation, which underscores the limitations of human nature. New religions instead tend to highlight the exemplary charisma manifested by the extraordinary personality of their leaders. Christians refuse to worship individuals, although they respect them. Christians argue that the power of devotion to a charismatic leader invites worshipful imitation rather than the sorts of tough choices called for by a belief in delegated power.

The essence of Christianity is trust. The essence of traditional and non-Western systems of magic and divination is a mixture of mistrust, jealousy, and suspicion—precisely the opposite of trust. The centrality of trust in Christianity gives it a unique psychology, evident already in the story of Adam and Eve. When they fell, the bond of trust between God and humanity was broken, and we began to doubt God. Doubt and mistrust ravaged human psychology. Men and women began to blame the evil they did on a vengeful or indifferent God. And yet no effort to thus free humans of blame was successful. As **Hans Küng** puts it, "Compelled to justify himself, emancipated man attempts to exonerate himself, to find an alibi and to shift blame with the aid of a variety of excuse mechanisms. He practices the art of showing 'that it was not him.'" As a society we have attempted to blame evil on our environment; genetic preprogramming; our instinctive urges; "individual, social, linguistic structures"—in short on anything but ourselves (Küng 1978:429–430).

Though humans may be emancipated, they remain burdened with a nagging feeling of guilt. If emancipation cannot free people of guilt, what can? Küng contends, and we agree, that the answer is redemption. Redemption and emancipation both mean liberation, but whereas "emancipation means liberation of man by man . . . self-liberation" (Küng 1978:430), redemption means liberation of humans by God, true liberation. God restores humans' sense of proportion. In the process of redeeming humankind, the resurrection distinguishes humans from God, redefines humans as finite but free. God's revelation of his infinity frees human beings from the delusion that they are or ever can be gods. Thus from a Christian perspective, people need to pause in the quest for meaning only to make certain that they have chosen the good rather than the bad and that they remain grounded in trust.

## Conclusion

The new mythology is opposed to modern science and Christianity as method and knowledge. Those who have accepted the new mythology venerate the human being and the fruits of high tech; at the same time, they are curiously intoxicated with the traditions of non-Western societies. New global religions resolve this paradox. It is in this sense that the new mythology can be said to produce modern versions of romanticism and pastoralism. Despite their nominal celebration of democratic ideals, the new mythmakers have embarked upon a reactionary adventure with the aim of reestablishing a hierarchical world based on the power of privilege and wealth, unrestrained by reason. They are willing to discard democratic traditions that have served Western culture for millennia. Instead, they favor a mystical revival reminiscent of the thirteenth century that put an end to the great advances made during a twelfth-century renaissance. Rather than bringing light, the new mythology ushers in a new dark age, complete with a priesthood of occult authorities who control power and limit knowledge.

It is the irony of our age that phenomena called futuristic are in fact conservative and even reactionary. As fragments of many diverse myths have combined into a general mythology of modernity and healing myths, they have followed a conservative impulse. What the new mythmakers and the disciples of some new religions have heralded as a step into a new era is in fact a retreat into the bitter past gilded by tales of imaginary old or non-Western civilizations. The highs from LSD, meditation, trance, or the touch of a "spiritual master" are in fact just different versions of techniques and talismans used by ancient shamans and diviners—the sorts of things we once dismissed as "primitive" and "constricting." Nevertheless, the new religions present them as the means by which we can be catapulted into global transformation and a new transcendent consciousness. New religionists and new mythmakers would have us believe that ancient practices that once served as desperate defenses against a narrow existence filled with monotonous routines are now a key to the future. Serious anthropological work has demonstrated how stressful the old communal life was, with its suspicions, jealousies, and above all its unrelenting pressures to conform. Popularizers who feel the need to romanticize the past simply ignore all this.

Although the contents of myths vary, their structures are remarkably uniform. Both public myth and private conversion dream have the same form: A vision of world catastrophe is followed by death and rebirth. These are given cosmic importance, and the mythmaker or dreamer becomes imbued with a sense of mission. Conversion and commitment, though private and mundane, are projected onto the world as an evolutionary process. Indeed the conversion process, once but a feature of adolescent development, has in our free society been extended into adulthood. We are now willing to entertain alternate ways of life and reach for imaginary higher levels of evolution throughout our lives.

And so we note, after all, the limitations of human imagination. Mythical structures, like the structures of dreams and fantasies, would appear to be as fixed as the instinctual behavior patterns of animals on the lower rungs of the evolutionary ladder. Fantasies, dreams, myths, and science-fiction stories are filled with an eclectic carousel of uniforms, sensualist high technology, lurid vapors, and ancient rituals that are sometimes violent, often pornographic, and always primitive, repressive, and deadening of reason and the critical sense. The new mythmakers would have us believe that this content is ultramodern, but it is quite the opposite. It is not possible to break through to modernity without the rigorous exercise of rational thought. The melodramatic fantasies that are so prominent a feature on the screens and in the novels of our culture only serve to jade our senses and numb our minds. We have come full circle.

Our journey through the world of new religions has led us to the realization that there are three important spheres of human reality that should not be mixed with, nor canceled by, one another. These spheres are the world of storytelling and mythmaking, the world of solid traditions, and the world of science. Although mythmakers borrow from the other two spheres to concoct something new, it would be foolish to believe that their creation could serve as a substitute for tradition and science. Tradition and science have stood the tests of time. They are the measuring rods that help us assess the value of all those exciting and exotic ideas that spring from our receptive imaginations.

## KEY TERMS

**Chesterton, Gilbert Keith** (1874–1936): English journalist and Roman Catholic layman whose *Orthodoxy* [1908] (1949) and other writings provided a popular defense of Christianity.

**Comte, Auguste** (1798–1857): French philosopher who argued that all knowledge should be based on positive, or observable, facts. His system is known as positivism.

**Copernicus, Nicolaus** (1473–1543): Roman Catholic priest and Polish astronomer known for his theory that the earth rotates around the sun.

**Drucker, Peter F.** (1909–): Austrian American thinker sometimes called the father of modern management. His first English book, *The End of Economic Man* (1939), is a brilliant analysis of the intellectual, moral, and social crisis facing the modern world.

**Empirical**: Relating to empiricism, the theory that knowledge is based on experience and observation.

**Galilei, Galileo** (1564–1642): Italian astronomer whose theories about the universality of motion and the mechanistic nature of the universe, attack on the philosophy of Aristotle, and confrontational personality brought him into conflict with the Roman Catholic Church.

**Huxley, Thomas Henry** (1825–1895): English biologist who advocated scientific education to remedy the intellectual, social, and moral needs of humanity. He coined the term "agnosticism" to describe his belief that knowledge of God or other spiritual things is impossible and can be neither proved nor disproved.

**Küng, Hans** (1928–): Swiss theologian who studied at the German College in Rome. He gained fame as a progressive but not radical thinker within the Roman Catholic Church and is an important figure in the discussions of the Second Vatican Council.

**Newton, Isaac** (1642–1727): English physicist and philosopher who formulated the law of gravity and helped create modern science.

**Quantum theory**: Newton's classical physics held that it was possible to know both the speed and position of any particle. With Heisenberg's uncertainty principle, modern physics recognized that we can know either the speed or the position of a particle but not both. Certainty gave way to probability, and Niels Bohr, Max Planck, and Albert Einstein created a new view of the universe based on the complex mathematical theories of quantum mechanics.

**Special revelation**: Divine revelation such as is found in the Bible, the Qur'ān, and other sacred books. It is opposed to general revelation, which may be learned from observing the world.

**Tillich, Paul** (1886–1965): German American philosopher-theologian and Christian socialist.

**Totalitarianism**: The organization of a state or society that allows no autonomous or independent institutions and denies the freedom of association to its members.

**Wittgenstein, Ludwig** (1889–1951): Austrian philosopher whose *Tractatus Logico-Philosophicus* and later works had a profound effect on Anglo-Saxon philosophy in the 1960s through his development of the idea of "language games."

# ❀ **9** ❀

# *How Dangerous Are New Religions?*

*Conversions occur at any time, but when they take place in a time of cultural transition to a new era, conversions as religious transformations become decisive acts. . . . During such a movement a change in the understanding of life's meaning takes place.*

Johannes Aagaard (1991:92)

## Full Circle

We began this book by criticizing some popular views about cults, sects, and new religions. First, we argued they tend to rely on ad hominem arguments that attack people rather than ideas. Second, we rejected the essentially ad hominem argument that invokes brainwashing as an explanation for conversion. Third, we pointed out that many of the critics are poor scholars. Finally, we agreed with Bochinger's argument in the context of the so-called New Age movement: The whole area of new religions is far more complex than is usually recognized (Bochinger 1994).

Having said this, we must admit that all human endeavors have a potential for corruption. It is always possible to find examples of people who were hurt by any institution, including a religion (Tobias and Lalich 1994). Further, there are some churches, sects, and new religions that clearly do harm some individuals (Kaihla and Laver 1993). Such harm, however, is not unique to these organizations. Rather, it is a common human failing.

Now we want to close this book by addressing the question, How dangerous are new religions? In Chapter 1 we referred to a court case in Germany that ruled that various groups, including the Hare Krishna movement and a local Christian charismatic church, were potentially dangerous. We also drew attention to the growth of new religions in Germany and the German anti-cult movement, with its network of "cult experts" (Klöcker and Tworuschka 1994; Haack 1993). In particular, we mentioned the concerns of the Berlin-Brandenburg cult specialist the Reverend Thomas Gandow.

We rejected Gandow's views because like most German "cult experts" he tends to associate all contemporary religious movements with "dangerous cults" (Usarski 1988). Nevertheless, he certainly has a point when he draws attention to the German past and the dangers of national socialism: Dave Hunt and Constance Cumby mention the Nazis in their attacks on contemporary religions. The problem with these comparisons is that they cast a very wide net. In other words, they tend to automatically characterize all new religions as proto-Nazi movements.

Such sweeping condemnations are of course wrong. Most new religions are genuine expressions of spirituality that grow out of profound spiritual experiences (Wiesberger 1990). Whether their spirituality is self-indulgent or philanthropic, mature or immature, sensible or unintelligent is another matter. What is important is that both founders and followers are inspired by real religious concerns that have nothing to do with the Nazis.

As we see it, the biggest problem with new religions is that because they are new they often lack the built-in safeguards that established religions have developed over time. Of course this criticism can also apply to sects. When a Buddhist, Hindu, or Islamic sect is transported to the West, it loses contact with the culture that nourished it and can easily go astray, acting as though it has no roots.

The danger of new religions is greater because most lack the restraints that even transplanted sects retain. Nevertheless, some new religions do adopt powerful mechanisms of social control that limit the ability of their members to act in socially destructive ways. For example, new religions such as Mormonism, the ama-Nazarites, and the Unification Church are firmly grounded in the moral teachings of great traditions. When Joseph Smith created a dynamic new religion, he rooted its ethics and social outlook in traditional Christianity; in moral terms, therefore, the Mormons are Christian. Isaiah Shembe, the founder of the ama-Nazarites, welded Christian ethics to traditional Zulu codes of behavior to create a clear moral framework for his followers. Similarly, Sun Myung Moon united Christian and Confucian ethics in a creative dialogue that his followers claim has maintained the best of both systems.

Other new religions, however, lack connections to established moral systems. Rather, they seek to create their own standard of values that they see as transcending all previous moralities. In many cases these values may be perfectly reasonable, indeed admirable. But cut loose from historical roots, they can easily become bizarre and socially destructive. Because something like this happened in Germany in the late nineteenth century that led to the growth of Nazism, the worries of men like Thomas Gandow are not unfounded.

## The Problem of Nazi Religion

To most people outside of Germany, the Nazi movement is an example of a political ideology gone mad. It was that. But as George Mosse pointed out in the early 1960s, Nazism was inspired by various new religions and at its core was deeply religious but violently anti-Christian (Mosse [1964] 1981). Of course for most Germans national socialism was a political movement that claimed to be able to solve the problem of unemployment and end the Great Depression. But behind the economic and political policies of national socialists lay a clearly articulated religious vision that was shared by the Nazi leadership. More than 73.4 percent of Hitler's elite guard, the SS, were adherents of a new German neo-paganism (Borst 1969; Ziegler 1989:87). Following the end of World War II, many historians played down the religious content of the Nazi vision. In doing so, they disparaged the work of its chief spokesman, Alfred Rosenberg, dismissing him as an eccentric. In their view he represented a fringe group that the party tolerated but that did not represent Nazi ideology.

More recent research, however, has shown the significance of Rosenberg and his religious ideology (Lixfeld 1994:131–149; Bramwell 1985:61–62; Cecil 1972:viii–ix, 134–161; Molau 1993). At various times Hitler played down Rosenberg's role, especially when speaking with Church leaders and the press. He did this to gain time and the support of Christians. But behind the scenes Hitler and the Nazi Party funneled vast funds to Rosenberg and his associates to enable them to implement an educational program that would eventually destroy the churches and establish a new Germanic religion (Lixfeld 1994:69–76, 85, 134, 136–137; Baumgartner 1977; Mosse 1981).

## New Religions or Magical Religions?

In their general theory of religion, Stark and Bainbridge predict that people who are denied access to desired rewards will tend to accept either specific or general "compensators" (Stark and Bainbridge 1985:7, 30, 172, 265, 285). Specific compensators include ritual procedures a shaman prescribes to cure a particular condition, such as a headache. General compensators involve such things as the promise of a happy life. Compensators usually entail promises of rewards in the distant future or in some other nonverifiable context.

Religion, says Stark, "is a system of general compensators based on supernatural assumptions," and he contends that those religious organizations that move "markedly in the direction of non-supernaturalism" will thereby "pursue the path to ruin" (Wilson 1981:159–177). Bainbridge and Daniel Jackson present evidence to the contrary: They found that transcendental meditation decreased in popularity as it stressed the supernatural (Wilson 1981:135–158). TM originally gained large numbers of recruits precisely because it emphasized its "scientific" status and sought to avoid the label of religion. It was presented as an intellectually respectable if novel technique of personal development. Although the later drop in recruitment is attributable to a number of factors, it seems quite clear that important among them was an inclination toward magic that belied its claim to being based in science: Recruiters promised potential followers everything from a knowledge of the past and the future to the ability to levitate. When its claim of offering a new state of consciousness was attacked TM lost those who had joined it for that reason. University students who had found it respectable to practice magic so long as everyone considered it a science dropped it once its true status was revealed.

In general, we agree with Stark and Bainbridge's market model of new religions. Indeed, we would go so far as to suggest that the secular-religious dichotomy is not vital in the discussion of new religions. In some ways the term "new religion" is a misnomer, since so-called new religions are not actually new products taking the place of old ones in a religious market. The thing that is "new" in new religions is the content of their mythological idioms and their conscious use of images, practices, and theories from anywhere in the world. Here again it is worth pointing out that whereas the Nazi cult was fanatically nationalistic, it borrowed its central symbol, the swastika, from India and used many other concepts from Yogic and pre-Christian religions. In this sense, its ideology was global.

New religions are more than simply recent versions of experiential healing religions. There has been a continuous waxing and waning of medico-moral, therapo-religious, or therapo-spiritual cults. They existed before the time of Christ, and they still exist in all parts of the world. If we want to make a distinction, we might better differentiate between *experiential* therapo-religious phenomena on one hand and *intellectual* therapo-religious phenomena on the other. Experience and magic predominate in the one, rationality and faith in the other. The former tends to be magical, the latter discursive. Each has borrowed from the other. It is because sociologists tend not to engage in comparative or historical studies that they have assigned an exaggerated importance to the newness of new religions in the West. As a result, they confuse contemporary religions, cults, and sects with genuinely new religions.

Throughout history, therapo-spiritual religions have had to steer a dangerous course—first between traditional medical practice and formal mainline religions, then between science and mainline religions, and finally between state and church. The legal battles in which today's new religions are embroiled—concerning issues of brainwashing, whether they are secular or religious, and so on—resemble those that certain cults faced centuries ago. Indeed, sectarian religions in all times and places have been caught up in such opposition. Given the current separation between state and church and between science and religion, we should not be surprised by the legal opposition new religions are up against today. Generally speaking, experiential therapo-spiritual religions are considered untidy religious mutants in our culture, and the courts seem to offer a perfectly rational context in which to handle the embarrassingly irrational problems.

In order to clarify our contention that most contemporary new religions follow a long line of therapo-moral cults that have stressed experience over doctrine, we should look at some historical examples of such cults—specifically, the Aesculapian cult of ancient Greece and the Mesmer cult of the eighteenth century. The Aesculapian cult of the Hippocratic period of ancient Greece (from the fifth century B.C. to the third century A.D.) was one of the therapo-moral cults that have existed for centuries in the interstices between the medical professions and religious institutions. At its center was the practice of "temple healing" facilitated by its god of medicine, Aesculapius. Like members of the Unification Church who have visions of the Reverend Sun Myung Moon, members of the Aesculapian cult had dreams and visions of Aesculapius that encouraged their belief in his cures and beneficence. And just as the Unification Church encourages its members to write up and circulate their dreams, so members of the Aesculapian cult recorded on votive tablets the dreams and visions patients experienced during their sleep at the temple sites.

Ilza Veith (1965) has argued that suggestion probably played a major part in the Aesculapian temple-healing process. There is good evidence that some temple priests impersonated Aesculapius in encounters with semiconscious patients. Veith also contends that priests may have enhanced the suggestibility of patients by staging dramatic rituals of sham surgery. Like today's faith healers, they may also have used hypnosis. Since many patients were suffering psychological problems, they were already receptive to mystical and ritualistic procedures of temple healing. Physicians in Europe throughout the centuries noted the need for "moral treatment" of or "moral therapy" for patients.

The Mesmer cult, which gained substantial popularity in Vienna and Paris in the late eighteenth century, is another interesting example of a therapo-moral cult. Central to mesmerism was the concept of "magnetic fluid"—a feature that has obvious counterparts in new religions, such as the "engrammic clearing" of Scientology, the "somatic clearing" of Zulu diviners, and the "energy" and "merging" of Rajneeshies. Indeed, if the notion of "magnetic fluid" is replaced with that of "energy," the resemblance between mesmerism and Rajneeshism is strong.

According to Veith, the German physician F. A. Mesmer believed that he communicated his healing powers to his patients by magnetic fluid. He did this during elaborate and highly ritualized ceremonies that attracted wealthy patients. Using a bath surrounded by curtains, iron filings, and rods to "direct" the magnetism, Mesmer appeared to the sound of melancholy music. As he inspected the patients, he draped them in lavender-colored silk robes, then he rubbed their bodies and touched them with an iron wand (Veith 1965:221–223). Occasionally, the healing ceremonies were held outside under "magnetized" oak trees or on the banks of "magnetized" brooks or fountains. Beguiled by Mesmer's impressive ritual, the participants, predominantly women, fell into a somnolent trance, or "mesmeric sleep," from which they awoke refreshed and healed.

Mesmer received hostile criticism from his medical colleagues, who succeeded in putting an end to Mesmer's séances. Veith notes that public opposition persuaded Louis XVI in 1784 to appoint a royal commission to examine the validity of "animal magnetism." The group included such leading scientific personalities as Benjamin Franklin and Antoine Lavoisier. It was their judgment that Mesmer's cures were entirely due to imagination. When his practices were prohibited by the medical faculty of the University of Paris, Mesmer withdrew into obscurity. His ideas, however, never quite died out (Darton 1968).

For our purposes, it will be important to note two central features of these cults: ritual drama and the manipulation of something either in the body or in the mind. Anthropologist E. E. Evans-Pritchard has classified these features as characteristics of sorcery. Distinguishing sorcery from witchcraft, Evans-Pritchard defines the former as the power to manipulate and alter natural and supernatural events or states with the proper magical knowledge and performance of ritual. It is typically understood that the magic of sorcery can be put to good or bad use. Witchcraft, by contrast, is the possession of an inherited power and is used primarily for evil ends. Sorcerers depend on magic to implement their power, whereas witches derive their power from their mystical inheritance (Evans-Pritchard 1937:8–11, 21–39). According to these definitions, we can conclude that most cults, including several recent new religions, are in fact systems of magical manipulation, and their leaders are modern-day magicians.

Of course we are not the first to reach this conclusion. Scholars such as Robin Horton have noted that magic, like religion, serves important philosophical and metaphysical functions for its practitioners. Horton argues that in the West magic serves much the same function that science serves. Both science and magic (and witchcraft and religion) are explanatory theories, at least in the sense that they reflect a quest "for unity underlying apparent diversity; for simplicity underlying apparent complexity; for order underlying apparent disorder; for regularity underlying apparent irregularity" (Wilson 1970a:131–171).

But this modern confluence of magic, reason, science, and religion poses dangers of a sort. Paul Tournier was probably right when he wrote about "the magic of Reason" and "the magic of Science" (Tournier 1960). The spirit of magic—which in the new religions is often called spirituality and which our scholarly community is now trying to reclassify as altered states of consciousness in the context of a "transpersonal psychology"—would appear to be inherent in human nature. Tournier defined magic as "the longing for the fairy tale, for the magic wand that will charm away the difficulties of life, the suffering, the limitations, and the uncertainties of our human condition" (Tournier 1960:118–120). Put more simply still, magic is the longing for simple solutions, for certitude. It is a condition to which idealistic middle-class youths are especially prone.

That the distinction between science and reason on the one hand and magic and myth on the other is becoming ever more vague in our culture is a good indication that we—and our religions with us—are drifting toward faith in magic. John Horgan recently made a similar point. Responding to critics of the argument he makes in his book *The End of Science* (1996), Horgan pointed out that highly complex theories of physics are "meaningless in human terms." What people want to know is "the purpose of the universe and our place in it" (*Globe and Mail*, 13 August 1996:A6).

Tournier answers this argument with the claim that the one holdout against the cultural tide toward magic is Christianity. He suggests that the dichotomy is no longer between reason and magic because reason itself is becoming magical as more and more people expect magical results from science. Instead, the key distinction is between all that is magical on the one hand and *faith* on the other.

## Magic, Cultural Condition, and Religious Cure

When Poewe was studying the Herero in Namibia, she found that they kept directing her attention to their problems. They were racked by severe and unrelenting anxiety. They described themselves as oppressed by suspicion, deceit, and jealousy; as overcome by hopelessness; as dazed into stuporous indifference. Several women had obvious symptoms that we associate with a preconversion state. Many were hypochondriacs. Among the Herero, with their emphasis on seniority even among women, it was as if discontent, social unease, and hypochondria formed a continuum—the first two finding expression in the younger, the latter becoming fixed in the older population.

These findings suggest to us the existence of what might best be called a condition of cultural anxiety and an anxious culture. As Poewe has pointed out, the Herero defeat by the Germans in 1904 was so severe that cultural anxiety and disillusionment became a universal phenomenon (Poewe 1985). Among women, somatic and psychological expressions of their anxiety predominate; among men, social ones predominate. We might define an anxious culture as a culture of disillusionment, with the proviso, however, that the disillusioned cannot and will not accept their condition. They live with, and pass on to their children, the need to find a sacred solution. Aching under the social imbalance with which they have to live, they become preoccupied with their condition. They begin to perceive their fate as sacred. Suffering ties them to the transcendent. Spiritually open, they are highly suggestible.

We might define cultural anxiety as the condition in which a people suffers from a sense of disillusionment so profound that their whole private and symbolic life comes to be centered on an idée fixe, a problem they can imagine being resolved only by an ultimate, dramatic, or sacred solution. The search for a sacred solution likewise makes the people peculiarly suggestible. The condition involves both social and psychological imbalances that may be further expressed in somatic or cultural imbalances. In some social settings, the people may express their condition in dramatic somatic form (individual paralyses, inability to speak, blindness, localized aches and pains) or in equally dramatic psychological form (identity crises, transient psychoses, spirit possession, trance, convulsions). In other social settings, the anxiety may be expressed socially (in relationship imbalances, drifting, and such sociopathies as victimization, theft, and rescue or rape themes) or culturally (in themes of suspicion, jealousy, death, chosen people, and holocaust). Some or all such forms of expression may be present in any one society. Indeed, they may systematically reinforce or echo one another. Alternatively, in some societies only certain forms may be given expression, and then rather sporadically.

Major elements of cultural anxiety—a deep sense of disillusionment with society and heightened suggestibility—are found in the case histories of those who have joined new religions as well. In contemporary America members of new religions tend to be in the midst of an identity crisis, homosexual panic, wife battering or wife swapping, bouts of shoplifting or drug abuse, depression, or emotional breakdown. We have observed such complaints above all among Rajneeshies and members of the Unification Church.

The road to conversion followed by middle-class people in particular exemplifies this pattern of cultural anxiety. Individuals often describe interpersonal relationships that are "repetitive, impulsive, and stereotyped" along child-parent themes, rescue themes, or sometimes victim-aggressor themes. Personal testimonies of converts always include one or another of these themes (Faber 1996). Some say that they feel as though they are not in control and not responsible, which in part explains their fascination with the occult. Many Rajneeshies, for example, describe having let the I Ching or chance meetings determine their next moves in life.

An assistant of ours who lived for a time among members of the Unification Church corroborated our observations of certain characteristics that Mardi Horowitz also describes—frequent "attention-seeking behaviour," "displays of variable emotions," "behavioural provocativeness with self-recognition of intent," and of course "suggestibility" (Horowitz 1977:3–6). These features are rarely found in sociologists' analyses of members of new religions. When they are, it is typically because the sociologist has reproduced verbatim the accounts of the people interviewed. By contrast, participant observers are more likely to relate such findings.

Another category of characteristics typically omitted from sociological descriptions of members of new religions is short-term patterns of information processing. Sociologists simply are not accustomed to making such relatively close observations. Nevertheless, some information of this sort is available to us. Bob Mullan's case histories give evidence of some of these characteristics, such as the use of language for effect on others rather than for meaning. Experiential and new religions almost seem to encourage "unclear verbal statements," "choice" of global rather than specific labels for "experience," and "failure to understand ideational implications," all of which tends to make members appear somewhat shallow (Mullan 1983:50–79).

It seems to us, then, that new religions are expressions of cultural anxiety in an increasingly global world. They amplify or produce disillusionment with the old order yet at the same time resolve personal problems and offer a new future for humankind.

## Conclusion

New religions are firmly based in religious experiences that are surprisingly common in the modern world. The mythologies and primal experiences of new religions involve the use of faculties like the receptive imagination. The existence of new religions reminds us that for many people reason and logic alone are not enough to live full lives (cf. Gray 1990). Reason cut through dead tradition in the Enlightenment of the seventeenth and eighteenth centuries. But the world recent generations have inherited is fragmented, so that once more people yearn for wholeness and are willing to bracket skepticism.

The operating system of new religions is a form of mythmaking that we call box myths, myths within myths that enable people to place themselves within a cosmic framework. The most famous founders of new religions are those mythmakers who have the creative talent to construct a labyrinthine box myth with the idea of sending their followers through it, as if they were embarked on a sacred adventure. This adventure is elaborated and given substance by numerous ideas, doctrines, and practices borrowed from the historic religious traditions of the world.

New religions open their members to highly creative lifestyles that enable them to envision themselves as citizens of the global city that our world has become. Like Christian missions, they are global movements that energize their followers with a new vision of the world (van der Heyden and Liebau 1996). By uprooting traditions from their social and historical contexts, new religions propose new ways of life that give members a reason for living and hope for the future. Whether any of today's new religions will become a world religion that embraces a large proportion of humanity is, as Rudyard Kipling would say, "another story."

# Bibliography

Aagaard, Johannes. 1991. "Conversion, Religious Change, and the Challenge of New Religious Movements." *Cultic Studies Journal* 8(2):91–121.

Abanes, Richard. 1996. *American Militias*. Downers Grove, Ill.: InterVarsity.

Able, Theodore. 1986. *Why Hitler Came into Power*. Cambridge: Harvard University Press. First edition 1938.

Adams, Daniel J. 1991. "Reflections on an Indigenous Christian Movement: The Yoido Full Gospel Church." *Japan Christian Quarterly* 57(1):36–45.

Adamski, George, and Desmond Leslie. 1953. *Flying Saucers Have Landed*. London: T. Warner Laurie.

Adler, Margot. 1986. *Drawing Down the Moon*. Boston: Beacon Press.

Anderson, Paul. 1981. *The Broken Sword*. New York: Ballantine.

Baird, Robert D., ed. 1981. *Religion in Modern India*. New Delhi: Manigar.

Balzer, Marjorie Mandelstam, ed. 1990. *Shamanism: Soviet Studies of Traditional Religion in Siberia and Central Asia*. London: M. E. Sharpe.

Bames, Sandra. 1989. *Africa's Ogun: Old World and New*. Bloomington: Indiana University Press.

Barborka, Geoffrey. 1966. *H. P. Blavatsky, Tibet and Tulku*. Adyar, India: Theosophical Publishing House.

Barker, Eileen, ed. 1982. *New Religious Movements*. New York: Edwin Mellen.

_____. 1984. *The Making of a Moonie*. Oxford: Basil Blackwell.

_____. 1989. *New Religious Movements: A Practical Introduction*. London: Her Majesty's Stationery Office.

Barkun, Michael. 1994. *Religion and the Racist Right*. Chapel Hill: University of North Carolina Press.

Barrett, David B. 1968. *Schism and Renewal in Africa: An Analysis of Six Thousand Contemporary Religious Movements*. Nairobi: Oxford University Press.

Barrett, David B., and T. John Padwick. 1989. *Rise Up and Walk! Conciliarism and the African Indigenous Churches, 1815–1987*. Nairobi: Oxford University Press.

Barrett, William. 1958. *Irrational Man*. Garden City, N.Y.: Doubleday.

Bastedo, Ralph W. 1978. "An Empirical Test of Popular Astrology." *Skeptical Inquirer* 3(1):17–38.

Bastian, Adolf. 1860. *Der Mensch in der Geschichte: Zur Begründung einer Psychologischen Weltanschauung*. 3 vols. Leipzig: Verlag Otto Wiegand. Reprint, Osnabrück: Biblioverlag, 1968.

Baumgartner, Raimund. 1977. *Weltanschauungskampf im Dritten Reich*. Mainz: Matthias-Grünewald.

Beaman, Edmund A. 1971. *Swedenborg and the New Age*. New York: AMS Press. First edition 1881.

Beattie, John, and John Middleton, eds. 1969. *Spirit Mediumship and Society in Africa.* New York: Africana.

Beck, Brenda E. F. 1978. "The Metaphor as a Mediator Between Semantic and Analogic Modes of Thought." *Current Anthropology* 19(1):83–97.

Beckford, James, ed. 1985. *New Religious Movements and Rapid Social Change.* Beverly Hills, Calif.: Sage.

Bede. 1965. *A History of the English Church and People.* Translated by Leo Sherley-Price. Harmondsworth: Penguin.

Bednarowski, Mary Farrell. 1989. *New Religions and the Theological Imagination in America.* Bloomington: Indiana University Press.

Bendix, Reinhard. 1962. *Max Weber: An Intellectual Portrait.* London: Methuen.

Berger, Peter. 1969. *The Sacred Canopy: Elements of a Sociological Theory of Religion.* New York: Anchor Books.

Berlin, Twenty-seventh Chamber of the Administrative Court. 1995. *Church on the Way vs. the Country of Berlin,* 24 March. V 27 A 320.94. Translated by Pamela T. Wood and Karla Poewe.

Beverley, James A. 1995. *Holy Laughter and the Toronto Blessing.* Grand Rapids, Mich.: Zondervan.

Bibby, Reginald. 1985. "Religionless Christianity: A Profile of Religion in the Canadian '80s." Department of Sociology, University of Lethbridge, Lethbridge, Alberta. Disk.

_____. 1987. *Fragmented Gods: The Poverty and Potential of Religion in Canada.* Toronto: Irwin.

_____. 1993. *Unknown Gods: The Ongoing Story of Religion in Canada.* Toronto: Stoddart.

_____. 1995. *The Bibby Report: Social Trends Canadian Style.* Toronto: Stoddart.

Blackmore, Susan. 1987. "The Elusive Open Mind: Ten Years of Research in Parapsychology." *Skeptical Inquirer* 11(3):244–255.

Blair, Lawrence. 1975. *Rhythms of Vision.* New York: Schocken.

Blavatsky, Helena. 1972a. *Isis Unveiled.* Pasadena: Theosophical University Press. First edition 1877.

_____. 1972b. *The Key to Theosophy.* Pasadena: Theosophical University Press. First edition 1888.

_____. 1974. *The Secret Doctrine.* Pasadena: Theosophical University Press. First edition 1888.

Block, Marguerite. 1968. *The New Church in the New World.* New York: Octagon Books.

Boas, Marie. 1962. *The Scientific Renaissance: 1450–1650.* London: Collins.

Bochinger, Christoph. 1994. *New Age und moderne Religion: Religionswissenschaftliche Analysen.* Gütersloh, Germany: Chr. Kaiser.

Boisen, Anton. 1971. *The Exploration of the Inner World: A Study of Mental Disorder and Religious Experience.* Philadelphia: University of Pennsylvania Press. First edition 1936.

Borst, Gert. 1969. *Die Ludendorff-Bewegung: 1919–1961.* Munich: Privately published.

Bourguignon, E. 1976. *Possession.* San Francisco: Chandler & Sharpe.

Bramwell, Anne. 1985. *Blood and Soil.* Bourne End, England: Kensal Press.

Brandon, Owen. 1960. *The Battle for the Soul: Aspects of Religious Conversion.* London: Hodder & Stoughton.

Brandt, Johanna. 1918. *The Millenium: A Prophetic Forecast.* Johannesburg: Privately published.

_____. 1936. *The Paraclete, or Coming World Mother.* Johannesburg: Privately published.

Brent, Peter. 1973. *Godmen of India*. Harmondsworth: Penguin.

Bright, John. 1962. *The History of Israel*. London: SCM.

Brodie, Fawn M. 1971. *No Man Knows My History*. New York: Knopf.

Bromley, David, and James T. Richardson. 1983. *The Brainwashing/Deprogramming Controversy: Sociological, Psychological, Legal and Historical Perspectives*. New York: Edwin Mellen.

Bromley, David, and Anson Shupe. 1980. "The Tnevnoc Cult." *Sociological Analysis* 40:361–366.

_____. 1981. *Strange Gods: The Great American Cult Scare*. Boston: Beacon.

Brown, Robert, and Rosemary Brown. 1986. *They Lie in Wait to Deceive*. Mesa, Ariz.: Brownsworth.

Bruce, Steve. 1990. *The Rise and Fall of the New Christian Right: Conservative Protestant Politics in America, 1978–1988*. Oxford: Clarendon Press.

Burger, Thomas. 1976. *Max Weber's Theory of Concept Formation*. Durham, N.C.: Duke University Press.

Burgess, Stanley M.; Gary B. McGee; and Patrick H. Alexander, eds. 1988. *Dictionary of Pentecostal and Charismatic Movements*. Grand Rapids, Mich.: Zondervan.

Burridge, Kenelm. 1971. *New Heaven, New Earth*. Oxford: Basil Blackwell.

_____. 1979. *Someone, No One: An Essay on Individuality*. Princeton: Princeton University Press.

_____. 1991. *In the Way*. Vancouver: University of British Columbia Press.

Butt, A.; S. Wavell; and N. Epton. 1966. *Trances*. London: Allen & Unwin.

Campbell, Bruce F. 1980. *Ancient Wisdom Revived: A History of the Theosophical Movement*. Berkeley: University of California Press.

Campbell, Robert, ed. 1968. *Spectrum of Protestant Beliefs*. Milwaukee: Bruce Publishing.

Capra, Fritjof. 1982. *The Turning Point: Science, Society and the Rising Culture*. New York: Simon & Schuster.

Caudill, William, and Tsung-Yi Lin, eds. 1969. *Mental Health Research in Asia and the Pacific*. Honolulu: East-West Center Press.

Cavendish, Richard. 1967. *The Black Arts*. New York: G. P. Putnam.

Cecil, Robert. 1972. *The Myth of the Master Race: Alfred Rosenberg and Nazi Ideology*. London: B. T. Batsford.

Cesara, Manda. 1982. *Reflections of a Woman Anthropologist*. London: Academic Press.

Chesterton, G. K. 1949. *Orthodoxy*. London: Bodley Head.

_____. 1957. *St. Francis of Assisi*. New York: ImageBooks.

Chidester, David. 1988. *Salvation and Suicide: An Interpretation of Jim Jones, the People's Temple, and Jonestown*. Bloomington: Indiana University Press.

Cho, Paul Yonggi. 1979. *The Fourth Dimension: The Key to Putting Your Faith to Work for a Successful Life*. Plainfield, N.J.: Logos International.

Chryssides, George D. 1991. *The Advent of Sun Myung Moon: The Origins, Beliefs and Practices of the Unification Church*. New York: St. Martin's Press.

Chull, Park; Hang Lee Nyong; Sheen Doh Sung; and Yoon Se Won. 1981. *Sun Myung Moon: The Man and His Ideal*. Seoul: Mirae Munhwa Sa.

Clark, David K., and Norman L. Geisler. 1990. *Apologetics in the New Age: A Christian Critique of Pantheism*. Grand Rapids, Mich.: Baker.

Clark, Donald N. 1986. *Christianity in Modern Korea*. New York: University Press of America.

Clark, Gordon H. 1957. *Thales to Dewey: A History of Philosophy*. Boston: Houghton Mifflin.

Clarke, Arthur C. 1963. *Childhood's End*. New York: Harcourt Brace Jovanovich.

Clarke, Peter B., and Jeffrey Somers. 1994. *Japanese New Religions in the West*. Sandgate, England: Japan Library.

Clifford, Ross, and Philip Johnson. 1993. *Shooting for the Stars*. Sutherland, Australia: Albatross.

Coker, Robina. 1995. *Alternative Medicine: Helpful or Harmful?* Crowborough, England: Monarch.

Cole, Michael; Jim Graham; Tony Higton; and David Lewis. 1990. *What Is the New Age? A Detailed Candid Look at This Fast Growing Movement*. London: Hodder and Stoughton.

Coleman, Simon. 1991. "Faith Which Conquers the World." *Ethnos* 56(1–2):9–18.

Concilium Legionis Mariae. 1959. *The Official Handbook of the Legion of Mary*. Shepherdsville, Ky.: Publishers Printing.

Connerton, Paul. 1989. *How Societies Remember*. Cambridge: Cambridge University Press.

Conway, Flo, and Jim Siegelman. 1978. *Snapping: America's Epidemic of Sudden Personality Change*. Philadelphia: J. B. Lippincott.

_____. 1984. *Holy Terror: The Fundamentalist War on America's Freedoms in Religion, Politics and Our Private Lives*. New York: Delta.

Conze, Edward. 1951. *Buddhism*. New York: Harper & Row.

_____. 1979. *The Memoirs of a Modern Gnostic*. Sherbourne, England: Samizdat Publishing.

Cumbey, Constance. 1983. *The Hidden Dangers of the Rainbow: The New Age Movement and Our Coming Age of Barbarism*. Shreveport, La.: Huntington House.

Daiber, Karl-Fritz. 1995. *Religion unter den Bedingungen der Moderne: Die Situation in der Bundesrepublik Deutschland*. Marburg, Germany: Diagonal.

Daneel, Inus. 1987. *Quest for Belonging*. Harare, Zimbabwe: Mambo Press.

_____. 1988. *Old and New in Southern Shona Independent Churches*. Gweru, Zambia: Mambo Press.

Darton, Robert. 1968. *Mesmerism and the End of the Enlightenment in France*. Cambridge: Harvard University Press.

Davidson, James Dale, and William Rees-Mogg. 1994. *The Great Reckoning*. New York: Simon & Schuster.

Davis, Winston. 1980. *Dojo: Magic and Exorcism in Modern Japan*. Stanford: Stanford University Press.

Day, Terence P. 1982. *The Conception of Punishment in Early Indian Literature*. Waterloo, Ontario: Wilfrid Laurier University Press.

de Camp, L. Sprague. 1970. *Lost Continents: The Atlantis Theme in History, Science and Literature*. New York: Dover.

Dick, Thomas. 1828. *Philosophy of a Future State*. Philadelphia: Key and Biddle.

Dinnage, Rosemary. 1986. *Annie Besant*. Harmondsworth: Penguin.

Dirven, Peter J. 1970. "The Maria Legio: The Dynamics of a Breakaway Church Among the Luo in East Africa." Doctor of Missiology thesis, Pontificia Universitas Gregoriana, Rome.

Dooyeweerd, Herman. 1953. *New Critique of Theoretical Thought*. Philadelphia: Presbyterian and Reformed.

Dow, James R., and Hannjost Lixfeld, eds. 1994. *The Nazification of an Academic Discipline: Folklore in the Third Reich*. Bloomington: Indiana University Press.

Droogers, André. 1990. "Macht in zin: Een drieluik van Braziliaanse religieuze verbeelding." Inaugural lecture, Vrije Universiteit, Amsterdam.

Droogers, André; Gerrit Huizer; and Hans Siebers. 1991. *Popular Power in Latin American Religions.* Saarbrücken, Germany: Breitenbach.

Drucker, Peter F. 1939. *The End of Economic Man: A Study of the New Totalitarianism.* New York: John Day.

_____. 1942. *The Future of Industrial Man: A Conservative Approach.* New York: John Day.

Dubb, Allie A. 1976. *Community of the Saved.* Johannesburg: Witwatersrand University Press.

Duddy, Neil. 1981. *The God-Men.* Downers Grove, Ill.: InterVarsity.

Earhart, Byron H. 1974. "The New Religions of Korea: A Preliminary Interpretation." *Transactions of the Korea Branch of the Royal Asiatic Society,* vol. 49.

Eddy, Mary Baker. 1880. *Science and Health with Key to the Scriptures.* Boston: Christian Science Publishing House. First published 1875.

Edwards, Jonathan. 1962. *Jonathan Edwards: Representative Selections.* Edited by Clarence H. Faust and Thomas H. Johnson. New York: Hill and Wang.

Eisenberg, Diane U., ed. 1990. *Transformations of Myth Through Time.* New York: Harcourt Brace Jovanovich.

Eliade, Mircea. 1965. *The Myth of the Eternal Return.* Princeton: Princeton University Press. First published 1954.

_____. 1969. *Yoga, Immortality and Freedom.* London: Routledge & Kegan Paul.

_____. 1972. *Shamanism.* Princeton: Princeton University Press.

Elliot, Gil. 1972. *Twentieth Century Book of the Dead.* London: Allen Lane.

Emery, Eugene, Jr. 1987. "Catching Geller in the Act." *Skeptical Inquirer* 12(1):75–80.

Enroth, Ron. 1978. *Youth Brainwashing and Extremist Cults.* Grand Rapids, Mich.: Zondervan.

Evans-Pritchard, E. E. 1937. *Witchcraft, Oracles, and Magic Among the Azande.* London: Oxford University Press.

Eysenck, Hans J., and Carl Sargent. 1982. *Explaining the Unexplained: Mysteries of the Paranormal.* London: Weidenfeld and Nicolson.

Faber, M. D. 1996. *New Age Thinking: A Psychoanalytic Critique.* Ottawa: University of Ottawa Press.

Fabian, Johannes. 1971. *Jamaa: A Charismatic Movement in Katanga.* Evanston, Ill.: Northwestern University Press.

Featherstone, Mike, ed. 1990. *Global Culture.* London: Sage.

Ferguson, Duncan S., ed. 1992. *New Age Spirituality.* Louisville, Ky.: Westminster/John Knox Press.

Ferguson, Marilyn. 1980. *The Aquarian Conspiracy.* Los Angeles: J. B. Tarcher.

Ferm, Robert O. N.d. *The Psychology of Christian Conversion.* London: Pickering & Inglis.

Fernandez, James W. 1965. "Politics and Prophecy." *Practical Anthropology* 12(2):71–75.

Fikes, Jay Courtney. 1993. *Carlos Castaneda, Academic Opportunism and the Psychedelic Sixties.* Victoria, B.C.: Millenia Press.

Finke, Roger, and Rodney Stark. 1992. *The Churching of America: 1776–1990.* New Brunswick, N.J.: Rutgers University Press.

Finney, Charles. 1989. *The Memoirs of Charles Finney: The Complete Restored Text.* Edited by Garth M. Rosell and Richard A. G. Dupuis. Grand Rapids, Mich.: Zondervan.

Flaherty, Gloria. 1992. *Shamanism and the Eighteenth Century.* Princeton: Princeton University Press.

Forem, Jack. 1973. *Transcendental Meditation*. London: George Allen.

Freed, Josh. 1980. *Moonwebs: Journey into the Mind of a Cult*. Toronto: Dorset Publishing.

Frye, Northrop. 1982. *The Great Code: The Bible and Literature*. New York: Harcourt Brace Jovanovich.

Gallup, George, and Jim Castelli. 1989. *The People's Religions: American Faith in the 90's*. New York: Harles.

Gardner, Gerald. 1982a. *The Meaning of Witchcraft*. New York: Magical Childe. First published 1959.

_____. 1982b. *Witchcraft Today*. New York: Magical Childe. First published 1954.

Gifford, Paul. 1988. *The Religious Right in South Africa*. Harare, Zimbabwe: Baobab Books.

Glock, Charles Y., and Bellah Robert N., eds. 1996. *The New Religious Consciousness*. Berkeley: University of California Press.

Goodman, Felicitas D. 1972. *Speaking in Tongues: A Cross-Cultural Study of Glossolalia*. Chicago: University of Chicago Press.

_____. 1988. *Ecstasy, Ritual and Alternative Reality: Religion in a Pluralistic World*. Bloomington: Indiana University Press.

Goodrick-Clarke, Nicholas. 1985. *The Occult Roots of Nazism*. Wellingborough, England: Aquarian Press.

Gordon, Sarah. 1984. *Hitler, Germans, and the "Jewish Question."* Princeton: Princeton University Press.

Goswami, Satsvarūpa Dās. 1983. *Prabhupada*. Los Angeles: Bhaktivedanta Book Trust.

Gray, William D. 1990. *Thinking Critically About New Age Ideas*. Belmont, Calif.: Wadsworth.

Grayson, James Huntley. 1985. *Early Buddhism and Christianity in Korea: A Study in the Emplantation of Religion*. Leiden: E. J. Brill.

_____. 1989. *Korea: A Religious History*. Oxford: Clarendon Press.

Greil, Arthur L., and Thomas Robbins, eds. 1994. *Religion and the Social Order*. Greenwich, Conn.: JAI Press.

Griffith-Thomas, W. H. 1930. *Principles of Theology*. London: Longman, Green.

Grim, P., ed. 1982. *Philosophy of Science and the Occult*. New York: State University of New York Press.

Groothuis, Douglas. 1986. *Unmasking the New Age: Is There a New Religious Movement Trying to Transform Society?* Downers Grove, Ill.: InterVarsity.

Gross, Martin L. 1978. The Psychological Society. New York: Random House.

Haack, Friedrich-Wilhelm. 1993. *Europas neue Religion: Sekten–Gurus–Satanskult*. Freiburg: Herder.

_____. 1994. *Sekten*. Munich: Münchener Reihe.

Hackett, Rosalind I. J., ed. 1987. *New Religious Movements in Nigeria*. Lewiston, N.Y.: Edwin Mellen.

Hall, John R. 1989. *Gone from the Promised Land: Jonestown in American Cultural History*. New Brunswick, N.J.: Transaction Publishers.

Hall, Rupert. 1963. *From Galileo to Newton: 1630–1720*. London: Collins.

Hammond, Phillip E., ed. 1985. *The Sacred in a Secular Age: Toward Revision in the Scientific Study of Religion*. Berkeley: University of California Press.

Hannegraff, Hank. 1993. *Christianity in Crisis*. Eugene, Ore.: Harvest House.

Hansen, Klaus J. 1981. *Mormonism and the American Experience*. Chicago: University of Chicago Press.

Hanson, J. W., ed. 1895. *The World's Congress of Religions: The Addresses and Papers*. Chicago: Mammoth.

Hardy, Alister. 1979. *The Spiritual Nature of Man*. Oxford: Clarendon Press.

Harrison, R. K. 1969. *Introduction to the Old Testament*. Grand Rapids, Mich.: Eerdmans.

Hassan, Steven. 1990. *Combatting Cult Mind Control*. Rochester, Vt.: Park Street Press.

Hay, David. 1975. "Reports of Religious Experiences by a Group of Postgraduate Students: A Pilot Study" and "Religious Experiences Among a Group of Postgraduate Students: A Qualitative Survey." Papers presented at the Colloquium on Psychology and Religion, Lancaster University.

_____. 1990. *Religious Experience Today: Studying the Facts*. London: Mowbray.

Hay, David, and Ann Morisy. 1978. "Reports of Ecstatic Paranormal or Religious Experiences in Great Britain and the United States: A Comparison of Trends." *Journal for the Scientific Study of Religion* 17(3):255–265.

Hayashi, Minoru. 1988. "Learning from the Japanese New Religions." Doctor of Missiology thesis, Fuller Theological Seminary, Pasadena, California.

Hayes, Stephen. 1990. *Black Charismatic Anglicans*. Pretoria: University of South Africa.

Hegel, G. W. F. 1961. *On Christianity: Early Theological Writings*. Translated by T. M. Knox. New York: Harper.

Heinze, Ruth-Inge. 1991. *Shamans of the 20th Century*. New York: Irvington.

Henry, Carl F. 1976. *God, Revelation and Authority*. 4 vols. Waco, Tex.: Word.

Hexham, Irving. 1981. *The Irony of Apartheid*. Lewiston, N.Y.: Edwin Mellen.

_____. 1991. "Charismatic Churches and Apartheid in South Africa and the Problem of Method in the Study of Religion." Paper presented at the Conference on Global Culture: Pentecostal/Charismatic Movements Worldwide, University of Calgary, 9–11 May.

_____, ed. 1994. *The Scriptures of the amaNazaretha of Ekuphakameni*. Translated by Londa Shembe and Hans-Jürgen Becken. Calgary: Calgary University Press.

_____, ed. 1996. *The Oral History and Sacred Traditions of the Nazareth Baptist Church: The Story of Isaiah Mdliwamafa Shembe*. Translated by Hans-Jürgen Becken. Lewiston, N.Y.: Edwin Mellen.

Hexham, Irving, and Karla Poewe. 1986. *Understanding Cults and New Religions*. Grand Rapids, Mich.: Eerdmans.

Hill, Christopher. 1965. *The Intellectual Origins of the English Revolution*. Oxford: Oxford University Press.

Hill, Michael. 1973. *A Sociology of Religion*. London: Heinemann Educational Books.

Hiro, Dilip. 1989. *Holy Wars: The Rise of Islamic Fundamentalism*. New York: Routledge.

Hiroko, Shiraizu. 1979. "Organizational Mediums: A Case Study of Shinnyo-en." *Japanese Journal of Religious Studies* 6(1):413–444.

Hittleman, Richard. 1969. *Guide to Yoga Meditation*. New York: Bantam Books.

Hodgson, Janet. 1980. *Ntsikana's Great Hymn*. Cape Town: Centre for African Studies.

Hoffmann, Banish. 1960. *The Strange Story of the Quantum*. London: Penguin.

Holmes, Arthur F. 1983. *Contours of a World View*. Grand Rapids, Mich.: Eerdmans.

Holy Spirit Association. 1973. *The Divine Principle*. Washington, D.C.: Holy Spirit Association for the Unification of World Christianity.

Hori, Ichir. 1968. *Folk Religion in Japan: Continuity and Change*. Edited by Joseph M. Kitagawa and Alan L. Miller. Chicago: University of Chicago Press.

Horowitz, Mardi J., ed. 1977. *The Hysterical Personality*. New York: Aronson.

Horton, Robin. 1967. "African Traditional Thought and Western Science." *Africa* 37(1):50–71; 37(2):155–187.

Howe, Ellic. 1972. *The Magicians of the Golden Dawn*. New York: Samuel Weiser.

Hoyt, Karen, ed. 1987. *The New Age Rage: A Probing Analysis of the Newest Religious Craze*. Old Tappan, N.J.: Fleming H. Revell.

Humphries, Christmas. 1964. *Buddhism*. Harmondsworth: Penguin.

Hunt, Dave, and T. A. McMahon. 1983. *Peace, Prosperity, and the Coming Holocaust: The New Age Movement in Prophecy*. Eugene, Ore.: Harvest House.

_____. 1985. *The Seduction of Christianity*. Eugene, Ore.: Harvest House.

_____. 1988. *America: The Sorcerer's New Apprentice–The Rise of New Age Shamanism*. Eugene, Ore.: Harvest House.

Ichirō, Hori; Ikado Fujio; Wakimoto Tsuneya; and Yanagawa Keiichi. 1972. *Japanese Religion*. Tokyo: Kodansha International.

Inglis, Brian. 1964. *Fringe Medicine*. London: Faber and Faber.

_____. 1979. *Natural Medicine*. Glasgow: Fontana Collins.

Ishida, Hōyū. 1989. "Otto's Theory of Religious Experience as Encounter with the Numinous and Its Application to Buddhism." *Japanese Religions* 15(3):19–33.

James, William. 1985. *The Varieties of Religious Experience. A Study in Human Nature*. London: Fontana. First published 1902.

Jenkins, Terrell R. N.d. "The Theology of Watchman Nee and Witness Lee." Mimeograph.

Johannes Institut. 1991. *Die Guten Seiten*. Wiesbaden, Germany: Johannes Institut.

Johnson, Benton. 1963. "On Church and Sect." *American Sociological Review* 28:539–549.

Jorgensen, Sven-Aage, ed. 1968. *Johann Georg Hamann: Sokratische Denkwürdigkeiten*. Stuttgart: Reclam.

Joshi, Vasant. 1982. *The Awakened One: The Life and Work of Bhagwan Shree Rajneesh*. San Francisco: Harper & Row.

Judah, J. Stilson. 1974. *Hare Krishna and the Counterculture*. New York: John Wiley and Sons.

Kaihla, Paul, and Ross Laver. 1993. *Savage Messiah*. Toronto: Doubleday.

Kakar, Sudhir. 1981. *The Inner World: A Psycho-analytic Study of Childhood and Society in India*. New York: Oxford University Press.

_____. 1982. *Shamans, Mystics and Doctors*. Boston: Beacon Press.

Kanai, Shinji. 1987. "The New Religious Situation in Japan." In Allan R. Brockway and J. Paul Rajashekar, eds., *New Religious Movements and the Churches*. Geneva: WCC Publications.

Kant, Immanuel. 1983. *Critique of Pure Reason*. Translated by Norman Kemp Smith. London: Macmillan. First published 1781.

Keel, John. 1970. *UFOs: Operation Trojan Horse*. New York: Putnam's Sons.

Kepel, Gilles. 1991. *Die Rache Gottes*. Munich: Piper.

Kershaw, Ian, ed. 1990. *Weimar: Why Did German Democracy Fail?* London: Weidenfeld and Nicolson.

Kim, Byong-Suh. 1985. "The Explosive Growth of the Korean Church Today: A Sociological Analysis." *International Review of Missions* 74:293.

Kim, Young Oon. 1980. *Unification Theology*. New York: Holy Spirit Association for the Unification of World Christianity.

King, George. 1961. *You Are Responsible*. London: Artherius.

King, Ursula. 1980. *Towards a New Mysticism*. London: Collins.

Klöcker, Michael, and Udo Tworuschka. 1994. *Religionen in Deutschland*. Munich: Olzog.

Koepping, Klaus-Peter. 1983. *Adolf Bastian and the Psychic Unity of Mankind*. St. Lucia, Australia: University of Queensland Press.

Koestler, Arthur. 1978. *Janus: A Summing Up*. New York: London House.

Kohl, Karl-Heinz. 1987. *Abwehr und Verlangen*. Frankfurt am Main: Qumran.

Kolnai, Aurel. 1938. *The War Against the West*. London: Victor Gollancz.

Kroll, Una. 1974. *TM: Signpost to the World*. London: Darton, Longman & Todd.

Kuhn, Thomas. 1962. *The Structure of Scientific Revolutions*. Chicago: University of Chicago Press.

Küng, Hans. 1978. *On Being a Christian*. London: Collins.

Laderman, Carol, and Marina Roseman, eds. 1996. *The Performance of Healing*. London: Routledge.

Laing, R. D. 1965. *The Divided Self*. Harmondsworth: Penguin.

Lam, Nora. 1980. *China Cry*. Waco, Tex.: Word.

Lange, Ingrid, ed. 1993. *Fundamentalismus in Africa und Amerika*. Hamburg: Evangelisches Missionswerk.

Langness, L. L. 1965. "Hysterical Psychosis in the New Guinea Highlands: A Bena Bena Example." *Psychiatry* 26:258–277.

Laqueur, Walter. 1962. *Young Germany: A History of the German Youth Movement*. London: Routledge & Kegan Paul.

Laslett, Peter. 1984. *The World We Have Lost*. New York: Charles Scribner's Sons.

Leary, Timothy. 1970. *The Politics of Ecstasy*. London: Paladin.

_____. 1982. *Changing My Mind, Among Others: Lifetime Writings*. Englewood Cliffs, N.J.: Prentice-Hall.

Lee, S. G. 1954. "A Study of Crying Hysteria and Dreaming in Zulu Women." Ph.D. dissertation, University of London.

Lee, Yohan. 1985. "An Analysis of the Christian Prayer Mountain Phenomenon in Korea." Ph.D. dissertation, Fuller Theological Seminary, Pasadena, California.

Leek, Sybil. 1968. *Diary of a Witch*. New York: Signet Books.

Leppard, David. 1993. *Fire and Blood: The True Story of David Koresh and the Waco Siege*. London: Fourth Estate.

Lepra, William P. 1966. *Okinawan Religion: Belief, Ritual and Social Structure*. Honolulu: University of Hawaii Press.

_____, ed. 1976. *Culture-Bound Syndromes, Ethnopsychiatry and Alternate Therapies*. Honolulu: University Press of Hawaii.

Levine, Saul. 1979. "The Role of Psychiatry in the Phenomenon of Cults." *Canadian Journal of Psychiatry* 24:593–603.

_____. 1984. *Radical Departures: Desperate Detours to Growing Up*. San Diego: Harcourt Brace Jovanovich.

Lévi-Strauss, Claude. 1978. *Myth and Meaning*. London: Routledge & Kegan Paul.

Leviton, Daniel, ed. 1991. *Horrendous Death, Health, and Well-Being*. New York: Hemisphere Books.

Lewis, C. S. 1964. *The Discarded Image*. Cambridge: Cambridge University Press.

_____. 1971. *Christian Reflections*. Edited by Walter Hooper. Grand Rapids, Mich.: Eerdmans.

Lewis, I. M. 1971. *Ecstatic Religion: An Anthropological Study of Spirit Possession and Shamanism*. Harmondsworth: Penguin.

_____. 1986. *Religion in Context: Cults and Charisma*. Cambridge: Cambridge University Press.

Lewis, James R., and J. Gordon Melton. 1992. *Perspectives on the New Age*. New York: SUNY Press.

Liebersohn, Harry. 1988. *Fate and Utopia in German Sociology, 1870–1923*. Cambridge: MIT Press.

Lifton, Robert Jay. 1968. "Protean Man." *Partisan Review* 35:13–27.

Liljegren, Sten Bodvar. 1957. *Bulwer-Lytton's Novels and Isis Unveiled*. Cambridge: Harvard University Press.

Lindsey, Hal. 1970. *The Late Great Planet Earth*. Grand Rapids, Mich.: Zondervan.

Lixfeld, Hannjost. 1994. *Folklore and Fascism: The Reich Institute for German Volkskunde*. Bloomington: Indiana University Press.

Lloyd-Jones, D. Martyn. 1959. *Conversions: Psychological and Spiritual*. London: InterVarsity.

_____. 1984. *Spiritual Depression: Its Cause and Its Cure*. Grand Rapids, Mich.: Eerdmans.

Lofland, John. 1984. *Doomsday Cult*. New York: Irvington.

Lovejoy, Arthur O. 1960. *The Great Chain of Being*. New York: Harper & Row.

Luckmann, Thomas. 1990. "Shrinking Transcendence, Expanding Religion?" *Sociological Analysis* 50(2):127–138.

Ludendorff, Mathilde. 1935. *Aus der Gotteskenntnis meiner Werke*. Munich: Ludendorffs Verlag.

_____. 1937. *Ein Blick in die Dunkelkammer der Geistersehe*. Berlin: Ludendorffs Verlag.

Luhrmann, T. M. 1989. *Persuasions of the Witch's Craft*. Cambridge: Harvard University Press.

Luthuli, Albert. 1962. *Let My People Go*. London: Fontana.

MacDougal, Curtis D. 1983. *Superstition and the Press*. Buffalo: Prometheus Books.

MacGaffey, Wyatt. 1983. *Modern Kongo Prophets*. Bloomington: Indiana University Press.

Macionis, John J.; Juanne Nancarrow Clarke; and Linda M. Gerber. 1994. *Sociology*. Scarborough, Ontario: Prentice-Hall.

MacLaine, Shirley. 1983. *Out on a Limb*. New York: Bantam Books.

Malinowski, Bronislaw. 1954. *Magic, Science and Religion*. New York: Anchor Books.

Malony, H. Newton, and A. Adams Lovekin. 1985. *Glossolalia: Behavioural Science Perspectives on Speaking in Tongues*. Oxford: Oxford University Press.

Mann, William E. 1955. *Sect, Cult and Church in Alberta*. Toronto: University of Toronto Press.

Maranda, Pierre, ed. 1972. *Mythology*. Harmondsworth: Penguin.

Marshall, Dorothy, ed. 1973. *Industrial England: 1776–1851*. London: Routledge & Kegan Paul.

Martin, Walter. 1976. *The Kingdom of the Cults*. 27th ed. Minneapolis: Bethany House. First published 1965.

Marty, Martin E., and Kenneth L. Vaux. 1982. *Health/Medicine and the Faith Traditions*. Philadelphia: Fortress Press.

Maslow, Abraham. 1968. *Toward a Psychology of Being*. New York: Van Nostrand Reinhold Books.

McAll, Kenneth. 1985. *Healing the Family Tree*. London: Sheldon Press.

McConnell, D. R. 1988. *A Different Gospel: A Historical and Biblical Analysis of the Modern Faith Movement*. Peabody, Mass.: Hendrickson Publishers.

McFarland, H. Neil. 1970. *The Rush Hour of the Gods.* New York: Harper & Row.

McGervey, John D. 1977. "A Statistical Test of Sun-Sign Astrology." *The Zetetic* 1(2):48–55.

McGuire, Meredith B. 1981. *Religion: The Social Context.* Belmont, Calif.: Wadsworth.

Meade, Marion. 1980. *Madame Blavatsky: The Woman Behind the Myth.* New York: G. P. Putnam's Sons.

Meadows, Donella H.; Denis L. Meadows; Jørgen Randers; and William W. Behrens III. 1972. *The Limits to Growth.* New York: Universe Books.

Melton, J. Gordon; Jerome Clark; and Aidan A. Kelly. 1990. *New Age Encyclopedia.* Detroit: Gale Research.

Metzke, Erwin. 1967. *J. G. Hamanns Stellung in der Philosophie des 18. Jahrhunderts.* Darmstadt: Wissenschaftliche Buchgesellschaft.

Meynell, Hugo. 1882. *The Intelligible Universe.* New York: Barnes & Noble.

Michell, John. 1967. *The Flying Saucer Vision: The Holy Grail Restored.* London: Sphere Books.

Middleton, John. 1960. *Lugbara Religion.* London: International African Institute.

_____, ed. 1967. *Myth and Cosmos.* New York: Natural History Press.

Milingo, Emmanuel. 1984. *The World in Between.* Maryknoll, N.Y.: Orbis Books.

Miller, Elliot. 1989. *A Crash Course on the New Age Movement.* Grand Rapids, Mich.: Baker.

Miller, Russell. 1987. *Bare-Faced Messiah: The True Story of L. Ron Hubbard.* Toronto: Key Porter Books.

Miller, Timothy, ed. 1995. *America's Alternative Religions.* New York: State University of New York Press.

Moerman, Daniel. 1979. "Anthropology of Symbolic Healing." *Current Anthropology* 20(1):59–80.

Molau, Andreas. 1993. *Alfred Rosenberg: Der Ideologe des Nationalsozialismus.* Koblenz, Germany: Siegfried Bublies.

Mommsen, Wolfgang J., ed. 1987. *The Political and Social Theory of Max Weber: Collected Essays.* Chicago: University of Chicago Press.

Moon, Sun Myung. 1973. *The Divine Principle.* New York: Holy Spirit Association for the Unification of World Christianity.

Moos, Felix. 1967. "Leadership and Organization in the Olive Tree Movement." *Transactions of the Korea Branch of the Royal Asiatic Society,* vol. 43.

Mosse, George L. 1981. *The Crisis of the German Ideology.* New York: Schocken. First edition 1964.

Mühlmann, W. E. 1984. *Geschichte der Anthropologie.* Wiesbaden, Germany: AULA-Verlag.

Mullan, Bob. 1983. *Life as Laughter.* London: Routledge & Kegan Paul.

Mullins, Mark R. 1989. "The Situation of Christianity in Contemporary Japanese Society." *Japan Christian Quarterly* 55(2):78–90.

_____. 1990. "Japan's New Age and Neo-New Religions: Sociological Interpretations." Paper presented at the annual conference of the Society for the Scientific Study of Religion, Virginia Beach.

_____, ed. 1991. "New Religions and Indigenous Christianity." Special edition of *Japan Christian Quarterly* 57(1).

Naipaul, Shiva. 1980. *Road to Nowhere: A New World Tragedy.* New York: Simon & Schuster.

Nanko, Ulrich. 1993. *Die Deutsche Glaubensbewegung.* Marburg, Germany: Diagonal.

Neil, Stephen. 1979. *A History of Christian Missions.* Harmondsworth: Penguin. First edition 1964.

Nethercott, Arthur. 1963. *The Last Four Lives of Annie Besant*. Madras, India: Theosophical Society Press.

Nicholls, William, ed. 1987. *Modernity and Religion*. Waterloo, Ontario: Wilfrid Laurier University Press.

Nickell, Joe, and John F. Fischer. 1987. "Incredible Cremations: Investigating Spontaneous Combustion Deaths." *Skeptical Inquirer* 11(4):352–357.

Niebuhr, H. Richard. 1957. *The Social Sources of Denominationalism*. New York: New America Library.

Noll, Richard. 1994. *The Jung Cult: Origins of a Charismatic Movement*. Princeton: Princeton University Press.

North, Douglass C., and Robert Paul Thomas. 1980. *The Rise of the Western World*. Cambridge: Cambridge University Press.

North, Gary. 1988. *Unholy Spirits: Occultism and New Age Humanism*. Fort Worth, Tex.: Dominion Press.

O'Dea, Thomas. 1964. *The Mormons*. Chicago: University of Chicago Press.

_____. 1966. *The Sociology of Religion*. Englewood Cliffs, N.J.: Prentice-Hall.

Offner, C. B., and H. van Straelen. 1963. *Modern Japanese Religions*. Leiden: E. J. Brill.

Olivier de Sardan, Jean-Pierre. 1992. "Occultism and the Ethnographic 'I': The Exoticizing of Magic from Durkheim to 'Postmodern' Anthropology." *Critique of Anthropology* 12(1):5–25.

Ooms, Emily Groszos. 1993. *Women and Millenarian Protest in Meiji, Japan*. Ithaca, N.Y.: Cornell University Press.

Oosthuizen, G. C. 1992. *The Healer-Prophet in Afro-Christian Churches*. Leiden: E. J. Brill.

Oosthuizen, G. C.; S. Edwards; W. H. Wessels; and I. Hexham. 1988. *Afro-Christian Religion and Healing in Southern Africa*. Lewiston, N.Y.: Edwin Mellen.

Otto, Rudolf. 1923. *The Idea of the Holy*. London: Oxford University Press.

Paine, Thomas. 1974. *The Age of Reason*. Secaucus, N.J.: Citadel Press. First edition 1794.

Palmer, Spencer J. 1967a. *Korea and Christianity*. Seoul: Hollym.

_____, ed. 1967b. *The New Religions of Korea*. Seoul: Royal Asiatic Society.

Parker, Gail Thain. 1973. *Mind Cures in New England: From the Civil War to World War I*. Hanover, N.H.: University Press of New England.

Parsons, Talcott. 1968. *The Structure of Social Action*. New York: Free Press. First edition 1937.

Peel, R. 1958. *Christian Science: Its Encounter with American Culture*. New York: Henry Holt.

Penati, Charles, ed. 1976. *The Geller Papers*. Boston: Houghton Mifflin.

Phillips, D. Z. 1966. *The Concept of Prayer*. New York: Schocken.

Phillips, Earl H., and Eui-Young Yu. 1982. *Religions of Korea*. Los Angeles: Center for Korean-American Studies.

Poewe, Karla. 1985. *The Namibian Herero: A History of Their Psychosocial Disintegration and Survival*. Lewiston, N.Y.: Edwin Mellen.

_____. 1993a. "From Dissonance and Prophecy to Nihilism and Blame: A Look at the Work of Modisane in the Context of Black South African Writing." *Literature and Theology* 7(4):381–396.

_____. 1993b. "Theologies of Black South Africans and the Rhetoric of Peace Versus Violence." *Canadian Journal of African Studies* 27(1):43–65.

_____, ed. 1994. *Charismatic Christianity as a Global Culture*. Columbia: University of South Carolina Press.

_____. 1996. "The Spell of National Socialism: The Berlin Mission and Its Struggle with the Völkisch Movement (1918–1936)." Department of Anthropology, University of Calgary, Alberta.

Polanyi, Michael. 1964. *Personal Knowledge: Towards a Postcritical Philosophy*. New York: Harper Torchbooks.

Porter, Andrew. 1985. "Commerce and Christianity: The Rise and Fall of a Nineteenth-Century Missionary Slogan." *Historical Journal* 28(3):597–621.

Prabhupāda, A. C. Bhaktivedanta, trans. 1968. *Bhagavad Gita*. New York: Macmillan.

_____. 1970. *Easy Journey to Other Planets*. New York: Iskon.

_____. 1982. *The Search for Liberation*. Los Angeles: Bhaktivedanta Book Trust.

Pratt, Parley P. 1973. *Key to the Science of Theology*. Salt Lake City: Deseret Book. First published 1855.

Prebish, Charles. 1979. *American Buddhism*. Belmont, Calif.: Duxbury Press.

Pretorius, H. L. 1985. *Sound the Trumpet of Zion*. Pretoria: University of Pretoria.

Puharich, Andrija. 1974. *Uri: A Journal of the Mystery of Uri Geller*. New York: Bantam Books.

Quebedeaux, Richard. 1978. *The Worldly Evangelicals*. San Francisco: Harper & Row.

_____. 1983. *The New Charismatics II*. San Francisco: Harper & Row.

Quebedeaux, Richard, and Rodney Sawatsky. 1978. *Unification-Evangelical Dialogue*. Barrytown, N.Y.: Rose of Sharon Press.

Radin, Paul. 1957. *Primitive Religion: Its Nature and Origin*. New York: Dover.

Rajneesh. 1983. *Guida Spirituale*. Rajneeshpuram, Ore.: Rajneesh Foundation International.

Rampa, T. Lobsang. 1967. *Chapters of Life*. London: Trans World Publishers.

Randi, James. 1980. *Flim-Flam! The Truth About Unicorns, Parapsychology and Other Delusions*. New York: Lippincott & Crowell.

_____. 1982. *The Truth About Uri Geller*. Buffalo, N.Y.: Prometheus.

Rankin-Box, Denise. 1995. *The Nurses' Handbook of Complementary Therapies*. Edinburgh: Churchill Livingstone.

Rao, B. Narahari. 1988. "Science: Search for Truths, or Way of Doing?" *Cultural Dynamics* 1(3):336–358.

Reader, Ian. 1991. *Religion in Contemporary Japan*. Honolulu: University of Hawaii Press.

Reavis, Dick J. 1995. *The Ashes of Waco: An Investigation*. New York: Simon & Schuster.

Redfield, James. 1993. *The Celestine Prophecy*. Hoover, Al.: Satori Publishers.

Reid, Thomas F.; Mark Virkler; James A. Laine; and Alan Langstaff. 1986. *Seduction?? A Biblical Response*. New Wilmington, Pa.: Son-Rise.

Reiser, Judy. 1979. *And I Thought I Was Crazy! Quirks, Idiosyncracies and Meshugas That People Are Into*. New York: Simon & Schuster.

Reisser, Paul C.; M. D. Teri; and John Weldon. 1983. *The Holistic Healers: A Christian Perspective on New-Age Health Care*. Downers Grove, Ill.: InterVarsity.

Reventlow, Henning Graf, and William Farmer, eds. 1995. *Biblical Studies and the Shifting of Paradigms, 1850-1914*. Sheffield, England: Sheffield Academic Press.

Rhodes, James M. 1980. *The Hitler Movement: A Modern Millenarian Revolution*. Stanford: Hoover Institution Press.

Rhys-Davids, C. A. F. 1894. *Buddhism*. London: SPCK.

Richardson, Alan. 1961. *The Bible in an Age of Science*. London: SCM.

Richardson, Herbert W. 1967. *Toward an American Theology*. New York: Harper & Row.

_____, ed. 1980. *New Religions and Mental Health.* Lewiston, N.Y.: Edwin Mellen.

Richardson, James T. 1980. "People's Temple and Jonestown." *Journal for the Scientific Study of Religion* 19(3):239–255.

Roberts, Dave. 1994. *The 'Toronto' Blessing.* Eastbourne, England: Kingsway Publications.

Romain, Rolland. 1965. *The Life of Vivekananda and the Universal Gospel.* Translated by E. F. Malcolm-Smith. Calcutta: Advaita Ashrama. First published 1931.

Rose, Steve. 1979. *Jesus and Jim Jones: Behind Jonestown.* New York: Pilgrim Press.

Roszak, Theodore. 1969. *The Making of a Counter-Culture.* Garden City, N.Y.: Doubleday.

_____. 1975. *Unfinished Animal: The Aquarian Frontier and Evolutionary Consciousness.* London: Faber & Faber.

_____. 1981. "In Search of the Miraculous." *Harper's* 262 (January):54–62.

Ruff, Howard J. 1980. *How to Prosper During the Coming Bad Years.* New York: Warner Books.

Russell, Bertrand. 1931. *The Scientific Outlook.* New York: Norton.

Ruthven, K. K. 1976. *Myth: The Critical Idiom.* London: Methuen.

Samuelsson, Kurt. 1957. *Religion and Economic Action.* New York: Harper & Row.

Sargant, William. 1957. *Battle for the Mind.* London: William Heinemann. Second revised edition, London: Pan Books, 1959.

Saunders, Christopher. 1970. "Tile and the Thembu Church." *Journal of African History* 11(4):553–570.

Saxena, Vinod Kumar. 1989. *The Brahmo Samaj Movement and Its Leaders.* New Delhi: Anmol.

Schaeffer, Edith. 1981. *The Tapestry: The Life and Times of Francis and Edith Schaeffer.* Waco, Tex.: Word.

Schipmann, Monika, ed. 1994. *Informationen über neue religiöse und weltanschauliche Bewegungen und sogenannte Psychogruppen.* Berlin: Senatsverwaltung für Jugend und Familie.

Scruton, Roger. 1983. *A Dictionary of Political Thought.* London: Pan Books.

Seaman, Gary, and Jane S. Day, eds. 1994. *Ancient Traditions: Shamanism in Central Asia and the Americas.* Niwot: University Press of Colorado.

Seat, Leroy. 1991. "Japan's Fastest-growing New Religions." *Japan Christian Quarterly* 57(1):12–17.

Shaw, William. 1995. *Spying in Guru Land.* London: Fourth Estate Books.

Sherrill, John L. 1964. *They Speak with Other Tongues.* New York: McGraw-Hill.

Shils, Edward. 1981. *Tradition.* Chicago: University of Chicago Press.

Shupe, Anson, and David Bromley. 1980. *The New Vigilantes: Deprogrammers, Anti-Cultists and the New Religions.* Beverly Hills, Calif.: Sage.

_____. 1981. *A Documentary History of the American Anti-Cult Movement.* Lewiston, N.Y.: Edwin Mellen.

_____, eds. 1994. *The Anti-Cult Movement in Cross-Cultural Perspective.* New York: Garland.

Sigstedt, Cyriel Odhner. 1952. *The Swedenborg Epic.* New York: New Church.

Silberman, Lou H. S. 1983. "Wellhausen and Judaism." *Semina* 23:75–82.

Singer, Margaret Thaler, with Janja Lalich. 1995. *Cults in Our Midst.* San Francisco: Jossey-Bass.

Singer, Milton. 1972. *When a Great Tradition Modernizes.* New York: Praeger.

Smart, Ninian. 1958. *Reasons and Faiths.* London: Routledge & Kegan Paul.

_____. 1969. *Religious Experience of Mankind*. New York: Scribner's.

Smith, E. E. 1971. *Triplanetary*. London: W. H. Allen. First published 1934.

Smith, Ethan. 1825. *A View of the Hebrews*. Poultney, Vt.: Smith and Shute.

Smuts, J. C. 1987. *Holism and Evolution*. Cape Town: N & S Press. First published 1926.

Spangler, David. 1976. *Revelation: The Birth of a New Age*. Middleton, England: Lorian Press.

_____. 1984. *Emergence: The Rebirth of the Sacred*. New York: Delta Books.

Stark, Rodney. 1996. "German and German-American Religiousness: Approximating a Crucial Experiment." Paper prepared for the workshop "Religion in the United States and Germany," sponsored by the German Sociological Association, Dresden, 7–11 October.

Stark, Rodney, and William Sims Bainbridge. 1985. *The Future of Religion: Secularization, Revival and Cult Formation*. Berkeley: University of California Press.

_____. 1987. *A Theory of Religion*. New York: Peter Lang.

Steiger, Rod. 1976. *Gods of Aquarius*. New York: Harcourt Brace Jovanovich.

Steyn, Chrissie. 1994. *Worldviews in Transition: An Investigation into the New Age Movement in South Africa*. Pretoria: UNISA.

Stoll, David. 1990. *Is Latin America Turning Protestant?* Berkeley: University of California Press.

Stoller, Paul, and Cheryl Olkes. 1987. *In Sorcery's Shadow*. Chicago: University of Chicago Press.

Sundkler, Bengt. 1961. *Bantu Prophets in South Africa*. London: Oxford University Press.

_____. 1976. *Zulu Zion and Some Swazi Zionists*. Oxford: Oxford University Press.

Symonds, John. 1960. *The Lady with the Magic Eyes: Madame Blavatsky*. New York: Thomas Yoseloff.

Talmage, James E. 1962. *A Study of the Articles of Faith*. London: Church of Jesus Christ of Latter-Day Saints.

Taylor, John V. 1963. *The Primal Vision*. London: SCM.

ter Haar, Gerrie. 1987. "Religion and Healing: The Case of Milingo." *Social Compass* 34(4):475–493.

Thomas, Madathilparampil M. 1969. *The Acknowledged Christ of the Indian Renaissance*. London: SCM.

Thompson, Judith, and Paul Heelas. 1986. *The Way of the Heart: The Rajneesh Movement*. Wellingborough, England: Aquarian Press.

Thompson, William Irwin. 1975. *The Findhorn Garden*. New York: Harper & Row.

Tillich, Paul. 1957. *The Dynamics of Faith*. London: Allen & Unwin.

Tipton, Steven M. 1981. *Getting Saved from the Sixties: Moral Meaning in Conversion and Cultural Change*. Berkeley: University of California Press.

Tobias, Madeleine, and Janja Lalich. 1994. *Captive Hearts: Captive Minds*. Alameda, Calif.: Hunter House.

Tolkien, J. R. R. 1966. *The Lord of the Rings*. London: Allen & Unwin.

Tournier, Paul. 1960. *A Doctor's Casebook in Light of the Bible*. Translated by Edwin Hudson. New York: Harper & Row.

Travis, Stephen. 1974. *The Jesus Hope*. Waco, Tex.: Word.

Treharne, R. F. 1971. *The Glastonbury Legends*. London: Sphere Books.

Troeltsch, Ernst. 1931. *The Social Teaching of the Christian Churches*. Translated by Olive Wyon. London: Allen & Unwin. First published 1911.

_____. 1991. *Religion in History*. Translated by James Luther Adams and Walter F. Bense. Minneapolis: Fortress Press.

Tudor, Henry. 1972. *Political Myth*. London: Hutchinson.

Turner, Victor W. 1969. *The Ritual Process: Structure and Anti-Structure*. Chicago: Aldine.

Underwood, Alfred Clair. 1925. *Conversion: Christian and Non-Christian*. London: Allen & Unwin.

Underwood, Barbara, and Betty Underwood. 1979. *Hostage to Heaven*. New York: Clarkson N. Potter.

Usarski, Frank. 1988. *Die Stigmatisierung neuer spiritueller Bewegungen in der Bundesrepublik Deutschland*. Cologne: Böhlau Verlag.

Vable, Dattatrey. 1983. *The Araya Samaj: Hindu Without Hinduism*. Delhi: Vikas.

van Baalen, Jan Karel. 1956. *The Chaos of the Cults*. Grand Rapids, Mich.: Eerdmans. First published 1938.

van der Heyden, Ulrich, and Heike Liebau. 1966. *Missionsgeschichte, Kirchengeschichte, Weltgeschichte*. Stuttgart: Franz Steiner Verlag.

Veith, Ilza. 1965. *Hysteria*. Chicago: University of Chicago Press.

Vickers, Brian. 1989. *In Defence of Rhetoric*. Oxford: Clarendon Press.

Vilakazi, Absolom, with Bongani Mthethwa and Mthembeni Mpanza. 1986. *Shembe: The Revitalization of African Society*. Johannesburg: Skotaville.

von Daniken, Erich. 1968. *Chariots of the Gods? Unsolved Mysteries of the Past*. Translated by Michael Heron. London: Souvenir Press.

von Wiese, Leopold. 1974. *Systematic Sociology*. Translated by Howard Becker. New York: Arno Press. First published 1932.

Wach, Joachim. 1944. *Sociology of Religion*. Chicago: University of Chicago Press. First German edition 1931.

Wallace, Anthony F. C. 1966. *Religion: An Anthropological View*. New York: Random House.

Wallis, Roy. 1976. *The Road to Total Freedom: A Sociological Analysis of Scientology*. London: Heinemann.

Walzer, Michael. 1965. *The Revolution of the Saints: A Study in the Origins of Radical Politics*. Cambridge: Harvard University Press.

Washington, Peter. 1993. *Madame Blavatsky's Baboon: Theosophy and the Emergence of the Western Guru*. London: Secker & Warburg.

Watkins, Arleen J., and William S. Bickel. 1986. "A Study of the Kirlian Effect." *Skeptical Inquirer* 10(2):244–257.

Watson, Lyle. 1974. *Supernature*. London: Hodder & Stoughton.

_____. 1987. *Lifetide*. New York: Simon & Schuster.

Watts, Frank, and Mark Williams. 1988. *The Psychology of Religious Knowing*. Cambridge: Cambridge University Press.

Wavell, Steward; Audrey Butt; and Nina Epton. 1967. *Trances*. New York: Dutton.

Webb, James. 1971. *The Flight from Reason*. London: Macdonald.

Weber, Max. 1956. *The Sociology of Religion*. Translated by Ephraim Fischoff. London: Methuen. First German edition 1922.

_____. 1964. *Wirtschaft und Gesellschaft*. Cologne: Kiepenheuer und Witsch.

_____. 1973. "Max Weber on Church, Sect and Mysticism." Translated by Jerome L. Gittleman. *Sociological Analysis* 34(2):140–149. First published 1910.

_____. 1985. "'Churches' and 'Sects' in North America: An Ecclesiastical Socio-Political Sketch." Translated by Colin Loader. *Sociological Theory* 3(1):7–13. First published 1906.

Weems, Benjamin. 1964. *Reform, Rebellion and the Heavenly Way.* Tucson: University of Arizona Press.

Wehr, Gerhard. 1987. *Jung: A Biography.* Boston: Shambhala.

Welbourn, Fred. 1961. *East African Rebels.* London: SCM.

Welbourn, Fred, and B. A. Ogot. 1966. *A Place to Feel at Home: A Study of Two Independent Churches in Western Kenya.* London: Oxford University Press.

Wessinger, Catherine Lowman. 1988. *Annie Besant and Progressive Messianism (1847–1933).* Lewiston, N.Y.: Edwin Mellen.

Wiesberger, Frank. 1990. *Baustein zu einer soziologischen Theorie der Konversion.* Berlin: Duncker & Humblot.

Wilkerson, David, with John Sherrill and Elizabeth Sherrill. 1963. *The Cross and the Switchblade.* New York: B. Geis.

Williams, Raymond B. 1984. *A New Face of Hinduism: The Swaminarayan Religion.* Cambridge: Cambridge University Press.

_____, ed. 1992. *A Sacred Thread: The Modern Transmission of Hindu Traditions in India and Abroad.* Chambersburg, Pa.: Anima Books.

Wilson, Bryan. 1970a. *Rationality.* Oxford: Blackwell.

_____, ed. 1970b. *Religious Sects.* Englewood Cliffs, N.J.: World University Library.

_____. 1981. *The Social Impact of New Religious Movements.* New York: Rose of Sharon Press.

Winch, Peter. 1958. *The Idea of a Social Science and Its Relation to Philosophy.* London: Routledge & Kegan Paul.

Wise, Robert, et al. 1986. *The Church Divided.* South Plainfield, N.J.: Bridge.

Wittgenstein, Ludwig. 1963. *Philosophical Investigations.* Edited by Kenneth Scott. New York: Macmillan.

Wuthnow, Robert. 1978. *Experimentation in American Religion: The New Mysticisms and Their Implications for the Churches.* Berkeley: University of California Press.

_____. 1988. *The Restructuring of American Religion.* Princeton: Princeton University Press.

Yap, P. M. 1960. "The Possession Syndrome: A Comparison of Hong Kong and French Findings." *Journal of Mental Science* 106:114–137.

Yinger, Milton J. 1970. *The Scientific Study of Religion.* London: Macmillan.

Yonggi Cho, Paul. 1979. *The Fourth Dimension.* Plainfield, N.J.: Logos International.

Yoo, Boo Wong. 1986. "Response to Korean Shamanism by the Pentecostal Church." *International Review of Missions* 75:297.

Young, Richard Fox. 1988. "From *Gokyō-dōgen* to *Bankyō-dōkon*: A Study in the Self-Realization of Ōmoto." Japanese Journal of Religious Studies 15(4):263–286.

_____. 1989. "Jesus, the 'Christ,' and Deguchi Onisaburō: A Study of Adversarial Syncretism in a Japanese World-Renewal Religion." *Japanese Religions* 15(4):26–49.

_____. 1991. "The 'Christ' of the Japanese New Religions." *Japan Christian Quarterly* 57(1):18–128.

Yu, Chai-shin, and R. Guisso, eds. 1988. *Shamanism: The Spirit World of Korea.* Berkeley: Asian Humanities Press.

Zaehner, R. C., ed. 1971. *The Concise Encyclopedia of Living Faiths.* London: Hutchinson.

Zaretsky, Irving I., and Mark P. Leone. 1974. *Religious Movements in Contemporary America.* Princeton: Princeton University Press.

Ziegler, Herbert F. 1989. *Nazi Germany's New Aristocracy: The SS Leadership, 1925-1939.* Princeton: Princeton University Press.

Zinzer, Hartmut. 1992. *Okkultismus unter Jugendlichen.* Berlin: Pädagogisches Zentrum.

Zipfel, Friedrich. 1965. *Kirchenkampf in Deutschland, 1933–1945.* Berlin: Walter de Gruyter.

Zulkowsky, Patricia. 1980. "Piety and Spirituality." Lecture delivered at the Bahama Conference on Unification Views of the Family.

# About the Book and Authors

*A*lthough the Great Anti-Cult Crusade links new religious movements to dangerous cults, brainwashing, and the need for deprogramming, Karla Poewe and Irving Hexham argue that many cults are the product of a dynamic interaction between folk religions and the teachings of traditional world religions. Drawing on examples from Africa, the United States, Asia, and Europe, they suggest that few new religions are really new. Most draw on rich, if localized, cultural traditions that are shaped anew by the influence of technological change and international linkages.

With the widespread loss of belief in biblical mythology in the nineteenth century, new mythologies based on science and elements derived from various non-Western religious traditions emerged, leading to the growth and popularity of new religions and cults.

Irving Hexham is professor of religious studies and Karla Poewe is professor of anthropology, both at the University of Calgary.

# Index